+ Are you ready to radically improve yourself . . . and your life?
+ Are you as confident and secure as you'd like to be?
+ Are you living in the moment—fully present for yourself and those around you?
+ Could you benefit from criticizing less and loving more?
+ Are your relationships as strong and sturdy as you want them to be?
+ Do you base your worth on what you do, rather than on who you are?
+ Want to shed anxiety and smoothly navigate any social situation?
+ Do you sometimes compare yourself to others . . . and find yourself lacking?
+ Have you let down your guard, taken off your mask, to feel safe in your own skin?
+ Wish you knew how to handle the "difficult people" in your life?
+ Do you obsess over past events—replaying what you could have done differently?
+ Ever wonder how to finally fulfill those "once upon a time" dreams?
+ Question if you're tapping into your strengths to maximize your personality?
+ Are the people in your life better people for having known you?
+ Want to shake restless feelings and find a deeper meaning and purpose that anchors your soul?
+ Are you living each day to the max, taking advantage of most of your moments?
+ Do you like your life—or love it?

+    +    +

*Discover the 3 secrets to feeling good—deep down in your soul.*
*They'll transform you, your life, and your relationships fo*

LOVE *the* **LIFE** *You* LIVE

# Resources by Dr. Les Parrott

High-Maintenance Relationships
The Control Freak
The Life You Want Your Kids to Live
Helping Your Struggling Teenager
7 Secrets of a Healthy Dating Relationship
Once Upon a Family

## BOOKS WRITTEN BY DR. LES PARROTT AND DR. LESLIE PARROTT

When Bad Things Happen to Good Marriages
Saving Your Marriage Before It Starts
Saving Your Second Marriage Before It Starts
The Love List
Pillow Talk
Relationships
Becoming Soul Mates
Proverbs for Couples
The Marriage Mentor Manual
Love Is . . .
Questions Couples Ask
Getting Ready for the Wedding
**Resources available at www.RealRelationships.com**

✦  ✦  ✦

# Resources by Dr. Neil Clark Warren

Finding the Love of Your Life
Make Anger Your Ally: Harnessing Our Most Baffling Emotion
Finding Contentment
Learning to Live with the Love of Your Life . . . and Loving It
God Said It, Don't Sweat It: Sound Encouragement to Keep the
    Little Things from Overwhelming You
Catching the Rhythm of Love: Experience Your Way to a
    Spectacular Marriage
Date—or Soul Mate? How to Know if Someone Is Worth Pursuing
    on Two Dates or Less
**Resources available at eHarmony.com**

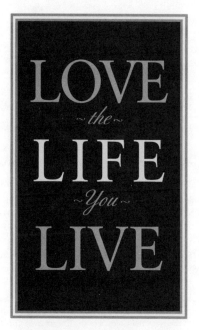

# LOVE ~the~ LIFE ~You~ LIVE

*3 Secrets to Feeling Good—*
*Deep Down in Your Soul*

## LES PARROTT, Ph.D.
## NEIL CLARK WARREN, Ph.D.
### Founder of eHarmony.com™

Tyndale House Publishers, Inc.
CAROL STREAM, ILLINOIS

Visit Tyndale's exciting Web site at www.tyndale.com

TYNDALE is a registered trademark of Tyndale House Publishers, Inc.

Tyndale's quill logo is a trademark of Tyndale House Publishers, Inc.

*Love the Life You Live*

Edited by Ramona Cramer Tucker

**Library of Congress Cataloging-in-Publication Data**

Parrott, Les.
    Love the life you live : 3 secrets to feeling good, deep down in your soul / Les Parrott and Neil Clark Warren.
        p. cm.
    Includes bibliographical references (p.    ).
    ISBN-13: 978-0-8423-8360-8 (hc)
    ISBN-10: 0-8423-8360-3 (hc)
    ISBN-13: 978-0-8423-8361-5 (sc)
    ISBN-10: 0-8423-8361-1 (sc)
    1. Success—Religious aspects—Christianity.  I. Warren, Neil Clark.  II. Title.
    BV4598.3 .P36 2003
    158—dc21                                                            2003012965

Printed in the United States of America

11  10  09  08  07  06
8   7   6   5   4   3   2

# TABLE OF CONTENTS

**Secret #3: Self-Giving Love**

**Conclusion: The Life of Your Dreams**

~

$\mathcal{O}$n a sunny day in Seattle, one of those pristine days when every Pacific Northwesterner forgives the rain for falling so much, the two of us were sitting around a table enjoying a leisurely lunch when an idea struck us like a ray of sunshine. The idea for this book was born.

Since we're both psychologists, we first got to know each other because we were focusing on the same area of psychology—mainly the building of healthy relationships. We've written books about the same subjects and repeatedly have found ourselves making the same points about the same issues.

And then we ended up on the same speaking team—leading weekend seminars about healthy relationships and healthy lives. Our wives became close friends, and our relationship as couples grew. We worked to maximize the times we had to talk about crucial issues.

That day in Seattle we suddenly recognized we had come to the same powerful place in our thinking. We both knew that relationships of every kind have virtually no chance in our culture until individuals within those relationships get healthy themselves first. For years we had said, separately and collectively, that relationships can only be as healthy as the least healthy person in them . . . and that individual wholeness is the backbone of a healthy relationship. In fact, that precise message runs through every counseling session, every seminar, and every book we have ever been a part of. So we both knew it made no sense to keep trying to help men and women build good relationships until we had first helped them discover peace and contentment at the center of their *individual* lives.

A single truth brought us together as authors: *Personal health, wholeness, and maturity are at the heart of every relationship that flourishes.* We realized that both of us were receiving similar letters, lots of them, from sincere people with the same key questions. After recounting their story, somewhere in their message they would ask, "You talk a lot about getting healthy and whole, but how do you do this? What are the tools?"

So that day in Seattle we began to talk like two people who were *convinced* we were on the edge of having the answer to the most critical question of our times. We could not shut up. Each of us was scribbling notes on napkins as we resonated with each other's thinking. It was at that luncheon that we decided to get more intentional about helping people answer these questions. As we talked excitedly, we became progressively more aware of our wholehearted agreement about what emotional and spiritual health is all about. We became, and remain, so convinced that emotional health is attainable in *every* life. That day we agreed—for the first time in either of our lives—to write a book with someone other than our wives, to partner in this deeply meaningful task of trying to shed light on this crucial subject.

This book is the result of many months of common labor on our parts. We have literally written this book from coast to coast. In the corner of a hotel lobby, set on the sands of Santa Monica Beach in California, we first began to structure our thoughts while discussing concepts and drawing diagrams on tablets of paper. We met again at a lodge in the foothills of Colorado Springs, where we refined our thoughts over the course of a couple of days. Another important session occurred months later when our travels brought us together on the deck of a high-rise in Miami Beach, Florida, overlooking Biscayne Bay. That's where we began to read aloud and critique each other's writing.

Sometimes we have agonized on the phone for hours in our

search for just the right words, just the right way to represent what we see as the clear path to health and wholeness. We have encouraged each other during difficult times, argued with each other now and then, laughed at our foibles, and all the time centered our attention on you, the reader. We deeply want you to love the life you live. Why? Because you will experience a transformation that will lift up not only yourself, but others, who will see your courage. And because of you, a fresh breeze of authenticity and optimism will encircle their life. You will, in fact, create a little heaven on earth . . . and few human experiences can compare to the sweetness of this. As Luciano de Cresenzo has said so poetically, "We are, each of us, angels with only one wing. And we can only fly embracing each other."

With every sentence we wrote, we genuinely thought of you. May your reading of our words be as satisfying and life changing as our own journeys to health and wholeness.

LES PARROTT
*Seattle, Washington*

NEIL CLARK WARREN
*Pasadena, California*

◇

*Healthy to the Core*

# IMPROVING YOU, YOUR LIFE, AND YOUR RELATIONSHIPS— FOREVER

*Life is my university, and I hope to graduate
from it with some distinction.*

LOUISA MAY ALCOTT

*A*t a renowned museum in Florence, Italy, you will find four partially finished sculptures. The famed sculptor Michelangelo had intended for each of them to be used on the tomb of Pope Julius. But midway through the project, he decided not to use them and ceased his work. Today anyone traveling to Florence can see the results—a hand protrudes here, a torso of a man there, a leg, a part of a head. None of them are finished.

If you stand in this great hall, looking at these fragmentary figures, you will sense the turmoil, the struggle embodied in these stones. It's as though the figures are crying to break free from their blocks of marble to become what they were intended to be.

Michelangelo called these figures "Captives." Study them for a time, and they are certain to stir up within you a deep longing to be completed yourself. Somehow these figures bring more consciously into your awareness the ache in your own soul to be free from anything that is holding you down and preventing the realization of your full potential. The incomplete figures eerily remind you of your *own* incompleteness. We know—both of us have stood there in that spot and quietly wondered if we were fully alive.

All of us, as humans, share a universal longing to be complete, to enjoy the fulfillment of realizing our God-given destiny.* But like Michelangelo's captive statues, we are often frozen in our efforts to experience who we are really meant to be. We never learn the secrets to chipping away at what holds us back. We never discover the parts of ourselves that are still in captivity. The result? We suffocate our calling and remain imprisoned in the jail cell of unfinished work. We are incomplete—never truly *loving* the life we live.

> **Destiny is not a matter of chance, it is a matter of choice; it is not a thing to be waited for, it is a thing to be achieved.**
> *William Jennings Bryan*

## WHAT WE KNOW ABOUT YOU

You may be single or married, young or old. You may have suffered unthinkable abuse or lived a charmed life. You may have a Ph.D. or be a high-school dropout. Whatever your baggage or background, we know at least one thing about you. Each moment of every day you are either moving away from or toward the person God designed you to be. And as a result, your inner self is either hemmed in and stuck, or it is quietly becoming a work of art. You are either maximizing your moments or allowing them to slip by without notice.

No matter our age, stage, faith, or career, all of us are searching for inner contentment—the kind that comes from being whole and complete. All of us want to love the life we live. This is exactly why we have filled this book with time-tested tools for seizing every moment of every day. We want you to learn the secrets of maximizing a simple moment in time by releasing the positive potential it contains for you and everyone around you. Once you begin to learn the simple skills we are about to teach you, the moments of your day will become consistently more meaningful, more exciting, until you realize you are growing. Thriving. Flour-

---

*See note at the beginning of "Sources" on page 253.

ishing. You are becoming healthier, more complete. You are unlocking parts of yourself you didn't know you had. You are freeing yourself and your relationships to be fully alive.

Since you are reading this book, we know that something within you has been stirred to move more intentionally toward health and wholeness. And we are going to do everything we can to help you experience it deeply and consistently. We are convinced that it is only when you achieve a deep level of emotional and spiritual health that you can find enduring inner peace and long-lasting joy. If you want to feel good, deep down in your soul, you've got to get yourself solidly healthy.

**A man too busy to take care of his health is like a mechanic too busy to take care of his tools.**
*Spanish proverb*

## HEALTHY TO THE CORE

When you achieve the level of health and wholeness we've been describing, you will begin to feel unusually good about yourself. Not the kind of good that is self-centered, but the kind of good that makes a positive, generous, caring human being out of you. Not only will you *feel* good, but you will *be* good. You'll catch yourself expressing all kinds of natural and free-flowing appreciation and love for others. And your newly found health will be so contagious that your whole community of friends and family—even strangers you encounter—will find their lives moving toward personal joy and self-giving love.

Goodness comes out of a solidly healthy inner place—and then it pours out of you in all directions. In the process of discovering new levels of personal effectiveness and fulfillment, you will inspire others to find those same new levels for themselves. As you learn to live serenely, above the grit of the daily grind, you will become committed to making this possible for every person you know. As you develop the skill of making wise decisions that define your life for the better, you will discover an inner passion to help others enjoy the same powerful and life-changing process. As you shake off your hurry-sickness and live in the now, being fully present for yourself and those around you, you will see the same thing beginning to happen for your dearest friends and family members. In short, as you love the life you live, this whole wonderful phenomenon will spread across the struggling society of eager human beings who make up your personal world.

## IT'S EASIER THAN YOU THINK

If this is what you want for your life—a positive transformation of you and your relationships—here's the good news: *You can have it!* This is exactly the kind of life you can live. At the risk of sounding like two slaphappy psychologists who are seemingly out of touch with the arduous work traditionally required for authentic wholeness, living the life you long for may be less complicated than you think.

We believe you can reach your most cherished goals for loving this life by following a relatively simple path.

An easy path? Not always. But simple nonetheless.

How can two veteran psychologists who have spent their professional lives in the hallowed halls of academia and in the clinical offices of mental-health centers make such a bold and seemingly naive claim? Because we believe wholeheartedly that all the answers to life's most challenging questions are available in ancient, time-tested principles—and our confidence in these truths is bolstered by new and powerful research in the social sciences. A contemporary generation of researchers with a fresh perspective in the sciences has shifted psychology's primary analyses of misery to an understanding of wellness. Psychology used to think it was critical to focus on—and then eliminate—negative emotions. Now we know there is a better way.

> There's a period of life when we swallow a knowledge of ourselves and it becomes either good or sour inside.
>
> *Pearl Bailey*

## YOU AND YOUR RELATIONSHIPS WILL NEVER BE THE SAME

The new research reveals that you can't be happy simply because you *aren't* encumbered by depression, stress, or anxiety. No—you can't be happy without being *healthy*. And there's a lot more to health than not being sick. Emotional health is more than the absence of dysfunctional emotions. Emotional health is at the center of a life you can love living.

You'll never be content in your career, at least not for long, if you're not emotionally fit. You can't enjoy being single until you like being you. You can't have a winning marriage if you are psychologically stuck. You can't be a good parent until you understand—and appreciate—who you are. You can't be well-adjusted if you're constantly comparing yourself to others or equating what you do with who you are. And you can't look into the face of death until you optimize your spiritual health.

It is nearly impossible to exaggerate the profound impact getting healthy and whole has on every aspect of your life. So it is certainly no exaggeration to say you will never, ever love the life you live until you become profoundly new and reborn emotionally, mentally, and spiritually at your very core.

The professional community knows more today about how to live a fulfilled life, no matter what your circumstances, than ever before. That's why we felt compelled to write this book. As psychologists specializing in relationships, we have seen more than 5,000 people in therapy. We have spoken to more than 300,000 people in seminars and appeared on several thousand radio and television talk shows. And we've written more than a dozen books—all in an effort to help people improve their lives and relationships. We are passionate about helping you do this too. But rather than give you tips and techniques (for improving communication, understanding gender differences, and all the rest), we've learned that until you get yourself healthy, the

> **Not life, but good life, is to be chiefly valued.**
>
> *Socrates*

tips and techniques are superficial. They eventually fall flat. Why? Because your relationships can only be as healthy as the least healthy person in them. For this very reason, we believe the most important goal you can ever accomplish is getting yourself healthy.

"Your life is like a coin," said writer Lillian Dickenson. "You can spend it any way you like, but you can spend it only once." The question is, how are you going to spend your capital? It is a question we have explored personally and thoroughly while writing this book, and because you are reading it, we know you want to make the very best investment you can. So in the next chapter, you will discover our plan for helping you become healthy and whole.

# HOW TO GET HEALTHY:
# A DEEP AND SIMPLE PLAN

*I saw the angel in the marble
and carved until I set him free.*

MICHELANGELO

*L*ife is deep and simple, and what our society gives us is shallow and complicated." Fred Rogers, the *Mister Rogers* of children's television, said this in a thoughtful interview shortly before he passed away. What a wise and compassionate man. And what an amazing and insightful sentence. Life *is* deep and simple. And yet we so often make it more complicated than it needs to be.

The scientific study of emotional wellness is new, but the principles it is excavating are ages old. How do we know? Because we've studied the pursuit of a life well lived from every vantage point we could, going far back into ancient history. The Greeks, for example, viewed the deep pleasures of life as being more of the mind than the body. Roman statesman Cicero proclaimed, "There is no fool who is happy, and no wise man who is not." The Greek philosopher Epicurus boiled fulfillment down to a straightforward thought: that the most contented people remember the past with gratitude and accept their present situation without coveting what someone else has. The Bible says the same thing, in so many words, and then drills down on the point that true fulfillment comes ultimately through love—through learning to love ourselves, one another, and our Creator.

Something about the truthful simplicity of this age-old wisdom got hold of our heart as well as our head as we set out to find a practical plan for helping ourselves and people like you be the best you can be.

## A DEEP AND SIMPLE PLAN

We've grown weary of seeing people spend inordinate amounts of time and money in the pursuit of wholeness, whatever their route, only to feel more confused and aimless as a result. So let us tell you what we know for sure. After surveying the pursuit of happiness throughout history, and after studying contemporary science's study of well-being, we know that profound health and wholeness, like life itself, is deep and simple. Don't be seduced by turning it into something shallow or complicated.

The only hard part about loving the life you live—about feeling good deep down in your soul—is figuring out precisely what it takes to get the job accomplished. In our opinion, it starts with (1) an insightful diagnosis, (2) a reasonable destination, and (3) a clear understanding of how to get from where you are to where you want to be. This road map is exactly what we offer you in the pages of this book. And once you see the route we have planned for getting you from here to there, we're convinced you will rave about the simplicity of becoming healthy and whole.

**This above all: To thine own self be true, and it must follow, as the night the day, thou canst not then be false to any man.**

*William Shakespeare*

## WHAT IS HEALTH AND WHOLENESS?

Beginning with the section "Secret #1: Profound Significance," each of the chapters will set you on a proven pathway for personal growth. By focusing on a unique and specific area, each of them will provide you with vital strategies for helping you become who you were designed to be and will show you how to maximize your moments and live your life at the highest peak.

Before we set off on our journey, however, we want to define our destination. It isn't enough to say we want you to realize an entirely new level of personal health and wholeness. We need to *define* exactly what we mean by health and wholeness.

Anyone who lives the good life, who *really* lives it, has found their way to what we call the three hallmarks of health. These people are defined by

1. Profound significance—They know they are loved unconditionally, to the center of their being.
2. Unswerving authenticity—They know who they are, and they are courageously committed to living out their *true* personality and God-given talents.
3. Self-giving love—They know others need them, and they are intent on giving of themselves to others on a daily basis.

If you want a complete list of the elements of health, we are convinced this list can be boiled down to these three. It's that simple. At the risk of sounding too colloquial on such a meaningful matter, you can also think of health and wholeness as getting right with God (significance), getting right with yourself (authenticity), and getting right with others (love). Simple? We hope so. But as you read more about these hallmarks later in this book, we think you will recognize just how profound they really are.

Obviously, we don't take credit for inventing these hallmarks. We are only attempting to breathe new life into these ancient principles as we provide you with numerous proven strategies for living them out.

This definition of emotional and spiritual health is as old as the ages and as fresh as contemporary research. Its simplicity can compel you to make it more complicated, but there's no need. The

> **The greater danger, for most of us, lies not in setting our aim too high and falling short; but in setting our aim too low, and achieving our mark. . . . Lord, grant that I may always desire more than I can accomplish.**
>
> *Michelangelo*

depth of these qualities, if properly understood, has been enough to propel the ultimate human quest throughout the ages.

These three hallmarks apply to everyone across cultures and over time. In fact, these hallmarks have been bandied about for centuries. Speaking of the value of *significance,* for example, Augustine, in A.D. 391 said, "God loves each of us as if there were only one of us." Speaking of *authenticity,* Jesus said to his followers, "What will it profit a man if he gains the whole world, and loses his own soul?" And speaking of *self-giving love,* Seneca, in 4 B.C., said, "If thou wishest to be loved, love."

Profound significance. Unswerving authenticity. Self-giving love. If you want to avoid what some call the "tragedy of being half formed," like Michelangelo's "Captives," and you want to become all that God designed you to be, these three keys will open the door.

Will you be perfect? No.

Healthy? Yes.

## PUTTING A FACE ON THE HALLMARKS OF HEALTH

Do you know someone who is psychologically and spiritually healthy? As we were discussing and writing this chapter together we often talked about various people and their healthy attributes. And when it came to identifying one person we both knew who most embodied health and wholeness, we easily identified our friend Lew.

Lewis B. Smedes is one of our most loved and respected friends. And right in the middle of our writing this chapter together, he fell from his ladder while installing his Christmas lights, hit the back of his head, and died a day or two later. We were stunned and saddened. I (Les) flew to Los Angeles from Seattle, and Neil and I attended the funeral together. Neil spoke at the service and said that Lew Smedes was a man of incredible gifts—the finest writer he had ever met, as well as the most powerful speaker he had ever heard. After the funeral, as we discussed the autobiography Lew had finished days before his fall, we said again that Lew was also one of the healthiest persons we have ever known.

He worked a lifetime to claim that level of *profound significance* about which he spoke and wrote so powerfully. His father died when he was two months old, and his mother, with five children, spoke little English and began cleaning houses for a barely minimal living. With such a stressful start, Lew struggled to claim his value. His incredible significance was sometimes much clearer to others than it was to himself. Knowing him so well, however, we knew he finally succeeded.

If he struggled to realize his intrinsic worth, he masterfully developed his *authenticity*. He lacked any knee-jerk defensiveness. He was eager for feedback and critique in an effort to minimize his blind spots. He embodied a kind of self-discipline that was free of legalism and rigidity. Lew was relentless about being authentic— and calling us to be the same. His life is packed with stories about the courage he needed in order to be the man he was when so many wanted to tell him what he should believe, how he should behave, and to whom and what he should remain captive.

Finally, he never doubted for a minute when it came to possessing *self-giving love*—and extending it to others. Lew could read a roomful of people like a book. He conveyed a warmth of understanding, and he could smell phoniness at a hundred paces. He was not focused as much on *doing* loving things as he was on *being* a loving person. He fully knew that the only thing better than being loved was to love. His care and kindness were contagious.

> **Ah, but a man's reach should exceed his grasp, or what's a heaven for?**
>
> *Robert Browning*

We tell you about our friend, Lew, because we want you to see that these three hallmarks of health are not academic. Significance, authenticity, and love are not theoretical abstractions. They can be lived out in flesh and blood. It is possible. It is simple. It is profound. We dedicate this book to helping you join the ranks of healthy people like Lewis B. Smedes.

For if you don't, as you are about to see in the next chapter, your life and your relationships become painfully shallow and needlessly complex.

# HOW HEALTHY ARE YOU?

*If a thing is worth doing,*

*it is worth doing badly.*

G. K. CHESTERTON

*W*hen it comes to getting healthy and whole, we couldn't agree more with English writer G. K. Chesterton. None of us ever fully arrive at psychological and spiritual health. We can never check it off our list and be done with it. Wholeness is a lifelong pursuit. Sometimes we pursue it with steady and strong determination; other times we limp.

But if we persevere and stay on the path, we discover that the road to health and wholeness runs straight through the center of our smallest daily tasks. We encounter it in minuscule moments. It runs directly through the heart of our fatigue and our times of inadequacy. It is not doled out only to the blessed, and it is not achieved quickly by anyone. So as you move in this positive direction, be aware that you will at times excel; at other times you will grope. But instead of feeling discouraged, take comfort in the fact that you are, at least, groping in the right direction.

Also, be aware that *all three* of the hallmarks of health we talked about in the last chapter—significance, authenticity, and love—are *essential* for wholeness to be realized. Think of them as a tripod. If one leg is missing, wholeness topples. Consider the facts:

- Without significance, you inevitably become needy, insecure, and vulnerable.
- Without authenticity, you are certain to become stagnant, superficial, and phony.
- Without love, you will definitely become self-consumed and insular.

The point is that unhealthy people, by default, suffer from being either insecure, stuck, and/or egocentric. They are very much like Michelangelo's "Captives"—developed in places but conspicuously incomplete.

Let's get honest. Do you sense that insecurity sometimes gets the better of you? Are you sometimes discouraged by being emotionally stuck or stagnant in certain relationships? Or in your honest moments, do you sometimes see that your self-centered motives drive you more than you'd like? If insecurity, exhaustion, or selfishness is keeping you down, you're not alone. And you're certainly not doomed.

> The desire for approval and recognition has been one of the major driving forces throughout my life.
>
> *Hans Selye*

## HOPE FOR THE CONSPICUOUSLY INCOMPLETE

There is hope—hope for *you!* You don't have to be one of the "Captives." We have helped thousands of people work their way out of captivity to achieve a joyful new level of psychological health. Your own journey toward wholeness—guided by significance, authenticity, and love—is the most important thing you will ever do for your relationships and for yourself. It will determine how far you go in your career, the depth of your relationship with God, the quality of your love life, the kind of friendships you cultivate, and your eventual level of well-being.

If you're skeptical, let me (Neil) tell you about a woman I know very well. I received a call from her just this week. She was reporting in. Fifteen years ago I saw her in psychotherapy. When she initially began her trek toward wholeness, she was incredibly confused and depressed. Now she has a vibrancy that's scintillating. Although she was a high-school dropout, today this thirty-five-year-old woman is a candidate for a Ph.D. Fifteen years ago she was totally unable to make decisions and articulate them to even the safest of her friends. Now she boldly determines where she stands, and she speaks up with confidence. She is sensitive, knows how to listen to others, and generously gives of herself. Her life has been transformed. She is *so* much healthier, and her enjoyment of living is beyond anything she ever expected.

**The difficulty in life is the choice.**
*George Moore*

Can this happen for you? We're convinced it can! You *can* reach the heights of emotional and spiritual health. And we can't wait to celebrate the process with you.

## ASSESSING YOUR PERSONAL HALLMARKS OF HEALTH

If you are like most people, you are probably wondering exactly where you stand in relation to our definition of health and wholeness. In an attempt to help you—and us—understand and use all three hallmarks of health, we developed a sophisticated instrument that will do just that.

Log on to the following address: **www.lovethelifeyoulive.com.** Follow the instructions and take the on-line self-assessment test before moving to the next chapter. Why? Because pinpointing where you stand on each of the hallmarks of health will be extremely valuable as you apply the information in the pages to come. For example, when you read the chapter on discovering your blind spots, you are far more likely to discover exactly how your particular blind spots may be preventing you from claiming your rightful significance or your personal freedom.

Measuring your personal health and wholeness is the first major step toward improving it. We hope you'll take a moment to do that right now, before you move into Secret #1.

The point is that measuring your personal health and wholeness is the first major step toward improving it. We hope you'll take a moment to do that right now, before you move into Secret #1.

*God loves each of us as if there is only one of us.*  AUGUSTINE

SECRET #1

TO FEELING GOOD—DEEP DOWN IN YOUR SOUL

◇

*Profound Significance*

Both of us had just stepped onto the platform in the Rose Garden Arena in Portland, Oregon, where nearly ten thousand people had assembled for a megamarriage seminar. That night each of the six speakers was to give a brief overview of what we would be speaking on over the next couple of days. Just before the rest of us went to the podium, our friend Gary Smalley captivated the crowd by holding up a crisp fifty-dollar bill and asking the massive audience, "Who would like this fifty-dollar bill?" Hands started going up everywhere. He said, "I am going to give this fifty dollars to one of you, but first let me do this." He proceeded to crumple up the bill. Then he asked, "Who still wants it?" The same hands went up in the air.

"Well," he replied, "what if I do this?" He dropped it on the ground and started to grind it into the floor with his shoe. He picked it up, all crumpled and dirty. "Now, who still wants it?" Again, hands went into the air. "You have all learned a valuable lesson," Gary said. "No matter what I do to the money, you still want it because it doesn't decrease in value. It is still worth fifty dollars."

Gary's simple illustration underscores a profound point. Many times in our lives we are dropped, crumpled, and ground into the dirt by the decisions we make or the circumstances that come our way. We may feel as though we are worthless, insignificant in our own and in others' eyes. But no matter what has happened or what will happen, we never lose our value if we choose to receive our significance.

Perhaps you've already internalized the message that crowd in Portland heard, and you already have a profound sense of significance. Maybe you already know at the center of your being, deep down in your soul, that your value is established for all time. Your *lovability,* and thus your significance, is rooted deep in God's unending love for you. You don't have to work harder, look better, or win prizes of any kind. You know and live the most crucial message ever articulated: that you have inestimable worth because you are a creation of the Creator.

Chances are, however, that even if you have experienced this significance at *some* time, you don't feel significant *all* the time. Research reveals that while many of us have heard this ancient truth about our worth, most of us, most of the time, don't incorporate it into our everyday lives. It doesn't really make a difference. We hear the message. We agree with it. And that's that. But instead of being unswervingly confident of our significance—feeling it resonate deep within our bones every day—we fall back into the habit of trying to earn it. Even if we agree that our Creator loves us, we still end up feeling better about ourselves only when we are winning the attention and approval of others.

We seem to be on a cosmic quest to *establish* our value—to prove it, earn it, deserve it—so we can *somehow* experience the ultimate feeling of inner well-being. And once we find what we're looking for, we relax—but only momentarily. Eventually the people we are pleasing—whether a parent, a spouse, a friend, an advisory board, or an audience—quit sending us *love messages*. Ultimately, we find ourselves back on our endless quest.

Finding the love of your life, for example, is a glorious experience, but it will not ultimately quench your thirst for significance. Neither will having children, as miraculous as that experience is. And neither will becoming famous, writing a best-seller, or building a successful company. Still, we run helter-skelter, always restless, desperate to find that next person, thing, or event that will satisfy our search. No wonder so many of us can identify with King Solomon's words: "Everything was meaningless, a chasing after the wind."

In all of our clinical work, we are astounded and saddened by the high majority of individuals who never experience their own deep sense of significance on a durable basis. It doesn't seem to matter how much they believe a set of doctrines, subscribe to a particular faith, or even share their *truth* with others. The fact is, they feel good about themselves when they *do* important things, *win* important promotions or prizes, *please* the crucial people, and thus *earn* the right to see themselves in a positive light. As soon as they quit doing, winning, pleasing, and earning, they feel awful about themselves.

You may, at times, feel positive about yourself. But if that feeling of significance comes and goes, and then you're back on the treadmill of *doing,* then you haven't yet grasped your true worth. And you're not alone. The most common addiction of all, we've found, is the endless internal compulsion to satisfy your frantic quest to feel good about yourself by simply making yourself worthy of positive self-assessments. In other words, you may have fallen for the "you have to *do* something in order to *be* someone" trap. You have to lose weight, climb the corporate ladder, birth a child, or become a leader.

But a deep, personal sense of significance is absolutely foundational to emotional health. Until you claim this significance at your core, you cannot be emotionally healthy. When you try to earn this significance and assume you deserve it because of your "success," you only gain an artificial and worthless variety of it. Such a gain really contributes *nothing* to your overall emotional health. In fact, it may well blind you to the fact that you don't feel intrinsically good about being you.

Why is it so hard to embrace the fact that profound personal significance is received, not achieved? Why are we so addicted to trying to prove our value? These questions have haunted the human race for centuries. Part of the answer, we believe, is that we are rarely given the tools to receive this truth in the deepest and most central parts of our beings—and this is exactly what we dedicate the next two chapters of this book to doing. We want you to have the time-tested tools for *really* embracing your personal significance. Whether you are starting from the ground up or are already well on your way, we want to show you exactly how to receive the greatest love of your life. It is the most important and foundational step to loving the life you live. It is the first time-tested step to feeling good—deep down in your soul.

Why? Because without profound significance you will be seduced by a cycle that is sure to leave you breathless. No matter how great the level of success, popularity, or power you achieve, the attention it garners will cause you to believe that whatever love has come your way is the result of what you do—not who you are. And you'll soon—inevitably—find yourself back where you started. Only this time little voices will conspire to keep you feeling anxious. However good you feel about yourself when you have achieved that good feeling, you are only a whisper away from feeling bad. When your work is criticized, your sense of value is directly affected. When you're left alone or abandoned, you see such situations as evidence of your worthlessness. Instead of trying to understand your limitations when you fall short, you blame yourself, ironically, not for what you *did,* but for who you *are.*

Feelings of inferiority make little distinction between who you are and what you do. And when you lack a profound sense of significance, you will spend at least half your time feeling inferior. Fundamentally, though, whether you feel momentarily good or bad, anxiety will haunt your life. You will never be far from despair.

But that doesn't have to be the life you choose. You *can* have a life you love—a life of profound significance—if you have the tools. So let's take a quick look at the two most important ones.

First, you will need to tune in to your "self-talk." Your internal dialogue is key to learning exactly how you feel about you. It is an indispensable tool in learning to let love capture your being. What you say to yourself is the most important conversation you have all day. Yet precious few pay attention to it. And only the most well-adjusted know how to monitor their inner voice for the sake of accepting their own significance. The next chapter will let you in on their secrets.

Second, we'll take a look at your past—the factors that have affected you and may still be affecting you. Why? Because this is the biggest obstacle to those wanting to embrace their significance. Pain from the past, for example, can keep some of us so stuck that we stay there forever. That's why, in chapter 5 we help you unpack your emotional baggage. You will be amazed by how the step-by-step exercises in this particular chapter can help you get unstuck and move more quickly than you imagined on your journey of personal growth. So get ready. We are going to help you identify any personal obstacles from your own history and then get you moving on, past whatever may be holding you down from your past.

We'll say it again. Personal significance is the first time-tested step to feeling good—deep down in your soul. It is the foundational prerequisite to loving the life you live. You can never live to the fullest, never enjoy relationships at their peak, until you experience a permanent and profound sense of significance deep in the core of your being. Only then will you hear a voice that reverberates in every corner of your personality saying, "I've known you from the beginning and have called you by name. I knitted you together in your mother's womb and counted every hair on your head. Wherever you go, I go with you, and I'll never abandon you or hide my face from you. You belong to me, and I belong to you. You are marked by my love, and you are the pride of my life. Nothing will ever separate us."

# 4

# TUNING IN TO YOUR SELF-TALK

*Thinking is the talking of the soul with itself.*

PLATO

*I*f you bugged yourself, what would you hear?

Can you imagine having an internal recorder that could actually replay what you say when no one else is listening? What would it do for you to come home at the end of the day and download the recordings of conversations you had with yourself over the last several hours? What phrases would you hear more than once? Would your self-statements be positive or negative? And if you could do such a thing, what would listening to these internal tapes teach you?

First, you would almost certainly be surprised, maybe even shocked, if you listened in. The fact is, most of the time we have little conscious awareness of our own internal dialogue. And yet this "self-talk" has a huge impact on how you feel about yourself. It is the single most important determiner of whether or not you feel profound significance at your core. Your self-talk is a primary tool for realizing your lovability and thus your significance—even in the most mundane moments of your daily life.

For example, imagine you're on your way home at the end of a long day. You can't stop thinking about a painful conversation you had with a colleague. The whole scene flashes before you again. Three or four sharply worded comments fly from your mouth, and your colleague's face gets red, her lips narrow, her eyes fill with tears, and her voice grows soft and quiet. She's genuinely hurt, and she doesn't know how to handle what you said. It bothers you all the way home and then, even when you are at home, you feel remorseful and embarrassed.

What was going on with you? Let's rerun your internal tape and find out.

Put yourself back in the lunchroom, back in the middle of the conversation. Listen in to what you were saying to yourself: *This conversation isn't going very well. I don't think she respects me much. I think she's coming down on me. I've got to straighten her out before I lose more of her respect.*

So *this* is why your words came out so fast—and so sharply?

What we know scientifically is that you *can* actually bug your own inner conversations. You can listen in to your internal dialogue and use it to bolster, like never before, your significance. We want to show you how.

## WHY IS SELF-TALK SO IMPORTANT?

When the two of us first began a serious exploration of psychological health and wholeness, we knew that a person's profound sense of significance was the most important foundational principle of all. And we were immediately aware that people cannot have a profound sense of their own significance until they develop a level of self-talk that generally promotes this indispensable inner conviction.

The fact is, if individuals do not have a durable sense of their profound significance, they will be vulnerable to *deals* with every false source of inner worth and significance. The only source of true significance is the one that emanates from a living and caring

God, but this *good news* about what is true in the larger reality does us no good at all until we accept it and continue to reinforce it through the way we speak to ourselves.

In a world that is so committed to the idea that self-worth is a consequence of various kinds of achievement, this idea of self-worth being a gift that merely needs to be accepted and held by faith is a difficult one to maintain. In every life circumstance, the challenge for every human being is to believe in the fact of their own intrinsic significance, given freely by God, and then to reinforce it moment by moment, day by day. Without this reinforcement, the constant message of the world about contingent worth is too hard to resist. Most of us, at one time or another, need to be encouraged or reminded about the powerful effect of the inner dialogue.

Healthy persons are keenly aware of what they say to themselves, how they say it, and when they say it. Moreover, they know that tuning in to self-talk unlocks the secret to emotional contentment, personal fulfillment, optimal performance, and profound significance. Healthy people use rational self-talk as their passport to new friendships, success, and dignity.

> **I have come that they may have life, and have it to the full.**
>
> *Jesus, in John 10:10*

So we dedicate this chapter to helping you tune in to your self-talk. We'll begin with its origins, revealing how your brain, deep down in its many folds and crevices, holds the most important conversations you ever have. We'll also explain, in a larger context, what self-talk is and why its value is difficult to exaggerate. Next we'll show you how to accurately assess your internal dialogue and discover precisely what you are saying to yourself in certain situations. We'll draw a line between the best and the worst kinds of self-talk so you can see the difference. And finally, we'll zero in on practical and meaningful ways to improve your self-talk. You'll learn how to monitor your inner voice and develop the mental muscle to make your self-talk work *for* you, rather than against you.

## THE ORIGINS OF SELF-TALK

On the campus of UCLA is a ten-story building called Slichter Hall, known by most as the Brain Research Institute (BRI). It houses 135 research laboratories where some of the world's most renowned neuroscientists do their brain research. And according to its director, its central mission involves one of the most fascinating tasks in the world—to train the human brain to scrutinize itself. The BRI attempts to use intelligence for the purpose of understanding the source and workings of the human mind. As they put it, "the human mind is what the brain does." So they study the brain to understand the mind.

It is a formidable undertaking. Not even the universe, with its countless billions of galaxies, represents greater wonder or complexity than the human brain. Consider this: If the brain of an average fifty-year-old could be fully emptied of all the impressions and memories it has stored, and if they could be recorded on tape, the length of the tape would reach to the moon and back several times! Truth be told, the contents of the human brain could never be fully inventoried or identified. The neurons of the human brain make the silicon chips and semiconductors that have been hailed as supreme technological achievements look like child's play.

As recently as 1950, brain researchers thought they were being extravagant when they guessed there might be as many as a billion neurons in the human brain. Today the estimates range from 50 to 100 billion. These neurons carry the traffic for millions of signals. As you read the words on this page, your brain sets off millions of electrochemical reactions to accurately understand and assimilate the information. When you visualize the face of a friend or recall what you had for lunch yesterday, the same process occurs. In short, numberless signals are flashing almost every second of our waking hours.

The brain is the only organ of the body that's totally essential for individual identity. If you have a defective kidney, liver, or heart, you can acquire a transplant and still retain your sense of self. But if you were to acquire a new brain, you would acquire a new personality. You would have a different set of memories, a different vocabulary, different aspirations. You'd also experience different emotions—a new way of thinking as well as feeling. With a new brain you would acquire a new mind. In short, assuming that medical science could solve the incredibly complex problems involved in a brain transplant, you would be somebody else in the same skin.

Clearly the power of the human brain is unmistakable. It does nothing less than preside over who you are.

And that is precisely why self-talk—what you say to yourself and how you interpret that inner dialogue—is paramount to personal growth and well-being. Self-talk not only originates in the mind, it could be argued that the human mind *is* self-talk. At the risk of oversimplifying the majesty of the mind, you can think of it as a composition of intricate internal conversations. The brain is a circuitry of complex communication, relaying millions of messages at any moment. And these messages determine who you are. They have a direct impact not only on your body, but on your psyche and your spirit as well. Your very personality is defined by your internal messages.

> I think,
> therefore I am.
> *Descartes*

Your psychological state—whether confident and hopeful or insecure and cynical—is played out through a series of electrochemical connections in your brain that determine your mental state. In other words, *you* prescribe, to a large degree, what your brain does by what you say when no one's listening. And, over time, the secret messages you shoot repeatedly through your mind begin to cut a groove or wear a path through your cortex. The routine and habitual nature of these messages make them prominent, so they achieve a higher priority than other messages. These governing messages, the ones that are heard most loudly, most often, and most quickly, are the ones that define your self-talk. These are the messages we intend to examine and understand and influence through this chapter.

## WHAT IS SELF-TALK?

On a downtown bus just pulling up to its stop, a woman stands, slaps the face of the man next to her, and hurries to the exit. Each passenger who sees this happen reacts in his or her own way. A middle-aged man feels sad for the man who was slapped. A younger woman is frightened. A teenage boy is angry. Another woman feels excited. How could the same event trigger such an array of varying emotions? The answer is found in self-talk.

The middle-aged man who reacts with sadness thinks, *He's lost her, and he'll never get her back.*

The fearful woman thinks, *She is really going to pay a price for that tonight when he sees her at home.*

The angry teenager says to himself, *She humiliated him; like most women, she must be a real jerk.*

The woman who feels excited says to herself, *Serves him right. What a strong woman; I wish I was more like that.*

In each case the event is almost instantaneously interpreted, judged, and labeled. And the individual's unique self-explanation results in a distinctive emotional experience—sadness, fear, anger, or excitement. Truth is, the emotional consequence of an event like this varies as much as the people observing it.

All of us, every minute of every hour, hold an unending dialogue with ourselves, a dialogue that colors every experience. You could compare this dialogue to a waterfall of thoughts cascading down the back of your mind. The thoughts are rarely noticed, but they continually shape your attitudes, emotions, and outlook.

> **Men are not worried by things, but by their ideas about things. When we meet difficulties, become anxious or troubled, let us not blame others, but rather ourselves, that is: our idea about things.**
>
> Epictetus, about A.D. 60

Self-talk is typically not spoken aloud, but its message is more piercing than any audible voice. What's more, it is reflexive. Automatic. Self-talk occurs without any prior reflection or reasoning, yet your brain instantly sees it as plausible and valid.

That means your self-talk need not be accurate. In fact, for many of us it rarely is. But that doesn't hinder the mind from acting as if it were.

In 1955 a little-known professor of psychology at Rutgers University was building a counseling practice. But he was also growing increasingly disillusioned with the traditional methods of treatment. Psychoanalysis, in his opinion, was too costly, too long, and too out of touch with how people change. So he gave up psychoanalysis entirely and began his own brand of therapy with the founding of his Institute for Rational Living. Albert Ellis, the now ninety-year-old founder, still travels the country holding workshops on his famed Rational-Emotive Therapy. Ellis was the first to use the term *self-talk*—a word that is part of our common vocabulary today.

But do we know what it really means—and how it profoundly impacts our significance?

To begin with, *self-talk is personal and specific.* Thomas, a college senior, has been sitting next to Tina in their English literature class all semester. And all semester Thomas has entertained thoughts of asking her out. On several occasions he has started to do just that but has been stopped in his tracks. *She doesn't want to go out with me,* he says to himself. And that puts an end to his efforts. Notice that Thomas is not saying, *Women are intimidating,* or even *Tina doesn't like going out.* He is zeroing in on one specific thought that relates to him: *Tina doesn't want to go out with me.*

*Self-talk is concise.* It is often composed of just a few words or even a brief visual image. Just two words—*Chico Way*—immediately engender inadequacy in me when I (Les) slip them into the crevices of my cortex. They tie into a miserable decision I made several years ago that eventually cost me a hefty financial price. It was one of the worst decisions I have ever made. Up to that point I had thought I was pretty good at making important decisions . . . until *Chico Way* shattered my confidence. And since then, when I am in the throes of a significant decision, such as how to invest money, those two words, *Chico Way,* creep up on me and immediately pull me down.

That's the nature of self-talk. It's concise. One word or a short phrase becomes shorthand for a group of self-reproaches, fears, or memories. And not one of us is immune to its power.

*Self-talk is quick and spontaneous.* While waiting at a red light you see a woman struggling to open the front door to an apartment while holding a baby in one arm and a bag of groceries in the other. At that very moment you see a man in a tailored suit walk right past her without even giving her a glance, let alone a helping hand. You quickly think, *Typical rich guy, not caring for anyone but himself.* The judgment is as real to you as your visual impression. When the light turns green, you're on your way. What you don't see is that the "rich guy" is completely blind. But after passing the woman, he hears the baby's cry and returns to offer help as best he can.

It's the nature of self-talk to waste no time in rushing to judgment.

*Self-talk is believed, no matter how irrational.* We both do a great deal of public speaking and more than once have shared the same platform with other speakers at a major arena event with thousands in the audience. This experience is always charged with eager excitement and anticipation. Backstage, there's a lot of laughter, prayer, encouragement, and a fair degree of nervous energy. Once the event is over and the speaker team is in a van headed to the airport, the predictable question eventually emerges: "So, how do you think it went?" That's when every professional speaker analyzes everything from the audience response to the temperature of the arena. The outline of the program is picked over, and the timing of our jokes is evaluated.

> **It is very obvious that we are not influenced by "facts" but by our interpretation of the facts.**
> *Alfred Adler*

And if any speaker is feeling insecure, this is when it shows. "I really missed the mark today," a speaker might say out loud. Of course we counter the comment with a heavy dose of praise. But if the speaker believes his own self-talk *(I did a terrible job)* it will do little good. He could literally have received a standing ovation from thousands, but if he feels he didn't meet his own standards, he genuinely thinks he's failed.

Irrational? You bet. But that's self-talk.

*Self-talk is learned.* When I (Neil) was growing up, I was treated like a prince. Although I was a total mistake, being born to parents when they had virtually finished raising two older sisters, my family members treated me like the only one who mattered. So naturally I learned to say to myself that I was a prince and the only one who mattered. The message was reinforced when I went to kindergarten in a tiny country school and was the only child in my class.

Then, when I was nine, our family moved to California. Soon the well-learned internal message was contradicted by a flood of experiences in a new and huge school. However, this early message never went totally away . . . at least not until Marylyn and I were married. In the early days of our marriage I didn't know how to tell her that I was a prince and the only one who mattered, but I showed her dozens of times by my self-centered behavior. Fortunately, Marylyn was far too healthy to put up with the consequences of my long-learned internal message. She carefully held a mirror up to me, made my selfishness crystal clear even to me, and the combination of my desire to be unselfish and Marylyn's unwillingness to enable my earlier behavior led to a sudden change in my approach. Even to this day, that old, learned, internal message—*you're a prince, and you're the only one who really matters*—whispers its false truths in my ear. But in partnership with Marylyn's sturdy resistance and my own deep wishes, I am able to mobilize my logical powers all over again.

> **Feelings are simply what we say to ourselves about our experiences.**
>
> *Charles T. Brown*

This aspect of self-talk, of course, is the most encouraging. Why? Because if irrational self-talk can be learned, it can be *unlearned* too.

To sum up, self-talk, the automatic thoughts that cut a groove in our brain, is personal and specific, concise, quick and spontaneous, believed, and learned. With this understanding, we'll explore next why these self-statements are so important.

## WHY SELF-TALK MATTERS

Take a few minutes to press the rewind button on your mental tape player. Review a conversation you had with someone today. It may have been early this morning, as your two-year-old woke you up from a sound sleep. Or it could have been as you arrived at work. Perhaps it was over lunch with a friend or at a family dinner. Replay as much of the conversation as you can. . . .

Now rewind your mental tape player to review the messages you sent yourself during that same interchange. . . .

Did those inner conversations come to mind as readily? Not if you are like most people. Most of us recall far more clearly the words we speak aloud than the words we speak to ourselves. So does that make our "outward dialogue" more important and lasting than our "inner dialogue"?

Consider the facts. Approximately 70 percent of our waking day is spent in one or more types of communication. You speak out loud at the rate of 150 to 200 words per minute. Research suggests that you talk privately to yourself, however, at the rate of approximately 1,300 words per minute. And this internal conversation is never turned off; it runs even while you sleep, monitoring your thoughts and feelings of significance and also influencing your hopes and dreams. In essence, your self-talk is forming *who you are.*

We are constantly feeding our brain with information. Most of it is reflexive—messages that coordinate our muscles to walk or reach for a pen, for example. And then there is the self-talk that serves our daily activities like, *I need to stop at the cleaners.* But the self-talk that impacts our psychological state is just as plentiful. At any given moment we say things to ourselves in rapid-fire succession that impact our well-being— our emotions, our energy level, our optimism or pessimism. Does this matter? You could say it is a matter of life or death, literally. And following are a couple of clear examples, taken from real-life stories.

## A MATTER OF LIFE AND DEATH

A man was traveling across the country by sneaking rides on freight trains. One particular night he climbed into what looked like a boxcar and closed the door. With the jolt of the train, the door locked shut, and he was trapped inside. As his eyes adjusted to the darkness, he must have noticed how chilly it was and then discovered he was inside a refrigerated boxcar. He probably hollered for help and pounded the walls, but all the noise he could make inside the car failed to attract anyone's attention. Eventually the man gave up and lay down on the floor of the railroad car, shivering.

Evidently believing he would soon freeze to death, he scratched part of a message on the floor of the car. He never finished. Sometime late the next day, repairmen from the railroad opened the door of the refrigerated boxcar and found the man dead. He appeared to have frozen to death. But the very reason for the repairmen's arrival was that the refrigeration units on the car were not working. It turns out the temperature inside the car never went below fifty degrees during the night—not nearly cold enough to kill a man. So why did the man die? Because he *told* himself he was freezing to death.

*Okay,* you say, *but that's just one dramatic story communicators use to illustrate a point.* Maybe so. But consider another example that's well-documented in research literature, one that has been replicated in different forms tens of thousands of times.

It all started nearly fifty years ago, when a team of doctors reported a single incident that stunned medical researchers. It all had to do with Mr. Wright, who was suffering from cancer of the lymph system and had developed large tumors throughout his body. At the time a group of physicians was studying a new chemical formula called krebiozen, which was being widely touted by the media as a miracle cure for cancer, although the medical establishment was less convinced. Wright's cancer was so far advanced that the physicians gave him the drug only as a compassionate exception—not because they expected any response. However, what happened next seemed nearly miraculous. Wright gained weight, looked and felt better, and his tumors shrank so drastically, they could hardly be detected.

Wright's improvement continued until the newspapers began reporting that krebiozen was not the great advance they had thought. After reading the negative coverage, Wright became discouraged and immediately began to lose weight. His tumors grew once more.

But the story doesn't end there. Mr. Wright's physicians quickly recognized the power of his self-talk and decided to influence it. They told him that the first batches of krebiozen had not been at full potency. The lab had corrected the problem, they assured him, and the new, stronger batch of the drug would soon be on its way. They continued to encourage Wright's hopes, finally announcing that the big day was here—the new batch of the drug had arrived. They then proceeded to give Wright injections just as before . . . but this time they used only sterile water.

Wright showed the same dramatic improvements that had occurred with the krebiozen. His remission lasted until, for a second time, the newspapers undermined the physicians, stating unequivocally, "AMA reports that krebiozen is worthless against cancer." Once again Mr. Wright began to sink physically and his tumors grew massive. Shortly thereafter, he died.

## THE UNDENIABLE POWER OF SELF-TALK

If you want proof that self-talk matters, you need look no further than the placebo effect. It definitively shows that what we say to ourselves holds unbridled power. Abundant medical research has proven that what we think commands the brain to produce unassailable changes in the body's chemistry, either setting the stage for intensified illness or quicker recovery. So it stands to reason that if what we say in our brain can influence our bodies, what we say in our brain can impact our soul as well. If our self-talk impacts our physical well-being, imagine how it impacts our emotional health . . . our feelings of significance.

Actually, you need not imagine it at all. The impact of self-talk on our emotions has been studied for decades from every angle, researched across cultures, and documented in countless scholarly journals and numerous professional presentations. A mountain of research has shown us that what you say to yourself, how you explain and interpret the world around you, creates your emotional state. In a very real sense, *what you say and think to yourself becomes what you feel.*

Imagine walking along a jungle path at twilight and hearing a lion roar. Your muscles tense, a knot forms in your stomach, and you can taste the fear rising in your throat. Why? Because in a split second, you say something to this effect: *I'm in extreme danger. I could be attacked by a lion!* This self-talk not only sets up a series of biological responses, it creates fright and even panic.

Now imagine walking along a path at the San Diego Zoo at the same time of the evening and hearing the same sound. This time, of course, you barely flinch. Why? Because in a split second, you say to yourself, *There's no cause for alarm. The lion is secured in his own cage.* The very same stimulus, the roar, elicits very different emotional responses because of your self-talk.

*This is all good and well,* you may be saying, *but what difference does this make in my desire to become a more psychologically whole individual?* We're glad you asked. For this is the bottom line: Healthy people have learned how to harness the power of self-talk to control and manage their emotions, stay in contact with reality, focus their intentions, and optimize their potential. How? It begins by assessing just what their self-talk is saying.

> **The first order of business of anyone who wants to enjoy success in all areas of his or her life is to take charge of the internal dialogue they have and only think, say, and behave in a manner consistent with the results they truly desire.**
>
> *Sidney Madwed*

✦ ✦ ✦

## ASSESSING YOUR SELF-TALK

You've probably heard the old adage: "There's nothing wrong with talking to yourself. But when you start answering back, it's time to worry." Whoever came up with this quip was wrong. Talking aloud to yourself in public isn't a sign of positive mental health, but holding an internal dialogue is not only normal, it's useful. Your inner conversations have a powerful impact on your emotional well-being. Becoming aware of exactly what you are saying *to* yourself *about* yourself can help you understand why you react the way you do to events and people in your life. It can help you figure out who you are, control your moods, repeat your successes, and short-circuit your shortcomings.

The key, of course, is to uncover exactly what you are saying when you talk to yourself. The following is a quick self-talk test that will help you zero in on your internal dialogue. Take as much time as you need to honestly answer these ten questions and when you are finished, we'll help you identify your self-talk style.

1. You are hosting a dinner party and everything goes pretty well, except for dessert, when you realize you forgot to pick up the pastry shells for the ice cream. At the end of the evening you are most likely to say to yourself:
   a. *Who cares? The evening was a great success.*
   b. *Sure, the dinner party went all right, but dessert was a failure.*
   c. *I ruined everything when I didn't remember to go to the bakery.*

2. You have a project at work that requires your team's support, and you are very eager and excited to get moving on it. At a meeting, however, one of your colleagues raises numerous questions about your idea and suggests you hold off until the team has more time to think about it. You most likely say to yourself:
   a. *He might have a good point.*
   b. *He doesn't trust me.*
   c. *He is either for me or against me.*

3. The words that most aptly describe your internal dialogue about yourself are
   a. Positive and upbeat

b. Neutral and on the fence

c. Negative and critical

4. You've just made a major mistake at work that potentially cost the company a major sale. You are most likely to say to yourself in the next day or two:

   a. *I may have made a mistake, but I'm still a worthwhile person.*

   b. *I never measure up to the person I want to be.*

   c. *I'm worthless.*

5. You enjoy a much needed outing with friends. When you arrive home, you find your spouse sprawled on the couch watching television, and leftover pizza and stacks of dirty plates and cups on the kitchen counter. You most likely say to yourself:

   a. *My spouse must be exhausted. I'll whip those dishes into shape and then relax on the couch too.*

   b. *I never get to go out by myself. Couldn't my spouse at least be courteous enough to clean up this one time?*

   c. *I should never have gone out. Things completely fall apart when I'm gone.*

6. When you were a kid, what kind of messages did you most often receive from your parents?

   a. Encouraging and loving messages

   b. An equal amount of encouraging and critical messages

   c. Critical and hurtful messages

7. You are headed out for the evening and want to wear one of your favorite shirts, which is in the final cycle in your washing machine. You put it in the dryer and the dryer shorts out. It's completely dead—no power. And your shirt is completely wet. You realize it won't be dry in time to wear. You most likely say to yourself:

   a. *No problem, I'll wear something else.*

   b. *It never fails. This always happens to me.*

   c. *I can't stand this. My whole evening is ruined.*

8. You are needing a helping hand to move some heavy furniture and wondering about asking a friend. What thought is most likely to shoot through your brain?

a. *I'm pretty sure he can help, and if not, he'll say so.*

b. *Am I pushing the limits of this friendship too far?*

c. *I don't deserve to have anyone help me, and I better not even ask.*

9. Your tennis opponent says out loud to himself, "What a lousy shot!" You are most likely to

a. Say, "You're being too hard on yourself"

b. Remain silent

c. Say, "You're right; I've seen better"

10. In general, the internal conversation you have with yourself most days tends to

a. Help you experience more fully and consistently your profound significance

b. Go back and forth between helping and hindering your experience of profound significance

c. Keep you from experiencing your profound significance

## SCORING

If you answered mainly *a,* it's safe to say that your self-talk is based on a solid sense of significance. You tend to consistently see things in their proper perspective and rarely punish yourself for mistakes. Your self-talk is based on the reality of the situation. If your shirt is wet, for example, you simply choose another shirt. No big deal. Also, your negative situations don't tend to elicit a negative emotional response. This is a sure sign of well-schooled self-talk. Plus if you make a mistake, you don't see *yourself* as a mistake—a sure sign of profound significance. In general, you are secure in yourself and enjoy a depth of self-worth. You have learned to use your self-talk as a tool to maintain your dignity and significance. Of course, if nearly every one of your answers was in this category, you may want to review how honest you are being with yourself. Rarely does a person answer every item like this.

If you answered mainly *b,* your self-talk tends to be more negative than is beneficial. While you are not likely to punish yourself for very long with a condemning internal dialogue, you certainly are not using your self-talk to maximize your experience of profound significance. You are literally talking yourself out of the full enjoyment of being loved at your core. There is much you can learn to improve your self-talk, and the remainder of this chapter will help you do just that.

If you answered mainly *c,* your self-talk shows signs of needing serious attention and repair. In all likelihood, you are suffering from a low sense of self-worth, and your self-talk is keeping at bay any chance of experiencing profound significance. Almost reflexively, you immediately equate any failure or bad experience to your own "badness." You have a very difficult time separating who you are from what you do. No doubt, you already know your internal dialogue is repeatedly sabotaging your ability to receive your significance and worth. What can you do? Plenty. The remainder of this chapter is dedicated to helping you improve your self-talk. We will show you how you can begin to maximize it in numerous ways.

Are the results of a self-test like this generalizations? Of course. Since we aren't meeting with you one-on-one, face-to-face, we don't have the luxury of examining unique nuances and subtleties of how you use or abuse your self through internal dialogue. However, this simple self-test can at least help you *identify* your general tendencies so that you can get the most possible out of this chapter.

✦   ✦   ✦

## THE BEST KIND OF SELF-TALK

Both of us are ardent admirers of Winston Churchill, and no one's self-talk contributed more to his eventual world leadership than Churchill's. Although his life was racked by emotional neglect, parental hypocrisy, and excessive expectations, he kept saying the right things to himself. He kept believing in himself and in his profound significance as a human being.

After slogging through failure after failure in his early education, Churchill's inner conversation eventually made a survivor of him. And this internal dialogue was best revealed in a commencement speech he made at Oxford. Approaching the podium with his trademark cigar, cane, and top hat, his entire speech consisted of only six words—six words that had clearly cut a groove and worn a path in his cortex. Gazing steadily at his waiting audience, Churchill finally shouted with the confidence of long experience, "Never give up!" Several seconds passed before he rose to his toes and shouted again, "Never give up!" Then he slowly reached for his top hat and his cigar, steadied himself with his cane, and left the platform. In those few words he had shared the most powerful advice he had to share— the personal self-talk that had carried him from mediocrity to maximum achievement.

> **Change your thoughts and you change your world.**
> *Norman Vincent Peale*

And those same words—"Never give up!"—can carry *you* to maximum achievement today.

But don't confuse positive self-talk with happy affirmations— or even worse, self-delusion. Let's say you can't carry a tune. You simply don't have much musical ability with your voice. If you tell yourself that if you only try harder, you can learn to be a virtuoso, that self-talk would be excessively positive . . . but flawed. If you tell yourself that you're no good at singing, your self-talk would be negative but not flawed. On the other hand, if you say to yourself that you can't do anything right (because you can't sing), that would be flawed, overgeneralized thinking.

The best kind of self-talk is not self-hype or excessively positive. Nor is it negative, flawed, or overgeneralized. It is logical, rational, and accurate.

In a landmark study, Stanford University's Albert Bandura, internationally known for his work in the study of personality, showed that while the vast majority of us spend lots of time worrying about things we can't control, healthy and successful people attend primarily to those things that are relevant and within their control.

So let's make this clear. The best kind of self-talk is the kind that says, *I choose my responses, they don't choose me.* It says, *No thought can dwell in my mind without my permission.* It says, *My value does not equal my performance.*

## THE WORST KIND OF SELF-TALK

While the news of Martin Luther King Jr.'s assassination in Memphis in 1968 understandably made headlines around the world, there was another death associated with his murder that few have heard about. It was the wife of the owner of the motel where King was staying. On hearing the news of the murder, the woman collapsed and died the next day.

Death from emotional shock is rare, but it underscores how lethal our internal thinking can be. Who knows what self-talk this poor woman invented upon learning this news? What we do know is that some forms of self-talk are far more damaging than others. These are the statements that stem from our negative inner voice, our pathological critic.

Rhonda, a twenty-nine-year-old mother of two, let herself have it the other night. "I was looking forward to a hot shower after a hectic day, but as I was getting undressed, I knocked over a bathroom plant. There was dirt and pottery everywhere, and I found myself saying, 'Rhonda, why are you so clumsy?' I don't even speak to my children that way!"

Most often this vicious and vocal critic compares you to others, their achievements and abilities. It sets up impossible standards and then tears you down for not meeting them. It calls you names: stupid, incompetent, ugly, selfish, weak. Your negative inner voice tells you your friends are bored, your spouse is annoyed, your parents are disappointed, your colleagues are disgusted. Your pathological critic, if not tamed, will undermine your dignity and significance at every turn. And according to some experts, as much as 77 percent of the average person's self-talk is negative.

Consider this scenario. Your boss calls you into his office and asks you to present your vision for the company's new advertising campaign. "I've called a special meeting of the board of directors and I want them to hear from you and a couple other of our employees." At first you are flattered. Then you start thinking, *I'm terrible in front of groups. I stumble all over my words. I'll end up a fool.* Your face doesn't show it. Your boss only knows he has just given you an enviable assignment.

Or did he? *Maybe he wants to see me fail,* you begin to reason. *Maybe he wants the board to see what an idiot I am so he can fire me.* Walking back to your office you snap out of it. *That's silly,* you say. *I'm overreacting—why do I do that? I'm so stupid.*

That night over dinner your spouse congratulates you on your opportunity, but you say to yourself, *She doesn't know the real me; I'm such a fraud.* You're up so late working on your remarks that you actually consider declining your boss's request. *But then he'd see me as the loser I really am,* you tell yourself.

This steady stream of poison feels normal and true if you have given credence to such internal lies. Your pathological critic could not be more toxic. Truly, it is more poisonous to your psychological health than almost any trauma or loss. That's because grief and pain normally diminish over time, but the critic, if not curbed, is always with you—judging, blaming, and finding fault. *There you go again,* says the internal critic, *being an idiot.*

If you too often fall victim to your pathological critic, if it is eroding your self-worth, there is hope. We have a plan. We have a way to shut your internal condemnation down for good. But first you need to be able to identify your self-talk style.

## MONITORING YOUR INNER VOICE

If you were to sum up all your self-talk statements and put the negative ones on one side of the scale and the positive ones on the other, which would win out? For many of us, it would be the negative statements.

But truth be told, how many are on each side of the scale may not matter. We've found that one negative self-statement can undo dozens of positive ones if it is expressed at an important moment. That's why it is particularly valuable to monitor your inner voice in situations that often elicit a negative tone.

A telltale sign of self-sabotage occurs when what is happening to you doesn't jibe with what you expect.

Here's an example. Kara, a single woman, goes to a party, hoping to find a date. But she expects men to approach her. Why? *Nice women don't start conversations with strange men.* On top of that, she tells herself, *I won't have to work at small talk if it's the right guy.* So she sits in one place most of the evening, never initiating conversation. And when a man approaches, she talks very little and waits for the proverbial sparks to fly. At the end of the party she goes home confused, insecure, and depressed. There are no dates in her future.

> This is my prayer: that your love may abound more and more in knowledge and depth of insight, so that you may be able to discern what is best and may be pure and blameless.
>
> *The apostle Paul, in Philippians 1:9-10*

If Kara examines her self-talk, she might realize she is her own worst enemy when it comes to finding a date. She might alter her self-talk to say, *There's nothing wrong with starting a conversation with a man I think might be interesting. It may take time to find a good match—and that's okay.* This kind of self-talk would completely change Kara's next party experience.

As clinical psychologists, we have talked intimately with several thousand individuals, couples, and families. They have told us all about their self-talk—times when it was constructive and times when it sabotaged their lives. While well over 90 percent of this self-talk was clearly beyond the borders of their consciousness, most of these people were shocked to discover the sneaky little tricks they played on themselves in these internal conversations.

Our collective memory as therapists can recall dozens of these dialogues.

Some people tried to take the risk out of every moment by telling themselves not to expect much. For instance, *If I don't expect her to like me, I won't get hurt.* Or, *I haven't seen my father in years. You'd think he'd at least phone me or send a card on my birthday. But I've learned not to expect much.* And by doing so, they reduced their chances significantly that much—if anything—would happen. In these scenarios, relationships don't have much of a chance for renewal because they are booby-trapped by self-talk before they can even get off the ground.

Others carried on loud shouting matches inside their heads. *You are so stupid! You never do anything right! Why don't you give up and just let someone else take over? Anybody would be better suited to this task than you!* These inner "words" were so overwhelming that these people couldn't even focus well on the complex matters confronting them.

Have you ever used the "low expectation" or "shouting match" self-talk techniques? When you begin monitoring your own inner voice, you almost always encounter a gold mine of crucial data that can explain your behavior, help you revolutionize your performance, and set you on the track of "cleaner" and more constructive relationships.

## HOW TO IMPROVE YOUR SELF-TALK

Once you recognize the potency of your self-talk, you are immediately motivated to maximize its contribution to your emotional, physical, and spiritual health. And we guarantee that you can use your inner conversations for your good, leading to some stunning personal growth. By identifying and correcting the messages in your self-talk, you will begin to feel, perhaps for the first time, your profound significance—to yourself, to others, and to God.

But your self-talk must directly reflect the primary decisions you have made about your life. If you don't say the right things to yourself, you'll go nowhere, or worse, you will travel like a rocket in the wrong direction.

Let us tell you precisely what we mean.

If you frequently say to yourself, *As soon as I . . .* , you may be in grave danger of doing yourself in. Far too often, *As soon as I* is followed by something like *get my weight under control,* or *get my husband communicating with me,* or *get married,* or *get the big promotion,* and then comes the telltale follow-up: *then I will feel good about myself,* or *then my life will be worth living,* or *then I will experience my value.*

> Until you value yourself, you won't value your time. Until you value your time, you will not do anything with it.
>
> M. Scott Peck

Our careful research with married people and single people, young people and old people, shy people and assertive people—in short, *all* people—reveals unmistakably that self-talk that emerges from a conditional sense of inner worth will lead you down a path to paralyzing anxiety and eventual disillusionment. Healthy people have a deep and confident sense of their own worth—at the most fundamental levels of their being. They believe wholeheartedly that God created them for a particular purpose ("All the days ordained for me were written in your book before one of them came to be"), and that he knows them intimately and loves them. They think of themselves as "wonderfully made." They have what we call *intrinsic* worth. And if you ask them how long they have had this uncompromising inner experience, they can tell you the very moment they first experienced it. Seldom, but sometimes, they have had it all their conscious life . . . and so they say "from the moment of my conception."

When a person who feels this way about her intrinsic value talks to herself, she doesn't focus on the good feeling about herself that she will have *if* . . . Her perceived value as a person is not conditional on anything. It simply *is,* and it influences everything about her inner experience.

And so she will frequently say to herself things like:

- *How can I do this in the best way?*
- *How can I make a decision about this that I will be comfortable with in the future?*
- *I want to live from moment to moment in a way that will be free of worry, brutally honest about the facts but maximally optimistic; and I want to deeply enjoy the process of my life.*

Note that all anxiety is stripped from this kind of self-talk. When you reach the point where you believe that your value and your worth are intrinsic, everything about your self-talk takes on a positive, future-focus sound. Anxiety vanishes.

Take time now to evaluate your own self-talk with the "Self-Talk Check" exercise on the next page.

Is monitoring your self-talk easy? Certainly not at the beginning. But be encouraged—with practice and reflection, you'll see gradual improvement. And over time, you'll become amazed at your skill. Your self-dialogue will become controlled but passionate, many-sided but ultimately unified.

Your primary relationships will become more rich and vital. You will be less defensive, more interpersonally caring, consistently generous, and maximally attractive for all the right reasons. The more you master your self-talk, the more you will embrace your profound significance—and you will be on your way to becoming *genuinely* healthy and whole.

———————————— S E L F - T A L K   C H E C K ————————————

The next time you feel yourself beginning to react emotionally to a situation or person, try the following first:

1. Identify the situation. For instance, *Here I am, stuck in traffic again.*
2. Identify what you're saying to yourself about that situation through your self-talk.

   ~ Is it realistic? *Of course. I should expect rush-hour traffic to slow me down at 4:30 P.M.*
   ~ Is it negative? *What's my problem? I should have left earlier—I knew better than this.*
   ~ Is it self-condemning? *I'm so dumb sometimes. Why didn't I take a different road? Now I'm going to be late for dinner, and they're going to be angry.*

3. Take a deep breath. Then say to yourself, *The reality is, I am stuck in traffic. There's nothing I can do about it. So why not just go with the flow?* If you follow such a self-talk style, you'll gain a calm, a peace (instead of a headache), and by the time you arrive home you'll be ready to tackle the rest of your evening in a much more healthy psychological state.

Continue this mini-exercise over the next week, and see what a difference it can start to make in how you feel about yourself, others, and your life situations.

———————————————————————————————

# 5

## MOVING PAST YOUR PAST

---

*Don't try to saw sawdust.*

DALE CARNEGIE

*T*hat's not the way I remember it!" Lauren exclaimed heatedly to her sister, Josey. "How could you think that? About *our father?*"

Josey narrowed her eyes in anger. It was the first "reunion" she'd had with her three sisters since her parents' death two years earlier. And this was why. Anytime she tried to talk with Lauren and Annette about their father and the way he had treated them, they could never see eye to eye. It was as if her sisters had lived in a different home and hadn't experienced his cutting remarks. (They called them his sense of humor, his sarcasm, and said that's the way he related to others.) It was as if they hadn't been hurt by him constantly missing their concerts and games. (They said it was because he had a strong work ethic and knew their family needed the money from his overtime.)

So who was right? Who had the real truth? The sisters may never know because they all remember their home life differently. But a kind friend who really cared about Josey finally shared with her what he saw: That she was using her anger against her father to keep her from becoming close to *any* man. Why? Because she was afraid of being hurt or feeling ignored again. That anger was poisoning her relationship with a man who loved her deeply and wanted to marry her. And it was also poisoning her relationship with her sisters, who longed to invite Josey more often into their homes.

Josey had to make a choice—to stay rooted in her anger against her father . . . or to let her bitterness go and move on, past her past. The choice would not be easy, but it was one she knew she would have to make.

And Josey isn't the only one who has a choice to make. All of us are shaped by our memories—whether factual or interpretations. These memories can either help us become individuals who are confident of our significance and our decisions . . . or individuals who plod through life, uncertain of our worth, anxious about our present, and too paralyzed to make decisions that could affect our future for the positive.

For this reason we are compelled to include this chapter in a book on becoming healthy and whole. Why? Because after conducting our own research on personal growth and after surveying a mountain of other studies on mental heath, we are unequivocally convinced that if you do not understand how your past—whether accurately recalled or simply imagined—is shaping your present, you will forever be stuck in it, never achieving the level of profound significance emotional health requires. As you saw in the last chapter, your self-talk is key to reinforcing the love that emanates from a caring God. But if you stop there, without learning to move past your past, you will forever be slowed down on your journey to wholeness. Your proverbial baggage is sure to weigh you down. It will keep you from fully reaching your significance at any meaningful level. Until you learn to move past your past, you will never be able to understand your incalculable value or experience profound significance at your very core.

> **One problem with gazing too frequently into the past is that we may turn around to find the future has run out on us.**
>
> *Michael Cibenko*

The bottom line? *The healthy person does not dwell excessively on the past.* He understands the past, but he doesn't get stuck in it. So we dedicate this chapter to helping you move past your past so you will more fully embrace your God-given significance. First we'll identify the elements of your past that are affecting you. Then we'll talk about why your memories may not be what you think they are. We'll explain why dwelling on that past can be self-defeating and give you solid advice on how to move on, past your past.

Before we get started on the rest of this chapter, take the self-test to see what factors from your past may be influencing your present.

✦ ✦ ✦

## CAN YOU REALLY FORGIVE AND FORGET?

Forgiveness is a crucial key to moving past your past. There is no way around it. Forgiveness is to a relationship what oxygen is to our lungs. Relationships cannot survive without it. The failure to give forgiveness is the primary reason people get stuck in their past. So do you have what it takes to forgive and forget? Take this quiz and find out.

> **Reflect on your present blessings, of which every man has many; not on your past misfortunes, of which all men have some.**
>
> *Charles Dickens*

1. Forgiveness is
   a. Easy to give to others
   b. Tough to give, but I can eventually do it
   c. Next to impossible to give to others

2. Peter Ustinov said, "Love is an act of endless forgiveness." Do you agree?
   a. Completely
   b. Not really
   c. For the most part

3. A radio talk show is taking calls from listeners. A good friend of yours phones the station to describe a falling-out the two of you had. She is likely to say:
   a. "I couldn't believe how quickly she gave me the benefit of the doubt. She's hardly mentioned the pain I caused her."
   b. "We had a lot of talking to do, but she came to a place where she was willing to start over."

c. "She really knows how to hold a grudge—it's been months now."

4. Which of these three statements do you agree with most?
    a. Love is letting go of the past.
    b. Love is never having to say you're sorry.
    c. Love hurts.

5. I've been known to carry a grudge
    a. Hardly ever
    b. For weeks and even months
    c. For years

6. When I hear the phrase "forgive and forget," I think,
    a. *It makes good sense.*
    b. *Forgiveness doesn't always require forgetting.*
    c. *If I've been hurt, you can forget forgiveness.*

7. If someone were to sum up a lesson learned from observing how I've forgiven others over the past decade, this person might say:
    a. "Forgiveness is not an act, it's a way of life."
    b. "Forgiveness keeps the past from interfering with the present."
    c. "It's easier to ask for forgiveness than give it."

8. The Beatles lyrics that come closest to capturing my personal view of forgiveness are
    a. All you need is love
    b. We can work it out
    c. Let it be

9. If someone I care deeply about has betrayed my trust, I
    a. Forgive quickly to get over the pain
    b. Count it as a lesson learned and never trust that person again
    c. Weigh the pain carefully and try to find forgiveness in my heart

10. When asked about forgiving people, John F. Kennedy once said, "Forgive your enemies but never forget their names."

   a. I'm not sure I agree. Forgiving means forgetting.

   b. You should not only remember your enemies' names, but where they live, too.

   c. He nailed it. Forgiving doesn't mean you're no longer smart.

## ANSWER KEY

Circle your responses. Then add up the number of ●'s, ■'s and ◆'s you have, per the chart below.

| Question | 1 | 2 | 3 | 4 | 5 | 6 | 7 | 8 | 9 | 10 |
|---|---|---|---|---|---|---|---|---|---|---|
| A | ● | ● | ● | ■ | ● | ● | ● | ● | ● | ● |
| B | ■ | ◆ | ■ | ● | ■ | ■ | ■ | ■ | ◆ | ◆ |
| C | ◆ | ■ | ◆ | ◆ | ◆ | ◆ | ◆ | ◆ | ■ | ■ |

### What Your Answers Mean

*Mostly ●'s*

You are a Rapid-Fire Forgiver. You avoid grudges like the plague and know the power of forgiveness. People who know you well, and even those who don't, know you to be a grace-full person. But sometimes your good intentions get in your way. You sometimes forgive too easily. Why? Maybe to avoid personal pain by quickly overlooking an injustice. Or without realizing it, you may even forgive others to one-up them—to outdo their forgiveness. And that induces guilt, the very opposite of what forgiveness is designed to do.

*What to Do*

❏ Keep trigger-happy forgiveness in check. The next time you feel compelled to say, "I forgive you," or "That's okay, I know you didn't mean it," stop yourself. Take some time to let it sink in. Forgive on your own schedule.

❏ Examine your motives. If you get hurt by a friend or family member, ask yourself this question: *Why do I forgive so easily?*

Could the fear of losing that person, for example, be driving you to premature forgiveness?

❑ Admit your pain in specific terms. Rapid-Fire Forgivers tend to gloss over the hurt that others have caused them. This is unhealthy for you and those around you. Before you know it, you'll have so many emotional time bombs ticking away, you won't know what you're really mad at.

*Mostly ■'s*

You are an Even-Keeled Forgiver. You seem to have achieved a healthy balance between being too quick or too slow to forgive the people who have hurt you. You neither rush into forgiveness, nor do you hold on to a grudge for very long. This trait has served you well in your relationships. When you forgive others they know it's genuine and they respect that.

*What to Do*

❑ Say thanks to your model of forgiveness. Who taught you to forgive so well? Did one of your parents model this quality? Maybe a friend did. Whoever it was, take some time to write that person a note. You have been given a treasure that must be acknowledged.

❑ Recognize the unimaginable power of forgiveness. Sometimes the pain of betrayal by a spouse has cut so deep that forgiveness is the only thing between a couple and their demise. Forgiveness is the ultimate healer—even in the worst of life's pain.

❑ Ratchet up your forgiveness. The pinnacle of forgiveness is achieved when you genuinely wish a former foe the very best. When you truly desire that your ex-boyfriend who broke your heart three years ago would find the love of his life and live happily, then you know you have mastered the fine art of forgiveness.

*Mostly ◆'s*
You are a Guarded Forgiver. You know it's the right thing to do, but sometimes you resist forgiving longer than you should. You're not always sure it's wise to pardon the person who has caused you pain. It's difficult for you to give up a grudge and even when your heart turns around, you still may wonder whether you should have given this person grace. The good news is that you are just a few steps away from becoming a much better forgiver.

*What to Do*

❏ Realize what forgiveness will do for you. When you carry a quiet rage against a former friend or even a family member, it eats you alive. Literally. Research shows that a lack of forgiveness increases our risk of all kinds of maladies, including cancer.

❏ Give up safeguards. Forgiveness means surrendering your desire to hurt the person who has hurt you. You can't do this without taking the risk that you will get hurt again. That's why forgiveness requires letting down your guard.

❏ Tap into humility. It's impossible to forgive without eating humble pie—that's what makes it tough. As the saying goes, "Humility is a pastry that's never tasty," but once you admit that you make mistakes too, you'll feast on the freedom of forgiveness.

✦   ✦   ✦

But beware—just as "self-talk" can be negative and false, so can your memories and what you think of as "your experiences."

## REAL OR FAKE?

For decades, neuroscientists assumed that long-lost experiences from our past were etched permanently on our brains—much like a computer's hard drive stores data that is entered into it. Why? Because anesthetized patients could recount experiences they were unaware of in their conscious state.

It was not until recently that this time-honored assumption was scientifically questioned. Memory researchers began scrutinizing medical reports that had been used as evidence for this assumption and made a surprising discovery. The flashbacks described by patients under anesthesia were extremely rare, occurring in only a handful of patients. Even more surprising, the content of these few recollections suggested that the experiences were not being relived at all—but were being invented!

The patients in these studies, it was found, were "recalling" occasions and settings they had never experienced or visited. Their memories were actually being reconstructed. How is this possible?

In many dozens of experiments involving more than twenty thousand people, Elizabeth Loftus and her colleagues have shown how eyewitnesses reconstruct their memories. In one experiment a film of a traffic accident was shown to subjects who were then quizzed about what they saw. Those asked, "How fast were the cars going when they *smashed* into each other?" gave higher speed estimates than those who were asked, "How fast were the cars going when they *hit* each other?" A week later, the researchers asked the viewers if they recalled seeing any broken glass. Compared to those who had been asked the question with *hit,* those asked the question with *smashed* were more than twice as likely to recall broken glass. In reality, there was no broken glass.

**Yesterday is but today's memory and tomorrow is today's dream.**
*Kahlil Gibran*

This is known as the *misinformation effect.* Even subtle misinformation causes people to misremember reality. So unwitting is the misinformation effect that people later find it nearly impossible to discriminate between their memories of real and suggested events. In recounting an experience from their past, people fill in their memory gaps with plausible guesses and assumptions. After retellings, they often recall these guessed details, now absorbed into their memories, as if they actually observed them.

In addition, other people's vivid retellings may implant false memories altogether. These are called *disputed memories* or *mem-*

*ory mergers* and they are most clearly illustrated with twins. Psychologist and twin Mercedes Sheen of the University of Canterbury in New Zealand was inspired to study disputed memories after hearing her twin sister describe her first kiss at summer camp at age twelve—especially since, as she told a reporter, "I know that I was the one it happened to." This belief set her on a course to examine similar muddied memories with twenty sets of twins, and later with sixty-nine close-in-age siblings. Her findings? Siblings who can't recall an event from their own history are very prone to use the memory of a brother or sister as a default.

All the accumulated recent research proves that, contrary to previous guesses, our mind doesn't store most information with the exactness of a computer. Rather, say memory researchers, we often conjure our recollections and shape our memories. And those memories can be very deceptive.

Why are we even bringing up this psychological research, and what does it all mean for you? Yes, difficult things may have happened to you—whether of your own or someone else's making. You may feel little or great pain as a result. However, it's important to know that "memory is a great betrayer," as novelist Anaïs Nin said. To remember our past is often to revise it. Deliberately or not, we rework, modify, and subtly change our memories to create a past that justifies our present. For instance, let's say you lash out in anger more than you like, so you recall how your father did that very same thing to you. No wonder you have issues with anger. Whether he did or not, your memory serves to say it was so.

> The past is a foreign country; they do things differently there.
>
> L. P. Hartley

If you're wondering why the human psyche works to revise one's past, the answer is simple. By recalling events in a desired manner, we are attempting to protect our self-image or explain our misfortune. So we slant a particular memory from adolescence to bolster our confidence or we may edit that same memory to explain our shyness. It all depends on what we are trying to say to ourselves through our self-talk (as we discussed in the last chapter).

The memory of an awkward date as a seventeen-year-old may trigger confidence in you because you remember your date (not you) as self-conscious and insecure. *I had my act together even though she didn't have a good time,* you explain to yourself. Or that memory may trigger timidity because you remember how you couldn't get your date to open up or laugh. *If I was more outgoing, she would have felt more comfortable and enjoyed our date,* you say.

Memories, whether true or false, provide the hooks upon which we can hang our history. Real or imagined, experienced or borrowed, our memories become the baggage we carry today. And that baggage either weighs us down or helps us move forward.

## WHY DWELLING ON THE PAST IS SELF-DEFEATING

Dwelling on the past is like driving your car with your foot on the brake, your eyes on the rearview mirror, and your gas tank empty. You're wondering why you aren't moving forward, and yet all the while you're focused on the wrong direction. Even if you want to make progress, dwelling on your past keeps you stuck and prevents you from embracing your profound significance.

For example, let's say you want to lose weight. But instead of being proactive—checking out exercise and diet programs—you blame your mother for "conditioning" you to clean your plate at every meal. Whether your mother did this or not isn't the real issue. The real issue is what you're going to do about it now. If you don't take steps to lose weight, you never will.

You may want to save money, but if your excuse is that you never had a father who modeled financial savvy (whether he did or not) you'll live from paycheck to paycheck.

You may want to be more intentional about dating and finding a potential spouse, but if you say you're shy because you were raised this way (whether you were or not) you'll probably stay home again this Friday night.

No matter how much you'd like to change, if you are blaming your real or imagined past for your present, you're not going anywhere. You'll be permanently stuck in your rut. Sitting in the same place may be "comfortable" because you don't have to take a risk, but is that really the way you want to live your life?

Let's make this perfectly clear: Bad things happen in this world. Sometimes they are of your own choosing—because you made a poor decision. Other times bad things happen because there is evil in the world, and even the most saintly among us are not promised an easy ride. Bad things happen to good people.

However, we want you to know that regret, blame, and excuses are a dead end. When your focus is on the lack of nurture your parents provided you as a child, or a mistake you made three years ago that plunged your finances into the red, or the devastating embarrassment your sister caused you as a teenager, or an opportunity you passed up six months ago to initiate a date with an attractive person, then you have a "good" excuse for giving up. After all, if you didn't get the lucky breaks or privileges others did, or you didn't receive the treatment you thought you deserved, or you were dealt a hand that could barely be played, or you made a choice that was clearly dim-witted, your situation is hopeless. Deep down, when you excavate your way through the layers of excuses, accusations, and blame, aren't you really asking a simple question: *Why try? It won't make any difference anyway.*

> **Those who stare at the past have their backs turned to the future.**
>
> Unknown

Truth be told, we know that's exactly what you're saying whenever you choose to be stuck in the past because research has clearly revealed it. Every time you make an excuse for not succeeding in the present, every time you cast your gaze to the past for an explanation of your current predicament, you are convincing yourself that your problem is more and more hopeless. In fact— and this is key—your excuses are actually *producing* the very kind of problem behavior you are attempting to explain.

Let's take Dave for an example. For years he's blamed his problems in relationships on his overbearing mother and his distant father. *I just can't get anybody to like me,* he tells himself—and he acts on that. Although he's physically attractive and has garnered many dates as a result, he booby-traps every date by showing up late, forgetting his wallet, or talking only about himself. *My parents just never taught me to relate to others,* he insists. Well, perhaps they did—and perhaps they didn't. But again, that isn't the issue. Because he thinks he can't relate to others, he isn't even trying—and as a result, he doesn't relate well to others.

At the University of Kansas, C. R. Snyder and Raymond L. Higgins have been studying for years the excuses for irresponsible, self-defeating behavior. And while much of their work has focused on the legal system and society at large, they are also concerned about the effects of excuses on individual health and well-being. What they have found may surprise you.

First of all, they have documented that excuses soften the link between you and an unfortunate action. That's the seduction of a good excuse. *I can't control my anger because I've always been this way. I'll never find my soul mate because I seem to attract only the most needy. I'll be in debt forever because my family could never save money.* All these excuses and millions more put a distance between you and your failures. They provide a modicum of comfort because you can explain your angry outbursts, your failed relationships, and your financial woes by pointing to something beyond yourself.

And that's why, for the short-term, we all need excuses. They protect our dignity and keep a fragile sense of self-esteem from crumbling. But these same excuses, when they linger too long, become our rationalizations for staying stuck.

In other words, an excuse that made you feel less guilty or less defeated at the onset of a poor choice will eventually explain who you are—not simply what you have done. And being at the receiving end of someone else's poor choice (such as childhood abuse or a marital affair) will eventually explain who you are—not simply what has been done to you.

For example, a woman who falls into a rut of blaming her disrespectful behavior toward her children on the depression she suffers over her divorce will soon attribute automatically all future transgressions with her children to her depression. It becomes habit, even compulsory. *If I weren't depressed I'd treat them better.* This excuses her behavior in the short-term, but in the long run it rattles her self-worth to the core. It undermines her sense of personal power, significance, and control. By blaming her insolent behavior on her depression, she gives up her freedom to change. *It won't make any difference, so why try?* In essence, she has moved from *making* the excuse to *being* the excuse. To justify her continued mistreatment of her kids, she has to remain depressed. And that's a vicious circle no one wants to be a part of. It won't help her to move past her past and confidently into the future—and it certainly won't help her children or anyone else who is part of her life.

> Look not mournfully into the past. It comes not back again. Wisely improve the present. It is thine. Go forth to meet the shadowy future, without fear.
>
> *Henry Wadsworth Longfellow*

All of us are vulnerable to this self-defeatism when we wallow in our personal history. Like this woman who hangs her poor choices on her reactive depression, we come to believe that we have no choice. We sacrifice our freedom to avoid taking responsibility. That's when dwelling on the past becomes toxic. And that's exactly why it is so self-defeating. We may want with all our hearts to change our current conditions, but because we fuse our past experiences into our present identity we "can't help" but be who we are. And unless we choose to make a change, we will continue making the same mistakes.

Dwelling on the past—whether real or imagined—is a road that will never lead to personal growth and health of mind. In fact, it clearly prevents it. You may never know, on this earth, if what you remember happening to you is the truth or not. However, you do have a choice now—to decide whether you will continue dragging around any past baggage or to remain stuck in a "poor me" victim mentality. Don't define yourself by your past. Don't allow yourself to continue as a "helpless slave" to a problem. For if you do, you will never actively take charge of your life. Instead, you will continually hand over control of the problem—and, thus, your future life—to others.

> **Who controls the past controls the future. Who controls the present controls the past.**
> *George Orwell*

As psychologists, we have treated countless clients who come into our offices after months or years of avoiding responsibility for their problems. "I can't help the way I am; my mother made me this way" is an ever popular refrain. Successful therapy, in these cases, depends on breaking down the person's self-deceptive, self-protective excuses. It depends on making him face the link—not between his past and his present—but between himself and his actions.

Frankly, it's a reality that not everyone wants to own. Some *want* to think of themselves as victims. After all, all of us, if we are honest, are tempted to play the victim on occasion. But that's what inevitably gets us into trouble . . . especially if we choose to remain stuck in that mode due to our emotional baggage.

## EXPLORING YOUR EMOTIONAL BAGGAGE

Ever thought about what's in the luggage that makes the rounds at the baggage-claim area in the airport? As you are waiting for your own bags to arrive, perhaps you think to yourself or say to a friend, "That monogrammed Louis Vuitton piece must surely contain valuables. That hot pink Samsonite number with the stickers on it looks intriguing. Wonder who owns that cardboard box held together with duct tape and string? Or how about that sleek silver case with the sturdy lock?"

Allow us to ask what may seem like a strange or even silly question: If your psychological baggage was traveling on that same conveyor belt at the airport, what kind of shape would it be in? How would it look? Would it be scuffed up? Tightly locked? Nondescript? How would you describe it?

We ask such a question because your answer reveals a bit

about how you consider your past. It provides a glimpse into your feelings about your personal history. And those feelings are what we psychologists are getting at when we talk about your proverbial baggage.

*History* is what has happened in our lives. *Baggage* is how we feel about it. Your psychological perspective on your past determines, to a great extent, your personal health and vitality.

We know a couple who has a huge heart for hurting kids. Ramona and Jeff have been foster parents to more than thirty struggling teenagers over the last dozen years. They have stories that don't quit. Recently, Ramona told us about two women, Marian and Andi, who are now in their early twenties. Both have been in counseling for childhood abuse, but the outcome for both could not be more divergent.

Marian repeatedly endured every-night assaults from a stepfather from the time she was eight years old until she ran away from home when she was fourteen. Andi was used multiple times in her uncle's sexual experimentation—all when he was supposedly "baby-sitting" her and her younger brother. As a result, both of these young women have suffered low self-worth, have distrusted any male, and have felt "used and dirty," unfit for anyone to love them for who they are. Through extensive counseling, both came to the same realization: that they had to unpack their baggage in order to move ahead in their lives.

Marian chose to do so—even though the baggage was tightly locked in her suitcase and even a slight peek was horrifying. Andi chose not to do so. She was not ready to let go of any of the items in her suitcase. Today, five years later, it's easy to see the huge impact that simple choice has made for both of them. Marian is now happily married to a loving man, has a beautiful baby (although she was told by several doctors that she could never conceive due to the massive internal damage from her early abuse),

> The farther behind I leave the past, the closer I am to forging my own character.
>
> *Isabelle Eberhardt*

and is actively involved in her church and community, helping other young women who have suffered such abuse as well. And Andi? She has chosen to flit from relationship to relationship, running away when any problem needed to be addressed, rather than facing it head-on. She has difficulty keeping a steady job, won't look anyone in the eye, and spends her nights alone—painting angry portraits.

By the way, you need not suffer a traumatic accident or something as dreadful as abuse to have baggage. We all have baggage. Even the most well-adjusted, healthiest people have baggage. No one is exempt. You may have childhood angst over parental divorce, conflicts with friends and family, or remorse over missteps and lost opportunities. Everyone has a history and an emotional response to it. What matters, when it comes to being a healthy, thriving human being, is whether or not you have deliberately unpacked your baggage. If not, it is bound to thwart your personal growth. You can never feel profoundly significant at your core until you make peace with this emotional baggage. The healthiest among us, you can be sure, have rummaged around in the contents of their own suitcases. They have explored what they feel and why they feel the way they do about their history. And this act of simply identifying and labeling their emotions as they explore their past serves as an amazing springboard to personal growth, self-insight, and maturity. It even impacts physical well-being.

Consider the following study, which is only one among hundreds that substantiate this point. Participants were asked to write for just fifteen minutes a day about a disturbing experience. They did this for three or four days in a row. Forget polish and politeness. The point was not to craft a wonderful essay but to dig deeply into one's emotional junkyard, then translate the experience onto the page. James Pennebaker, a psychology professor at the University of Texas at Austin and author of the study, then compared a group of college students who wrote about trauma with a group who wrote about trivial things (how they named their pet or the kinds of clothes they like). Before the study, the forty-six students in the study had visited the campus health clinic at similar rates. But after the exercise, the trauma writers' visits dropped by 50 percent relative to the others. Other studies have found that identifying one's feelings about past events actually increases the level of disease-fighting lymphocytes circulating in the bloodstream. It also lowers blood pressure.

Notice an important distinction. Spending time with your past, coming to terms with it, putting it in perspective, is different than wallowing in your past and using it as a scapegoat. In order to get *beyond* your past, you sometimes need to get *into* your past.

At this point you may be shaking your head vehemently. *No way am I going to relive that again. Especially when I'll get hurt all over again—and it won't change a thing!*

You're right—reliving your past may hurt. And that's not fun. But you're also wrong—spending time with your past does change things. In fact, it can change your entire life perspective. So hang in there with the process. Coming to terms with your past isn't easy, but it's necessary in order for you to move on. It will free you not only to like your current life, but to love your current life and have great hope for the future. The very process of exploring, identifying, and owning your emotional response to your history is what will allow you to move past your past. Contrary to what many of us may think, healthy people are not blessed with an unblemished history. Rather, they suffer the same struggles as you do. But they carry their negative history with little ill effect because they understand it to be part of their story. They have come to grips with the hurtful emotions a family member engenders, for example, and they acknowledge when those emotions arise. Because they have traced back the source of their hurt and examined it from different angles, they are able to set it aside. Their emotional baggage no longer pulls them down. In fact, they may even learn

**Shut out all of your past except that which will help you weather your tomorrows.**

*Sir William Osler*

to joke about it in a healthy way. (Think about it: One person's dysfunctional family background is another's entertaining tale or comedy routine.)

If you want to become the person you were meant to be, you've got to unpack your baggage. Here's our step-by-step plan for doing just that.

## HOW TO MOVE PAST YOUR PAST

Before we even get started, we want to be clear and up-front about one thing: It would be deceptive to say that if you follow our suggestions for gaining control over your emotional baggage, you will never struggle with it again or its tyranny will be completely erased. There is no "magic bullet" or "miracle cure" for overcoming the effects of your past. But it's no exaggeration to tell you that the plan we set forth below has proved to be both motivating and useful to countless people who have wanted to gain voluntary control over their emotional reactions to past events and live at a higher level of psychological health by embracing their profound significance. It's an easy-to-follow prescription for moving past one's past that has proved effective time and time again.

> When you make a mistake, don't look back at it long. Take the reason of the thing into your mind and then look forward. Mistakes are lessons of wisdom. The past cannot be changed. The future is yet in your power.
>
> *Hugh White*

The steps below look innocent—and simple. But don't be deceived. These four steps may prove more powerful than anything you have ever encountered to get you going in a positive direction.

### 1. Pinpoint your thinking

Judy says her divorce has long been put to rest. After all, it has been nearly twenty years. But whenever Judy hears Ken's name, she immediately remembers that he bitterly betrayed her, and she still feels that old anger rise up within her. Twenty years after the fact, Judy is allowing the baggage of her divorce to determine her emotional state. Why? Because she has never put her finger on exactly what triggers her anger. She has never owned the fact that she still wants Ken to pay a painful price for what he put her through. "He deserves at least as much hurt as I have experienced," she confides to her counselor. "Ken turned his back on me and our two children and he deserves to suffer for that."

Maybe so. But guess who has been suffering more for two decades—Ken or Judy? There's no contest. Judy has been carrying this emotional baggage so long she has forgotten that there is any other way. She has stayed stuck, hung up on her divorce, because she continues to focus her thinking on what Ken did to her. She has every right to be angry and hurt. But that's not the issue. If she wants to change, if she wants to live beyond such torture and feel profoundly significant again, she will have to face the fact that how she thinks about what happened to her is ruling her emotions.

Like Judy, we all must pinpoint our thoughts about our past.

How are *your* emotions doing? Take time now to do the "Emotion Check" exercise.

———————————— E M O T I O N   C H E C K ————————————

Grab a pen and paper, and find a quiet place. Take a few deep breaths to clear out your "to-do" list and help you focus on the task at hand. Then ask yourself:

~ What relationships or experiences from my past still make me emotional?

~ What strong negative emotions do I feel? (Label the emotions one by one, and write them down.)

~ What does my "self-talk" say about this relationship or experience? (In other words, how are you interpreting this memory?)

Such an exercise is the first step to escaping the dogmas that have made you a prisoner of your own memories. It will help you begin to pinpoint your thinking.

## 2. Shake off excuses

Before we even start to talk about this next step, we want you to try "The Excuse Finder." It's a simple little "fill-in-the-blank exercise."

────────────── THE EXCUSE FINDER ──────────────

Think of situations you've been in either in your distant past or recent past. Then fill in the blank with what you'd tell yourself about the situation.

~ I only messed up because _____.
~ If that wouldn't have happened, I'd never have done _____.
~ It's _____'s fault, not mine. I only did it to please him/her, and see where it got me?
~ I'd never have fallen for _____ if I hadn't been pushed into it.
~ I'm like this because _____.
~ I know [name an experience] _____
  wasn't my fault. I'm just a victim of my circumstances.

───────────────────────────────────────────────

One of the most popular self-help movements of recent years has focused on a deterministic perspective that revolves around the "inner child." This theory says that the traumas of childhood—rather than our own decisions or our character—have caused all the problems we are experiencing today as adults. The purported cure, in this line of thinking, is to overcome our "victimization" by delving into these early traumas, sometimes reexperiencing them, with an inner-child guru who will help us scream through the pain or imagine different outcomes.

We take a different point of view. Maybe you were traumatized as a child. Maybe you were mistreated and emotionally harmed. If so, you have reason to be angry and resentful. Every child deserves better. And that never should have happened to you. But all the wishing in the world cannot change the fact: You have baggage as a result.

However, if your bad childhood events have become the hook upon which to hang your adult problems, you're not going to be able to move forward in life. You won't become that healthy, happy, significant self you long to be. Nor will you have lasting, satisfying relationships.

It all comes down to choice. Your choice. Just because you've had a difficult personal history doesn't mandate that you have to be a troubled adult. If you're dubious of this statement, consider the research.

> **Do not look back and grieve over the past, for it is gone. Live in the present, and make it so beautiful that it will be worth remembering.**
>
> *Ida Scott Taylor*

Psychology has always considered the relationship between childhood events and adult development, but those in the know realize that the mass of research in this area lends little support to taking this relationship too seriously. One might expect to find massive evidence for the destructive effect of neglect, beatings, parental death or divorce, physical illness, and sexual abuse on the adulthood of the victims. But large-scale, costly surveys of adult mental health and childhood events, for the most part, have revealed the truth: People who have suffered terrible things are not predestined to live in misery. Do some choose to? Yes, stories abound in the media of people who have made that choice. But stories also abound of those who have made vastly different choices—choices that show they believe in their own profound significance and want to affect others' lives, for the good.

Such stories abound of people who have risen above their circumstances. People like Todd and Lisa Beamer. On that fateful day of September 11, 2001, Todd became a hero of United Flight 93—the only terrorist-controlled plane that didn't hit its target—when he gathered with fellow passengers to rush the cockpit. He knew by doing so that he would die, but he was certain of his destination—heaven. In the wake of incredible personal pain and grief, his wife, Lisa, has become a spokesperson of hope for our tumultuous world.

Other people have overcome their past to do incredible good in this world. Take Jackie Joyner-Kersee, for instance, who grew up in such poverty that she ate mayonnaise sandwiches and lived in a tiny house with paper-thin walls. But this determined young woman became an Olympic gold medalist who has inspired countless youth across the world. And not only that, she is integrally involved with the children and teens in her old hometown—providing a safe center they can go to for guidance and interaction with role models, and to fine-tune their skills in school basics and sports activities.

> **Realize that if you have time to whine and complain about something then you have the time to do something about it.**
> *Anthony J. D'Angelo*

Studies do not justify blaming your adult depression, anxiety, bad marriage, drug use, sexual problems, unemployment, aggression against your children, alcoholism, or anger on what happened to you in your earlier years. That means the struggles of your past—although painful—have been overrated. If you sincerely want to move past the pain and anger your past engenders, you can no longer lean on it to explain your problems, whatever they are. You've got to shake off excuses, take responsibility for your current choices, and embrace the freedom you now have to do so.

### 3. Excavate your feelings

In all our combined hours of psychotherapy experience, in our one-on-one work with individuals and couples, we have often seen a powerful emotional breakthrough when a client agrees to an exercise we and other therapists have been suggesting for decades: Write about your feelings. The "Write Your Feelings!" exercise is simple, but so worth the time it takes.

When a client actually follows through on this "Write Your Feelings!" exercise, the response is fairly predictable. The first entry is relatively incoherent. But by the third, the person is gaining a sense of empowerment and freedom from their past. On many occasions, we have heard a grateful client say, "Doc, the writing changed my life."

——————— WRITE YOUR FEELINGS! ———————

This exercise will take you about thirty minutes. You can either sit at your computer or with a pad of paper—whatever is most comfortable for you.

~ Reread your "Emotion Check" exercise and pinpoint one relationship or experience that still causes you emotional pain.
~ For the next thirty minutes, write intensively about your feelings. (For some of you, this amount of time may seem like an eternity, but hang in there! The results will be worth it!) Don't worry about making it sound like a school essay. Just jot down your feelings, however they come out. For some people, feelings come in a list; others simply write disjointed thoughts and emotions. But don't stop—write until you've put down as much of your pain, regret, loss, and grief as you possibly can.

---

How can writing accomplish all this? Research suggests that it's far more therapeutic than anyone ever knew. Since the mid-1980s, studies have found that people who write about their most upsetting experiences are more emotionally balanced, more confident, and less worried. And you can experience those benefits too (in fact, you probably already did, if you completed the "Write Your Feelings!" exercise).

This exercise isn't merely a simple catharsis. It's more than that. Putting your emotions on paper transforms the ruminations cluttering your mind into coherent stories—information that will help you make sense of the experiences you otherwise have avoided. Writing your feelings not only clarifies your experience, it dulls its impact. How is this possible through a little ink and paper? Because, perhaps for the first time, you articulate what used to lurk in murky emotional waters beneath the surface.

If you really want to see the benefits of this, write

> **The only use of a knowledge of the past is to equip us for the present. The present contains all that there is. It is holy ground; for it is the past, and it is the future.**
>
> *Alfred North Whitehead*

intensely for thirty minutes about your emotions over the course of a few days. This is a simple, but time-tested, process for getting your emotional hydraulics to work *for* you rather than against you. We urge you to give it a try!

## 4. Cultivate a different outlook

It's difficult to imagine a person who has more justification for being angry and bitter than Karen Scherer of Kansas City. A few years ago she was a thriving businesswoman with a fast-paced executive lifestyle. But everything in her life came to a screeching halt through a series of rapid-fire jolts. Her marriage of twenty-five years disintegrated and ended in an ugly divorce as her husband revealed he had betrayed her on numerous occasions and wanted out. A few months later her father was diagnosed with non-Hodgkin's lymphoma. And barely a week after that she got the news about her own health: inflammatory breast cancer.

> *The golden moments in the stream of life rush past us and we see nothing but sand; the angels come to visit us, and we only know them when they are gone.*
>
> *George Eliot*

Karen was angry at her ex-husband and now she was angry with God. *Why me?* she thought. *Why did I have to have the worst kind of breast cancer?* Then, through her hospitalization and treatment and the support of her friends and her church, Scherer's attitude turned more optimistic. She gained insight. "Every time something difficult came up," she told a reporter, "something good came out of it. When I was sick in the hospital, I had wonderful nurses and a wonderful doctor. I believed in those people, and they gave me hope." So Karen made a decision. She would not give up. And she would accentuate her gratitude. "Every day I try to look at something positive," she said. "Even when things seem very bad."

And as for her ex-husband, she said, her gratitude for the good around her helped her "not to let my emotions drive my train."

Karen Scherer's attitude shift may have saved her life, if not physically, certainly emotionally. Insufficient appreciation undermines serenity, contentment, and satisfaction every time. So it only stands to reason that savoring the good events in your past and present will loosen the grip of negativity and bitterness.

Take a few minutes now to complete "Your Emotion Quotient" exercise.

—————— YOUR EMOTION QUOTIENT ——————

Do you let emotions "drive your train"? Try this quick exercise to find out. What's your immediate response if

~ Someone cuts you off in traffic?
~ Your child "sasses" you?
~ A coworker claims credit for your work?
~ Your husband puts the last of the milk on *his* cereal?
~ Someone else is chosen over you?
~ A friend shares your embarrassing secret with someone else?

If you were honest about your responses to "Your Emotion Quotient" exercise, you *know* whether or not you're letting emotions "drive your train." How? Because even answering the questions turned up the heat of your emotions.

Having emotions is not wrong, however. It's what we *do* with those emotions that makes them wrong or right because they result in actions that can hurt ourselves or others.

The most compelling question is this: The next time you feel your emotions heating up, what will you do? Will you let them take off, in a huff? Or will you take a deep breath, think through the situation and your self-talk, realize how your background may be affecting you, and choose to cultivate a different outlook?

## A TRANSFORMED LIFE

"Freedom is what you do with what's been done to you," said philosopher Jean-Paul Sartre. We couldn't agree more. While moving past your past will certainly increase your energy, buoy your confidence, empower your outlook, and much more, the greatest payoff for exploring your emotional baggage is the new freedom you will enjoy to be yourself, as God created you to be.

Once you begin to cut the ties that bind you to irrational thinking, unruly emotions, senseless decisions, painful memories, and all the rest, each day becomes an opportunity for positive choices. You are no longer governed by what *has been* but, instead, by what *can* be. You are now sitting in the driver's seat. You are now having a say in the direction of your life and are no longer leaving it to the ghosts of your past.

**The past is but the beginning of a beginning, and all that is and has been is but the twilight of the dawn.**

*H. G. Wells*

After all, your emotional baggage, if not identified and claimed, can ruin a perfectly good day. While you're sitting there ruminating about the terrible things your mother or ex-spouse did to you last month or ten years ago, that person may be having a wonderful day at the beach, and you're the one suffering. It's predictably painful when your brain wraps around this kind of negativity. Why? Because unless you are intentional, you will become attached not only to your pain, but to the idea that if you stay angry enough at the person who caused your pain, then maybe that person will realize how terrible he or she has been.

But that's a false hope. Many times the people who have hurt you continue in their own blind way. If you continue to hang on to your pain and anger, hoping and wishing they will see it and repent, you will continue to carry your emotions around with you. You will become overfocused, even obsessed, with what the other party has done wrong. And when this happens, your own creative options to move beyond the pain from your past, to live differently, dissipate more quickly than a vapor.

On the other hand, when you step back and look at your own behavior and how it may contribute to conflict and negativity, and when you try to understand the person who has caused you pain, you will become more mature. You will grow emotionally. You will understand more about your profound significance.

And you will be well on the road toward a healthy life. When you move past your past you will feel as footloose as an alpine deer. You will breathe oxygen into your lungs more deeply than you ever have. Colors will seem more vibrant. Your actions will be more deliberate and your decisions more tuned. Your attitude will be more upbeat and your soul more contented. You will be at the top of your game, living in the upper reaches of your potential.

In summarizing the University of Michigan's nationwide surveys, Angus Campbell commented that "having a strong sense of controlling one's life is a more dependable predictor of positive feelings of well-being than any of the objective conditions of life we have considered." In other words, after all the research on personal fulfillment is reviewed and tabulated, moving beyond the dead weight of your past and gaining control over your future is turning out to be one of the single most powerful predictors of positive mental health we have.

It's clear that in order to be healthy, to be content, to be fulfilled, to realize the truth about your inner significance, you must tune in to your self-talk and move past the baggage of your past.

Profound significance is the first of the three secrets to health because you can never maintain an abiding sense of meaningful contentment—you can never feel good deep down in your soul—until you know at the center of your being that your value is established for all time. You don't have to work harder or look better. Significance is not about *achieving;* it's about *receiving.* It's not a task to be done, but an experience to be lived.

In this section, we gave you the two most effective tools we know of for *experiencing* profound significance: your ability to tune in to self-talk (and discover how you really feel about yourself) and your capacity to move past your past (and be freed from whatever may keep you from being loved). As you now know, healthy people continually lean on these two tools to more powerfully receive their profound significance.

Before we close this section of the book, however, we have a confession to make. These two tools will fall flat if you do not prepare and provide the space within your personhood to hold the profound significance we are talking about. And your spirit or your soul is the cradle of this secret. Perhaps we have taken this fact for granted, but we aren't about to leave this first section without making it abundantly clear that profound significance is not the result of thinking good thoughts. And it's not about recovering from difficulties in your past. These are the mere tools for embracing the greatest gift of all—the love of a Creator whose devotion and care for you is immeasurable. This is a gift that can only be received when you optimize your soul.

We have waded literally through stacks of scientific research studies that are recognizing and talking about the mysterious value and transforming power of a strong personal faith and a positive relationship with God. But rather than give you our summary of these studies at this point (you will find them in appendix A: "Optimizing Your Spirit"), we want to "put skin on" what is too often treated as an abstraction and show you how people literally receive significance deep down in their soul.

## A STORY OF UNLIKELY TRANSFORMATION

Lee Edward Travis was the greatest person I (Neil) ever knew. Possessed with a luminous mind, sparkling wit, and an unassuming demeanor, he left an indelible impression on nearly everyone he met.

Born on June 23, 1896, in a sod house built by his father on a Nebraska homestead, Lee was the second of twelve children, ten of whom earned advanced degrees from some of America's most distinguished universities. Lee's own academic career was meteoric: After returning from military duty in World War I, he graduated Phi Beta Kappa from the State University in Iowa in 1922, and two years later earned a Ph.D. He became a full professor in 1928 when he was only thirty-one.

During those years, he studied intensively in anatomy, physiology, neurology, and psychiatry. Eventually, he published 225 articles and numerous books, was voted one of the thirteen most influential psychologists in U.S. history, was a pioneer in the study of brainwaves and the reduction of speech disorders, and was one of the most prolific researchers and research supervisors in the history of American academia.

Quite a résumé, to be sure. But all of these achievements had little to do with my high esteem for Lee. Instead, his greatness flowed from within—from his *spirit*. He had a radiance that seemed to be magnetically charged. People simply gravitated toward him.

What was it about his spirit that exuded such dignity, kindness, and appeal? Was it his warm, penetrating eyes and his soft, deep voice? Perhaps it was the way he took hold of your hand, looked in your eyes, and said, "How are you *doing?*" with such genuineness that you knew he was really interested. His lively sense of humor was never at someone else's expense, and his way of listening to your thoughts and feelings made you feel utterly embraced and valued.

I didn't meet Lee Edward Travis until he was nearly seventy years old, but he seemed decades younger. (Les took a graduate class from Lee when he was eighty!) His spirit was timeless. When he offered me a job, I jumped at the opportunity—largely because I felt totally safe with him and wanted to be more like him. I eagerly moved our family from Chicago to California to take my first teaching position under his guidance, and he served as my mentor for more than fifteen years.

## WHAT MAKES THE DIFFERENCE?

Have you had the privilege of knowing someone like Lee Edward Travis—someone who emanated security, grace, goodness, and gentleness? Someone who felt so good in his own skin that he made you feel great about living in yours? If so, then you probably wondered what exactly made that person so extraordinarily special. What about that individual's inner spirit could manifest itself in such compelling outer qualities?

It's difficult to come up with definitive answers, but here's what I concluded about Dr. Travis. He was genuinely comfortable with himself—free, natural, and unguarded. He had a high degree of self-acceptance and appreciation for who he was. He knew, at his core, that he had profound significance. And, not surprisingly, he seemed equally at ease with a wide range of people. I never got the feeling that he appraised me or sized me up in any way. I *never* had the sense that he tried to impress me—or needed me to impress him. Quite the opposite. He seemed eager to establish a sense of equality with every person he encountered.

Surely Lee's interpersonal genius was made possible by the mastery of his internal world. Because he was not emotionally needy, he had no furious drive for recognition, adulation, or power. His needs for significance already met, he was free to simply enjoy those with whom he interacted.

## THE REST OF THE STORY

But the question still remains, where did Lee's high degree of self-acceptance and significance come from? Let me tell you the rest of the story. When Lee was sixty-five years old, after a lifetime of major professional and scientific achievement, he and his wife attended a church service for the first time in forty years. It happened to be at the Bel Air Presbyterian Church in Los Angeles, and the minister, Dr. Louis Evans Jr., was known for his thoughtful ways of applying Christian principles to contemporary issues of life.

Lee had a powerful psychological experience that day, a spiritual conversion. But because he was confused by it, he told no one of it, not even his wife. Like a true scientist, he went back the next week in an effort to "replicate his findings"—and he had an even more powerful experience than before.

"This time I was overwhelmed with emotion and attending physical reactions," he explained. "I didn't ask immediately what exactly was occurring. I felt only that it was something of great consequence, and that I would have to accept it and live with it as *me.*"

So Lee went on to tell us the dramatic story of the powerful spiritual encounter of a man who had previously given his whole life to science, rationality, the most precise kind of measurement, and a belief in the total sufficiency of material explanations for every question about the mystery of life. He was already a remarkable man, but the changes in his life were stunning.

We want you to hear Lee's own words . . . the way he summed up the consequences of his spiritual transformation:

> Absurdities have given way to the discovery of values and meaning in the experience of transcendence. A reverential awe has transcended to the throne of self-hood. It fosters a quest for the contemplative, the observational and the worshipful solution rather than the manipulative, the controlling and the unsettling.

When *you* optimize *your* spirit, it will almost always be in response to a spiritual event of great relevance to your life. This spiritual event will inevitably have to do with your search for significance on your journey to wholeness and health.

Preparing your spirit and exploring your soul gives you access to an empowering relationship with God that will affirm your significance for all eternity. This new power supply will provide a never-before-experienced vitality for your life. And the sooner you gain access to this power source, the sooner you will discover at the deepest levels of your being what it means to be *profoundly* significant. For further information, consult appendix A of this book. It provides you not only with the scientific studies supporting this point, but also will show you how to receive your significance from God by peeling away the religious clichés that sometimes cloud the process.

*What does it profit a man if he gains the whole world and loses his own soul?* JESUS

SECRET #2

TO FEELING GOOD—DEEP DOWN IN YOUR SOUL

◇

# *Unswerving Authenticity*

"Real isn't how you are made," said the Skin Horse. "It's a thing that happens to you. When a child loves you for a long, long time, not just to play with, but REALLY loves you, then you become Real."

This old toy horse in Margery Williams's classic children's story, *The Velveteen Rabbit,* not only squarely identifies the second essential step to health and wholeness, he wisely notes that it is the result of being loved.

Profound significance—which we've just explored in chapters 4 and 5—is the precursor to unswerving authenticity. Without the foundation of knowing we are unconditionally loved we cannot risk being authentic, or real. But once we claim our significance and recognize its durability over time, we cultivate the rich soil of our soul for authenticity to take root.

What is *authenticity*? It's what separates the genuinely loving person from the person who merely wants to be *seen* as loving. It makes no room for imitation or fakery. No space for "phoning it in." There's no going through the motions. Authenticity divides those who walk the walk from those who merely talk it. When you are real, your head and heart work in harmony. You are the same person behind the curtain as you are on stage. You no longer perform to win love—that was settled when you embraced your significance. No. You've dismissed the audience from your life and tossed the script. Instead, who you are determines what you do. You are genuine.

Authenticity is all about *being* rather than *doing*. When you focus on being genuinely loving, for example, the actions naturally follow. They are not contrived. There's no pretense. You don't wonder what you should do. Your doing flows naturally from your being. Health and wholeness matures at a remarkable rate as this important process unfolds.

And vulnerability, we are convinced, is key to unswerving authenticity. Consider this statement: "You're the first person I have ever been completely honest with."

These words are ones both of us, as psychologists, have heard hundreds of times. Every psychologist has. But it was Sidney Jourard who made sense of them in his in-depth book *The Transparent Self*. He was puzzled over the frequency with which patients were more honest and authentic with a clinician than they were with family or friends. After much study, he concluded that each of us has a natural, built-in desire to be known, but we often stifle our vulnerability with the significant people in our lives out of fear. We're afraid of being seen as too emotional or not emotional enough, as too assertive or not assertive enough. We're afraid of rejection.

The result? We wear masks. We put up our guard. In Margery Williams's story, the toy rabbit didn't know real rabbits existed. He thought they were all stuffed with sawdust like himself. "And he understood that sawdust was quite out-of-date and should never be mentioned in modern circles." The rabbit kept authenticity at bay through his fear of being found out. He never wanted to risk vulnerability.

But we are never authentic until we admit our frustrations, acknowledge our weaknesses, and disclose our insecurities. We are never real until we open our wounded hearts. Everyone's heart has been wounded. But most people would rather protect their wounds than divulge them. Healthy people, however, make personal wounds available to others when needed.

No one has written more sensitively on the gift of vulnerability than Henri Nouwen in his book *The Wounded Healer*. He points out that "making one's own wounds a source of healing does not call for a sharing of superficial personal pains but for a constant willingness to see one's own pain and suffering as rising from the depth of the human condition."

The point is that healthy, authentic people do not pretend to have it all together. They do not present themselves as something they are not. They are honest about their imperfections, problems, inadequacies, and pain. They do not relegate their dark side to the basement of their personality. They do not try to disown their failings or ignore their weaknesses. Instead, they use them to propel themselves forward.

Think of it this way. If four people had to push a car in need of gas across a street, what would be the best way for them to push? Obviously, all four of them pushing together in the same direction would maximize their likelihood of reaching the common goal. When they align their efforts, they multiply their power and optimize their efficiency.

Now imagine that this car represents your personality. And what you think, feel, say, and do are the four people trying to get the car across the street. In order for you to reach your highest goals, these four separate parts of you must work in alignment, all headed in the same direction. *Together.*

Being who you really are means lowering your defenses. It may even mean a few acts of daring vulnerability now and then. It's the only way to grow. If you are pushing and pulling in all sorts of directions, not at all in alignment within yourself, your progress will be painfully slow. But if you find your way to inner harmony, if you get real, you will begin to move on a sure and steady course to a deeply meaningful and satisfying life.

Abraham Maslow called this working together of the separate parts of you *congruency.* He considered it a major requirement for attaining the top level of his hierarchy of needs: fulfillment. We experience the peak of fulfillment when we become congruent. When we are *all of a piece.* Our thoughts, feelings, words, and actions are in sync. All the parts of us are striving together to help us reach our potential.

In every moment, then, our focus remains fixed on being the person we truly are. This unflinching determination to be authentic may lose us some friends, cost us some memberships or jobs, but the gains of being true to ourselves far outweigh the cost.

The first order of business in becoming more authentic is to take a quantum leap in self-awareness. You don't know yourself as well as you think you do. Surprised? It's a fact, not our opinion. Everyone has blind spots—and the more you have, the less authentic you are and the more your relationships will suffer. That's why chapter 6 will open your eyes to what you have not yet seen in yourself. Once you take off your blinders and face the truth about the real you, you won't believe how extraordinary your life will become. Why? Because discovering your blind spots, the first step toward authenticity, pays numerous rewards, as you will soon see.

Next we'll look at your "wild side." Everyone has something in their life that is wild, unrestrained, and needs to be harnessed. In chapter 7 we'll show you how to rein in what may be hurting you or others you love by taking a close look at the two most common areas of human struggle: anger and sexuality. These two drives will certainly control you, if you don't learn to control them. Every human being who prizes authenticity holds the reins of these two drives in a skillful hand. The key, of course, is to keep from squelching them out completely in your pursuit to manage them. For this very reason, we will give you a time-tested program for gently harnessing these wild horses so they work *for* you rather than *against* you.

When you are confident of your profound significance and you are unswervingly authentic, your contentment level will be stunningly high. Your primary relationships will be rich and vital. Your emotions will be deep and genuine. You'll no longer ask, *What* should *I be feeling?* but instead, *What* am *I feeling?* You will rely on an internal gyroscope that keeps your psychological bearings steady instead of trying to tiptoe around, guessing what you think others want you to be. You will be more sure of yourself, and others will respect you for it. In fact, unswerving authenticity, when coupled with profound significance, makes you maximally attractive for all the right reasons. You will be *genuinely* healthy.

# DISCOVERING YOUR BLIND SPOTS

*There are things which a man is afraid to tell*

*even to himself, and every decent man has a number*

*of such things stored away in his mind.*

FYODOR DOSTOYEVSKY

*A* minister, a Boy Scout, and a computer executive were flying to a meeting in a small private plane. About halfway to their destination, the pilot came back and announced that the plane was going to crash and that there were only three parachutes and four people.

The pilot said, "I am going to use one of the parachutes because I have a wife and four small children," and he jumped.

The computer executive said, "I should have one of the parachutes because I am the smartest man in the world and my company needs me," and he jumped.

The minister turned to the Boy Scout and, smiling sadly, said, "You are young and I have lived a good, long life. So you take the last parachute, and I'll go down with the plane."

"Relax, Reverend," the Boy Scout said. "The smartest man in the world just strapped on my backpack and jumped out of the plane!"

A high IQ has never guaranteed good decisions. No matter how superior one's intelligence, even a genius may not see what is obvious to others. You need not look far to find breathtaking acts of stupidity committed by people who are smart. You may be quick-witted, clever, and intellectually brilliant, but these enviable traits don't ensure wise judgments or accurate assessments, especially about yourself.

Blind spots. We all have them. And research shows that we don't know ourselves as well as we think we do. Psychological blind spots keep us from seeing the truth. They distort our perceptions. They trick us into believing in a reality that may not be true. And they feed us misinformation. Like the physical blind spots in automobiles, our personal blind spots steer us into danger if we're not careful.

Take thirty-year-old Michael, for instance, who complained to a friend that his wife didn't ever want him to go out with "the boys" . . . or have any fun. In reality, Michael was out with "the boys" at least two nights a week. His wife, as the mother of three young children, was simply asking him to limit his nights with the boys to *one* night a week so he could spend more time with the children, who only saw him for a couple of hours a day, due to his current work schedule. It took that wise friend, who had grown up with Michael, to ask a question that finally opened his eyes: "Do you think you might be reacting to your wife as if she were your mother? Remember how your mom kept such tight control on you as a teenager that she barely let you go out on a Friday night?"

Michael was stunned. He'd never considered the connection. Truly, this was a blind spot. But when Michael took off the blinders of anger and defensiveness, he realized *exactly* what was going on. He *was* penalizing his wife for the feelings he harbored against his mother. Because of this realization, he was able to talk with his wife, apologize for his defensiveness, explain how he felt, and come up with a solution that worked well for the entire family: Michael still went out with "the boys" one night a week, but his family regularly had a "Daddy" night each week too when he focused on nothing but the kids.

When the blinders come off, we see the truth. A new reality literally sets in, just as it did for Michael. A transforming truth about who we are and how we are responding materializes where before we only saw an illusion. This is why discovering your blind spots is so crucial to getting and staying psychologically healthy. It's not easy work, but the payoffs are certainly sweet. It heightens your self-awareness, as we'll soon see in more detail, lowers your stress, revolutionizes your relationships, and frees your spirit for optimal fulfillment.

In short, self-awareness—"an awareness of one's own personality or individuality," according to *Merriam-Webster's*—is curative. It means you know yourself well. You have the ability to see past your blind spots to who you really are. Dr. Steven Pinker, professor of cognitive science at the Massachusetts Institute of Technology and author of *How the Mind Works,* says that self-awareness helps us maximize who we are. "We have the ability to float above ourselves and look down at ourselves, to play back tapes of our own behavior to evaluate and manipulate it. Knowing thyself is a way of making thyself as palatable as possible to others."

> It is the person who is blind to what goes on around him [who] is most surprised when the same things happen to him.
>
> M. Thompson

Healthy people know themselves well. They know their strengths and limits, their likes and dislikes. They know what ticks them off and what soothes their spirit. They know their dark side and how to combat it. They monitor their feelings and learn how to manage them. They are aware of their motivations. They are aware of how they come off to others. Healthy people know, for the most part, what other people know about them. They work to keep their blind spots to a minimum.

Does this mean that awareness guarantees psychological health? No—but psychological health is impossible without knowing who you are. If you are in denial, you see yourself without any flaws and exaggerate your own abilities. You also dodge feedback at all cost. But if you are self-aware, you know the benefit of continuous critique. You know you can always improve by being more conscious, more alert to your emotions, your motives, your thinking, and your behavior.

So we dedicate this chapter to raising your level of awareness about you, the real you. First we'll look at why so many of us are blind to who we really are . . . to aspects of our personality that others can so readily identify. You'll find out how much you *really* know about yourself. Then we'll describe the five most common—and seductive—blind spots, so you can identify the ones that could be impacting you. We'll reveal the high price we humans pay for our blind spots (believe us, what you can't see *does* hurt you) and then the three main payoffs, the priceless rewards, for raising your level of self-awareness. And finally we'll give you strategies that *work* for diminishing your blind spots.

## THE UNEXAMINED LIFE

Few would dispute the enormous impact of Greek philosopher Plato, pupil of Socrates and teacher of Aristotle. In his various dialogues he touched upon virtually every problem that has occupied subsequent philosophers. His teachings have been among the most influential in the history of Western civilization, and his works are counted among the world's finest literature. And if you were to ask anyone "in the know" to quote him, more often than not you would hear a simple sentence that has become his trademark, something he must certainly have learned from Socrates: "The unexamined life is not worth living."

> **Become aware of internal experiences so that it immediately becomes possible for a certain amount of control to be exerted over these hither unconscious and uncontrollable processes.**
>
> *Abraham Harold Maslow*

This ancient adage has extolled the virtues of self-exploration and heightened self-awareness for centuries. You'd think by now we humans would have it down. But we don't. Every generation of individuals must learn to examine their lives, to make their unconscious more conscious, to diminish their blind spots in order to become unswervingly authentic. Why? Because we have a way of missing what's right in front of our noses.

Consider the fable of the Coloradoan who moved to Texas and built a house with a large picture window from which he could view hundreds of miles of rangeland. "The only problem is," he said, "there's nothing to see." About the same time, a Texan moved to Colorado and built a house with a large picture window overlooking the Rockies. "The only problem is I can't see anything," he said. "The mountains are in the way."

Like we said, people can be blind to what others see clearly. And this is most true when it comes to viewing ourselves. We may think we know ourselves well, but all of us, to some degree, are oblivious to things that others easily see in us. And most likely, we don't see these obvious aspects of who we are by our own design. We forget to recognize them in ourselves and then we forget that we've forgotten. In other words, we unconsciously deny ourselves access to certain aspects of our personality because we wish they weren't there. We reflexively avoid them because they cause fear, anxiety, or pain.

Is becoming unswervingly authentic always easy and pain-free? No. In fact, the anxiety of coming to terms with who we really are caused comedienne Lily Tomlin to quip on numerous occasions, "Reality is the leading cause of stress amongst those in touch with it." To get in touch with the real you can cause stress. We are the first to admit it. Realizing who you really are may not be fun—but it is the only way to become the person you'd like to be. It's the only way to have a life you not only like, but a life you love.

There is a saying in India: "When a pickpocket meets a saint, all he sees are the pockets." Our motives shape what we see—and don't see—around us.

We all share a tendency toward denial, an emotionally comfortable strategy that protects us from the distress that recognizing the harsh truth would bring. So we resort to filtering out information, rationalizing mistakes, avoiding responsibility. Many of us will do just about anything to steer clear of the truth if it might hurt. Because—let's be honest—who *wants* to be hurt? To make the matter worse, the people around us—whether close friends, family members, bosses, or coworkers—may avoid honest, constructive feedback because they fear hurting or angering us. So they act as though everything is fine . . . when in fact it is not.

Such behavior patterns set up a vicious circle. If we are not intentional, we buy the illusion of harmony at the cost of the truth.

And we miss the path that could take us to emotional maturity and psychological health. Finding the path is worth it. But in order to do so, you have to know *you*.

## FIVE COMMON BLIND SPOTS

Have you ever been surprised by others' descriptions of you? Maybe they said you were outgoing when you thought of yourself as shy. Or perhaps they said you were insensitive when you thought you were compassionate. When a surprising description emerges it almost always gives you pause. It may also give you a glimpse into an aspect of yourself you've never acknowledged.

For example, you may think of yourself as hardworking, but others may see you as hard-driving. You may think of yourself as straightforward and honest with people, but others may see you as self-righteous. You may think you handle your money well, but others may call you a tightwad. You may think you handle criticism well, but your body language tells others you are defensive. You may think you are aggressive and productive at work, but coworkers may see in you an insatiable need for recognition. You may think you're just staying in shape and "improving your looks," but your friends are convinced you are obsessed with your appearance, and they worry about your health.

> Oh, that God would give us the gift to see ourselves as others see us.
>
> *Robert Burns*

And these are just a few examples. The list of potential blind spots seems endless. But some areas that are most commonly pushed out of our awareness deserve to be highlighted. And that's exactly what we want to do next—take a glimpse at the five most common blind spots to see if any are blinding you. Consider the following list not as exhaustive, but instead as a jumping-off place. Ask yourself if any of the following five areas might apply to you.

### We are blind to our dark side

The best people, the healthiest, are not exempt from miserable parts. Everyone has tendencies toward meanness, selfishness, envy, materialism, cruelty, dishonesty, lust, and irresponsibility. In fact, the more of these miserable parts we have, the stronger our potential for greatness. Why? Because your character is hammered out not in the *absence* of negative traits, but *because* of them. Your struggle to overcome selfishness, for example, will make your generous spirit, once honed, far more prized, meaningful, and valuable than if it had come more easily or more naturally to you. There is no virtue in not acting on a desire that doesn't exist.

Yet so many, especially well-intentioned religious people, work diligently to block out or bury their baser parts. They operate under the false assumption that if they ignore such bad tendencies, their dark side will disappear. Healthy people take a different approach. They come to terms with the rotten parts of their nature, eventually learn why they have them, and most importantly, they learn how to subdue, control, and even transform them. At the end of this chapter, we'll give you proven strategies for doing just that.

In the meantime, steel your courage and risk delving into your own "dark side." Try the "Exploring Your 'Dark Side' " exercise now.

## EXPLORING YOUR "DARK SIDE"

Everyone has a side of themselves they wish wasn't there. In an effort to help you expose this side of yourself and to bring it more out into the open, take a few minutes to ponder these simple questions.

~ What part of yourself are you most ashamed of, and how do you hide it from yourself and others?
~ What "personality traits" or emotions tend to repeatedly get you in trouble (such as pride, jealousy, a need to please, anxiety, etc.)?
~ How do you currently deal with these personality traits and emotions when they crop up, and what are the results?
~ How motivated are you to learn better ways of coping with your dark side? Are you content to let it be, or do you truly desire a change?

## We are blind to our strengths

People who thrive, who excel to the highest levels—personally and professionally—have at least one thing in common: They know what they do best. Warren Buffett, "the world's greatest investor," is an easy professional example. This down-home, slightly disheveled financial titan from Nebraska may not seem like one of the wealthiest men ever, but he certainly knows how to sniff out a good investment. His patient and practical mind make this his signature strength. What makes him special, according to Marcus Buckingham and Donald Clifton of the Gallup International Research and Education Center, is that "he became aware of it." Buffet knows what he's not so good at (so he leaves that to others) and he knows what he does best. And he loves doing it every day he wakes up.

> **Most of us do not monitor our thoughts with the care needed so that we can create in our lives the results we say we want.**
> *Sidney Madwed*

Authors of a landmark study and the book, *Now, Discover Your Strengths,* Buckingham and Clifton have revealed that most people do not know what their strengths are. Business guru Peter Drucker echoes their point: "When you ask [people about their strengths] they look at you with a blank stare, or they respond in terms of subject knowledge, which is the wrong answer."

The tragedy of life for many people is not that we don't have enough strengths; it's that we are unaware of the ones we have. Benjamin Franklin aptly called these wasted strengths "sundials in the shade." After all, how can you best position your strengths or maximize them if you don't know what they are?

## We are blind to our limits

The converse of being unaware of our strengths is being blind to our limits. Many of us can also be clueless when it comes to our shortcomings and incompetencies.

Both of us have done a great deal of marriage therapy and one of the deficiencies we've seen in couples with unnecessary problems is their lack of accurate assessment. Every couple has deficits. But these struggling couples don't know what theirs are. "We just don't know how to communicate," they might say. In a sense, this may be true, but their real deficit is that they don't know how to make time for meaningful communication or they may have kept their feelings boxed up or any number of things. Communication breakdowns are only a symptom of their real problem. And if they weren't blind to this fact, they could do something about it.

The same holds true in work settings. In a comparison of executives who floundered and those who succeeded, both groups had weaknesses; the critical difference was that those who did not succeed failed to learn from their mistakes and accurately assess and accept their shortcomings. The unsuccessful executives ignored their faults, often rebuffing those who tried to point them out. Among several hundred managers from twelve different organizations, "accuracy in self-assessment was a hallmark of superior performance," according to author Daniel Goleman. "It's not that top performers have no limits," he says, but "they are *aware* of their limits."

Are you aware of your limits? Try the exercise now to find out.

## ARE YOU AWARE OF YOUR LIMITS?

One of the hallmarks of authenticity is knowing your deficiencies, your areas for growth. Countless blind spots are spurred on by this lack of acknowledgment. To help you face up to yours, try this simple exercise.

First, *note your top three deficiencies.* Survey your personality over the last few weeks and ask yourself, *What three deficiencies have been the most blatant?* These may have to do with relationships (criticizing more than is necessary), work performance (not giving proper credit to people), parenting (losing your patience because you are expecting more than is possible), or any number of areas.

Now, *consider how a good friend or spouse would answer this same question for you.* In other words, what would he or she say are your top three deficiencies?

~

~

~

Finally, take a deep breath. This last step is not for cowards. Ready? *Consider asking a friend or spouse how they perceive your top three areas for growth.* You need not do this immediately, but if you muster up the courage to ask for this kind of feedback in the next few days (before moving to the next chapter), you will take a quantum leap in self-awareness. Sure, it's risky. You've got to remain nondefensive. But this exercise is a true eye-opener that's sure to speed up your progress toward authenticity.

---

## We are blind to our egoism

You have just returned from an amazing vacation to the Galápagos Islands, but after the obligatory "How was your trip?" the conversation with some friends turns to and remains on them. They tell you about a deadline they are under at work, a conversation with their spouse, or a movie they just saw. They seem oblivious to you and your recent experience—and they are. How does this happen? Egoism. Think of these people as wearing mirrored sunglasses with the lenses flipped around. Everywhere they look they see a reflection of themselves and their own needs. They think they are looking at you, but they aren't. Their egoism pushes them to project feelings and thoughts on to you that have far more to do with their own emotions than yours.

Welcome to the world of the oblivious egotists who, if reading these words, would have a very difficult time acknowledging that this is them. But we still have to ask: Is there any possibility this might describe you?

> **The greatest of faults . . . is to be conscious of none.**
> *Thomas Carlyle*

Both of us have worked in academic institutions where peer evaluations of one's work are commonplace. And after reviewing countless performance appraisals we have seen a phenomenon we've now come to expect. The people whose work is lacking invariably have significant discrepancies between how they rate themselves on abilities like listening and adaptability and how their peers rate them on these same qualities. Of course, how our peers see us is almost always the more accurate predictor of our actual performance. Some people simply cannot imagine that they are not as good as they think they are.

Psychologists David Dunning and Justin Kruger tested students at Cornell University on a range of subjects from logical reasoning to grammar to the ability to spot a funny joke. They compared how well people thought they did versus how well they actually did. "Overall, people overestimated themselves," said Dunning, a professor of psychology at Cornell. "And those who did worst were most likely to think they had outperformed everyone else. Incompetent people don't know they're incompetent."

With results like these, it seems we'd all do well to examine our leanings toward egoism. To find out how you're doing, try the "Ego Check" exercise now.

———————————— EGO CHECK ————————————

1. Do you adapt well to new situations?
   ~ Definitely, and always
   ~ Most of the time
   ~ Sometimes
   ~ Rarely

Give an example of why you rated yourself as you did above.

2. When interacting with others or starting a conversation, do you tend to
   ~ Have an agenda of what you're going to say?
   ~ Ask questions to get to know others?
   ~ Make conversation by talking about what interests you?
   ~ Focus on making sure the other person is comfortable?

Think about the last conversation you had before you read this. Then ask yourself again, *Did I focus on myself—or the other person?* The answer will tell you how much you lean toward egoism.

3. On a scale of 1–10, with 1 being a "poor" listener and 10 being a "terrific" listener, where would you place yourself, and why? Give an example of a recent interaction you've had.

4. Have you ever been surprised by a person's response to you (whether in words or body language)? Describe the situation. Can you identify anything that you might have done to give that person that impression?

---

**We are blind to our emotions**

Scientists call it *metamood,* the ability to pull back and recognize that "what I'm feeling is anger," or sorrow, or shame. It's a difficult skill because our emotions so often appear in disguise. A person in mourning may know she is sad, but she may not recognize that she is also angry at the person for dying—because this seems somehow inappropriate. A parent who yells at the child who ran into the street is expressing anger at disobedience, but the degree of anger may owe more to the fear the parent feels at what could have happened. The boss who feels attacked by an employee's question about a new policy may be completely unaware that the innocent question seems aggressive to him only because his father used to ask the same kinds of things to point out his shortcomings.

Not recognizing how we really feel is one of the most common and troubling blind spots. When we don't see how we really feel, our emotions start to manage *us,* rather than the other way around. We literally begin to mask our emotions. We may be ticked off at a friend who's late, but if anger is too threatening, we simply smile and ignore our churning stomach. Later that evening we find ourselves snapping at our spouse for no good reason at all. *Where did that come from?* you both wonder.

**An anxious heart weighs a man down.**
*Proverbs 12:25*

When you are blind to your emotions, you give up your ability to control them. They bleed into other areas of your life where they have no right to be. You may start your day badly at home because your morning paper wasn't delivered and your coffee was weak. But if you don't know it—if you don't pull back and recognize that what you are feeling is disappointment or frustration—you'll be grouchy at work, never quite knowing why.

Once an emotional response comes into awareness—you acknowledge your metamood—the chances of handling it appropriately greatly improve . . . an impossibility if you are blind to your true emotions.

Can you identify your true emotions? Try the "Are You Aware of Your Emotions?" exercise now.

─────── ARE YOU AWARE OF YOUR EMOTIONS? ───────

1. Describe the last time you were really upset or angry. What was the situation? How did you respond?

2. Think about the factors "around" the incident. Why did that particular situation lead to that emotion? Has it happened to you before—with the same person or another person?

3. Identify the "true" emotion behind your anger. Was it
   ~ Disappointment?
   ~ Fear?
   ~ Shame or embarrassment?
   ~ The shock of betrayal?
   ~ Guilt?

4. How will knowing this help you respond differently in other "emotional" situations in the future?

─────────────────────────────────────────────

When we live in denial of our dark side, our strengths, our limits, our egoism, and our emotions, we pay a price. And more often than not, the price is staggering, as we are about to see.

✦　✦　✦

## EXPLORING YOUR PERSONAL BLIND SPOTS

Now that you have read about the five most common blind spots, take a moment to consider how each of them relates specifically to you. Take your time and be as honest as possible.

## Your Dark Side

**T    F**    I struggle with parts of myself that are materialistic or selfish.

**T    F**    I try to ignore or bury my baser parts—pretending I don't
really struggle with things like irresponsibility or dishonesty.

**T    F**    I rarely, if ever, reveal my struggles with such things as
selfishness or envy to even my closest friends.

**T    F**    If I'm honest, there is a little imp within me that enjoys
another person's suffering on occasion.

If you answered mostly "True" to these items, you are in touch with your
dark side. You are not blind to the parts of your self that you wish weren't
there. This self-awareness will serve you well on the path to wholeness.

## Your Strengths

**T    F**    I'm comfortable receiving a compliment for something I do
well.

**T    F**    I know what I do best.

**T    F**    I could readily identify my top three strengths.

**T    F**    I work to maximize what I'm good at rather than bolster
my weaknesses.

If you answered mostly "True" to this set of items, you tend to be in
touch with your personal strengths. You know what your personal assets
are and you are probably using them to your full advantage. This will help
you immeasurably as you journey toward unswerving authenticity.

## Your Limits

**T    F**    I can't really think of too many incompetencies I might
have.

**T    F**    I rarely make mistakes and when I do, I can usually find
a person who is also to blame.

**T    F**    If I have a goal to reach, nothing is going to stand in my way.

**T    F**    The word *failure* is not in my vocabulary.

If you answered mostly "False" to this set of items, you tend to
be in touch with your personal limits. You know you can't do every-

thing well, and you probably have a fair degree of humility as a result. This quality will move you along more speedily in your attempt to become more congruent and authentic.

## Your Egoism

T   F   In social settings, I am very deliberate and conscious of trying to find out about other people and make them feel comfortable.

T   F   I often ask for other people's input on my performance at work and I'm genuinely interested in what they think I can do to improve.

T   F   When someone has a problem with me, I immediately try to examine what I am doing to cause the problem—rather than assuming that they are the one with the problem.

T   F   I'm not always comfortable with the proverbial spotlight on me.

If you answered mostly "True" to this set of items, you have probably worked hard to look beyond your own life and put yourself in the place of others. Your empathy and your ability to step beyond your own needs will pay big dividends when it comes to cultivating authenticity.

## Your Emotions

T   F   I'm very aware of my angry impulses and can tell you when I feel the internal pressure rising to boil.

T   F   I could easily label the emotions I am feeling at this very moment without giving it more than a few seconds of thought.

T   F   I can recall times in my life when I have shifted the anger I feel onto a person or object that is less threatening than the real target of my anger.

T   F   I can often calm my nerves by simply identifying how I feel and why I feel it.

If you answered mostly "True" to this set of items, you are in touch with your feelings. You are good at identifying them and acknowledging why you feel the way you do. This emotional self-awareness is a terrific benefit, one of the most important, for becoming unswervingly authentic.

✦ ✦ ✦

## THE HIGH PRICE OF THE UNEXAMINED LIFE

The creators of the *Titanic* spared no expense to make sure it would be unsinkable. The ship's officers were unconcerned by their inability to get accurate information on possible hazards that might lie in its course. The ship had two lookouts on her masts, but the lookouts had no binoculars. The crew couldn't see far enough ahead to react to danger, and they had no way to get their information to the captain if they did see a problem approaching.

We all know what happened. The unsinkable ocean liner went to her death, along with most of her passengers, on her maiden voyage from Europe to New York, the victim of a disastrous collision with an iceberg.

What you don't see *can* hurt you. For example, you can convince yourself that if you submerge the dark side of your personality, ignoring its presence, it won't bother you. But you're wrong. Dead wrong. What you bury has a high rate of resurrection. Somehow, somewhere, it will pop up through the surface and be uglier than when you first buried it.

Let's say you abhor envy and petty jealousy in others. It's the last thing you would like to find in yourself so you turn a blind eye. You act as if envy would never *ever* take up residence in you. But it has. It may not live on the main floor but, like the rest of your dark side, it is locked away in the basement. Left alone long enough, unchecked, envy grows. And when you least expect it—maybe when your child has a great success or your friend gets a huge promotion—it bursts through the basement door of your personality and wreaks havoc throughout your whole house, fracturing the relationships you prize the most.

Sometimes the price we pay for our blind spots is not seen in an abrupt eruption, but it is paid more slowly over time. Say you are blind to your egoism. You may be charismatic and likable, but you haven't a clue how to really enter another person's world—and you don't know it. The emotional capability to walk in someone else's shoes, to imagine what their experience must be like, is foreign to you. But the people in your life put up with this "quirk." They don't expect you to invest emotionally in them. Your enthusiasm or your business savvy or your humor makes up for this interpersonal deficiency. People may come to respect you and your talent, but, sadly, they may not like you.

We've all seen an influential person who enjoys business success but pays the price for it, over time, by losing a deep and genuine connection with friends and family. The people in his or her life learn they have been used or viewed as peripheral. They were simply a stepping-stone or a decoration in this person's warped world. And if anyone dares confront the egotists, they are most likely "amazed" that anyone could even think it—for they cannot think it of themselves. They refuse to look at any evidence that contradicts their fantasy.

> **Your paradigm is so intrinsic to your mental process that you are hardly aware of its existence, until you try to communicate with someone with a different paradigm.**
> *Donella Meadows*

Let's make this plain. The price you pay for too many blind spots is a distortion of reality. You trade the truth for a false sense of security. By avoiding the facts of a negative trait you possess, you numb yourself to critics who point it out. In the short-term your blind spots guard against the incumbent anxiety and pain that accepting the truth might bring. You avoid, temporarily, this mental anguish. But this tactic comes with a high price: skewed perceptions and a warped personality. It is no exaggeration to say that your blind spots, if unchecked, may eventually cost you a friendship, a job, a marriage, and, most certainly, your peace of mind. And that's a high price even for the most wealthy.

However, if you choose not to shield yourself from the truth about your blind spots, if you choose to gather the information you need to become healthy, balanced, and whole, you will also experience profound significance, become unswervingly authentic, and begin to exhibit self-giving love—the very qualities of a fulfilled life with rich relationships.

## THREE PAYOFFS FOR INCREASING SELF-AWARENESS

As we've seen, it's easy to "go blind" to information that is so troubling, so frightening, or so riddled with anxiety that to see it clearly would require us to alter our view of ourselves or the world. But when we gain our sight, when we absorb reality, feeling what we really feel and knowing what we really think, we "become conscious." And that is the definition of *awakening*. To say that increasing our self-awareness does anything less would be a lie. Healthy self-awareness creates a virtually indestructible foundation for meaningful relationships, inner harmony, and personal freedom to choose our next step. Each moment becomes a miracle when you see more clearly.

> Let us resolve to be masters, not the victims, of our history, controlling our own destiny without giving way to blind suspicions and emotions.
> *John Fitzgerald Kennedy*

Hunting down your blind spots can be a bumpy adventure, but it leads to sublime destinations. Let's take a look at each of them.

### 1. Self-awareness lowers your stress

Want to rid yourself of undue stress? Decrease your blind spots. Why? For starters, self-awareness diminishes the time you spend stewing over stressful emotions. When you accurately identify how you feel, for example, you recover from distress more quickly. An experiment requiring people to watch a graphic anti-drunk-driving film depicting bloody automobile accidents lends credence. In the half hour after viewing the film many subjects reported feelings of tension, distress, and depression. They found themselves repeatedly thinking of upsetting scenes they had just witnessed. Those viewers who were aware of their emotions, who could identify more precisely what their experience was, however, recovered from their feelings of distress far more quickly.

Another study focused on people who were laid off. Many were, understandably, angry. Half were told to keep a journal for five days, spending twenty minutes writing out their deepest feelings (a common exercise in raising self-awareness). Those who kept journals found new jobs faster than those who didn't. Their heightened self-awareness lowered stress and more quickly enabled productivity.

Emotional clarity enables you to manage bad moods. It soothes your frustrations, calms your annoyances. In short, self-awareness lowers your stress. Richard Lazarus, in his book *Emotion and Adaptation,* reports on a college professor who was given a portable heart-rate monitor to wear because of his heart problems. Doctors feared that little oxygen was reaching the professor's heart muscle, but they needed to accurately assess how his heart was beating throughout a typical day. On this day the professor attended one of his regular and far-too-frequent departmental meetings—something he considered a waste of time.

But this typical day revealed something the professor was surprised to find . . . something he was completely unaware of. He learned from the monitor that, while he thought he was cynically detached from the discussions, his heart was pounding away at dangerous levels during his meetings. He had not realized until then how distressed he was by the daily scuffle of departmental politics—even when he felt uninvolved.

Without self-awareness, we are surprisingly oblivious to stress. Like the professor with heart problems or the laid-off workers, we allow stress to quietly creep in and dismantle our contentment. We allow it to sabotage our efforts and elongate our suffering. But once we diminish our blind spots, stress fades more quickly and keeps its distance more often.

## 2. Self-awareness improves your relationships

It all came to a head one day for Linda, a paralegal, as she sat alone in the work lunchroom for the third time that week. A year earlier she and a group of coworkers had always planned to take their lunches together. That half hour had been the highlight of her day since it was always filled with lively discussion. But lately her friends had been taking their lunches together, elsewhere—and they weren't inviting her.

On her drive home after work, Linda agonized, *Why? Don't my friends care about me anymore? What's wrong with them? Or is it me?*

What Linda didn't know is that she had been quietly poisoning her relationships over the entire past year until no one wanted to be around her anymore. When Janice, one of the women in the group, had become engaged, Linda was still single—and the only one who didn't congratulate Janice. Linda had made it clear, through her body language and sarcastic tone, that she didn't appreciate hearing about wedding plans or romantic dinners. And most certainly, she didn't want to accompany the group on any shopping trips for bridal paraphernalia. Her bitterness had made her a difficult—and embarrassing—friend to be around. So as time went on, the group left her out of more and more activities.

It took a caring, kind, but firm pastor to help Linda identify her blind spots and uncover what she didn't even realize herself—that she considered herself a "half" person until she found "her other half" and that she was deeply angry at God because she had just turned forty and didn't yet have her "soul mate."

Until Linda was able to acknowledge her blind spots and her hidden emotions, she could not be a real friend to Janice, who had been single for almost as many years as Linda and was excited but also nervous about linking her life permanently with another person's.

Being self-aware is a prerequisite for empathy. *Empathy*—*Merriam-Webster's* calls it "the action of understanding, being aware of, being sensitive to, and vicariously experiencing the feelings, thoughts, and experience of another"—is a key ingredient for healthy relationships. If we are not self-aware—and on the road to becoming unswervingly authentic—it is impossible to step into another's shoes or to become a true friend. But as you become more aware of who you are and the factors that have influenced you, you can begin to work through those issues in your life. And that will leave you more time and emotional energy to improve your relationships.

> As iron sharpens iron, so one man sharpens another.
>
> *Proverbs 27:17*

### 3. Self-awareness unlocks personal freedom

In 1997, when Oprah Winfrey was preparing to play Sethe in the movie *Beloved,* she arranged a trip along a portion of the Underground Railroad. "I wanted to connect with what it felt like to be a slave wandering through the woods," she said, "making the way north to a life beyond slavery—a life where being free, at its most basic level, meant not having a master telling you what to do every minute." To immerse herself in the experience Oprah was blindfolded and taken into the woods where she was left alone to contemplate how she would find her way to the next safe house. "I understood for the first time that freedom isn't about not having a master. Freedom is about having a choice."

The freedom to choose one's way in life is beyond compare. Without it, we are doomed to a life with limits at every turn. Consider Martha Chapman, a twenty-eight-year-old secretary to a grocery-store buyer. Martha was convinced she'd soon be promoted to assistant buyer, even though several younger women had been promoted ahead of her during the preceding three years. Martha's friends had been urging her to find a new job for years, but she turned down job offers, continuing to believe she had a future with the store. When her boss bluntly told her she was never going to be promoted, Martha was devastated.

"I had no idea at the time why I had been so blind to the truth," she recalls, "but I went into therapy because I felt absolutely worthless." Through therapy Martha realized that her blindness was rooted in unconscious fears. When she was a child, her father had moved the family across the country to take a new job. Soon afterward, he died of a heart attack.

"My father's death was a huge and horrible event in my childhood," Martha says, "but I didn't connect it with my own unwillingness to look for a better job in another company. In therapy, it became obvious to me that I associated my father's dying with his getting a new job and moving. In fact, I was unwilling to move, too. For years I lived in a horrible one-room apartment in a crumbling neighborhood, telling my friends it had charm and character. I warped my life to avoid facing down my own fears and I sacrificed my freedom to make my own choices."

If you feel stuck, stagnant, without options, then you've been boxed in by your blind spots. Once the blinders come off, a new perspective sets in. You see the horizon of possibilities. You recognize choices you didn't know you had. Self-awareness unlocks personal freedom.

> Man's capacity to experience himself as both subject and object at the same time [is] necessary for gratifying living.
>
> *Rolo May*

## HOW TO BECOME MORE SELF-AWARE

Neuroscientists, especially at Harvard University in Boston and Temple University in Philadelphia, are excited. A recent study they conducted shed significant light on the biology of self-awareness and tapped into the physical foundations of consciousness itself. Although their findings are based on investigations of only five patients, the results are compelling.

The five patients were injected with amobarbital to selectively anesthetize either the left or the right hemisphere of their brain. They were then shown a photograph of a face generated by "morphing" the patient's face with a famous celebrity.

Following anesthesia, each of the patients was asked which face was presented: the self-face or the famous face. "With the right hemisphere anesthetized," explains Julian Keenan of Harvard Medical School, the lead investigator of the study, "the patients selected the famous face. With the left hemisphere anesthetized the patients selected the self-face."

This small study is helping to solve one of the enduring mysteries of neuropsychology, namely the role of the right prefrontal cortex in self-awareness. This area of the brain has long been the "silent area" because researchers could not clearly explain its function—until now. The assignment of self-consciousness to this region is a breakthrough in brain work.

If you are not a neuroscientist, this recent discovery may not be all that thrilling. You're probably more concerned with the relevance of this study to your own level of self-awareness, and rightly so. After all, this is the promise of our chapter: To help you become increasingly self-aware, today and every day.

It is our hope that just as these scientists have discovered the location of consciousness in the brain, that you would tap into this area and discover your own breakthrough in personal self-awareness. That's what we'll help you do next.

## Be forewarned . . .

While self-awareness can be heightened through a variety of means, the one we are about to reveal is the most fundamental and effective.

Before we explore it, however, we have two important warnings:

1. *Its effectiveness will either sink or swim based on your mind-set.* The heightening of self-awareness demands a nonreactive, nonjudgmental attitude. It requires you to step back from your experience and explore it with an eagerness to accurately see it. Objectivity is the key. "A second self," says novelist William Styron, "is able to watch with dispassionate curiosity as his companion struggles."

> The awareness of the ambiguity of one's highest achievements (as well as one's deepest failures) is a definite symptom of maturity.
>
> *Paul Tillich*

Are you up to this? Your mission, as we see it, is a direct seek-and-destroy attack on your own pockets of denial.

2. *The nearer to the core of your personality you probe, the stronger will be your resistance.* But you *can* do it if you decide to. So we urge you to make a decision at the outset that you will pursue this path of finding the truth. If you don't want to find it, the strategy that follows will serve no purpose. If, on the other hand, you'd like to take this exciting journey of self-discovery, we are convinced it may be one of the most important things you ever do. So here goes.

## A time-tested strategy that works

Danish writer Hans Christian Andersen, famous for his fairy tales, revealed a powerful message for all of us who are tracking down our blind spots. You heard the story as a child, but it bears repeating in this context. "The Emperor's New Clothes" is the story of a conceited emperor who surrounds himself with people who only say what he wants to hear. Even the browbeaten citizens of the empire are so cowering and timid that they dare not disagree with the emperor's edicts, nor will they criticize anything he says or does.

Then two con men appear on the scene. They realize the ridiculous situation in the empire and are looking to make a fast buck. They announce that they are the world's best tailors and offer to make wonderful garments for the emperor—clothing such as has never been seen before. The catch is that the price tag for such royal garments is exorbitant. And as vanity will have it, the emperor insists that they make him new clothes.

After collecting a huge fee, the con men go to work, miming the actions of tailors. The emperor is measured and fitted, refitted and remeasured. The kingdom awaits breathlessly the day when the emperor will appear in his new duds, for word has it that only men of the purest of hearts will be able to see the glorious clothing in which the emperor will make his debut.

Finally the day comes, and the emperor is dressed in his new clothes. Everyone compliments the emperor on his stunning appearance as he strolls regally through his capital city.

Unbeknownst to his people, however, the emperor is having some doubts about his own purity of heart. He can't see his new clothes. Knowing that he cannot allow his people to see his own consternation, he goes along with the ploy. The crowd becomes more and more enthralled with his new outfit. Then suddenly, from somewhere back in the crowd, a young boy shouts, "The emperor has no clothes!"

The emperor is horrified. The crowd is dismayed. But slowly it begins to dawn on everyone present: Who has a more pure heart than a child? Sure enough, the emperor *is* naked.

And so was born a lesson for ages, a lesson especially for all of us seeking the truth: Without honest feedback we live an illusion.

Hunting for your own blind spots is like trying to examine the back of your own head. You can arrange mirrors at just the right angle and contort your neck as much as you like, but the easiest solution is to *solicit feedback from others.*

We can almost feel some of you about to close the covers of this book. *I don't want to ask people for feedback,* you may be thinking. But hear us out. The exercise we are about to outline just may be one of the single most important things you ever do to become healthy. It holds great potential for redefining you as a mature, well-balanced person.

You can work this mindful exercise in a couple of different ways.

1. *A common strategy is to list half a dozen people in your life whom you respect.* Tell each of them what you are doing and arrange a one-on-one meeting where they agree to talk about you. Ask them about their perceptions of you—your strengths, yes—but mostly your areas for growth. Invite them to give you specific examples that illustrate their perceptions. Of course, you'll want to take notes and compile a summary from all of these sessions.

2. *Another way to go is less intense, but also helpful.* For the next week or so, ask one or two people every day, never asking the same person twice, a simple question: "Is there anything about me that I don't seem to see but you do?" You can ask it of family members as well as people on the periphery of your life. If you have the courage, you could even ask relative strangers to give you their perception of you. Their insights might surprise you.

## Processing feedback

Whatever path you choose for gathering feedback—scheduled one-on-ones or more spontaneous encounters or both—you will need to make a three-point plan:

1. *Brace yourself for receiving it.* Nobody likes feedback on their foibles. Hearing that you come off as aloof or insensitive can easily elicit a defensive emotional reaction. Curb this impulse by simply saying, "Thanks." You are on a fact-finding expedition, so don't launch into an argument, even if you think the person is off base. You can decide later whether or not the person's feedback is useful.

2. *Make a plan for processing it.* Sometimes feedback will be objective; other times the information may be viewed through that person's own particular lens and motives. One of the reasons for gathering feedback from several people, in fact, is to filter out perceptions that have more to do with the speaker's dysfunction than yours. Typically, this is feedback that's vague—where the person can't think of an example to back it up. Useful feedback is specific and focused. It may hurt, but it leads to insight. So instead of ruminating on it, dismiss useless feedback and focus on the information your gut tells you is valuable.

Part of your processing plan, of course, must incorporate what you will do with this feedback. Neurologist Oliver Sacks wrote about a man who, virtually blind from early childhood, had an operation that restored his sight when he was middle-aged. Though the man's eyes now took in visual information, his brain wasn't used to making sense of it. You may feel the same way as you consider this feedback. You're not used to your new set of eyes. So give it time. Don't expect to always correctly gauge how you are coming across to others as you work on being more sensitive or more assertive, for example. Be patient with yourself. You'll soon see your behavior more clearly as the false image of yourself gives way to a more accurate self-perception.

3. *Realize that this exercise is not a one-shot proposition.* Asking others for feedback should be an ongoing exercise. Six months after you initially receive feedback, you'll want to go back to many of these same people and ask again how they view you. It's the only true way to track your progress in making sure your blind spots don't blind you from becoming unswervingly authentic. As the wise proverb says, "Wounds from a friend can be trusted, but an enemy multiplies kisses."

We have a friend who starts each new year with this exercise. During the first week of January, he mails out a simple feedback form to about ten people, asking them to point out his blind spots from the previous year. You may wish to start your year the same way.

But the most important thing to remember is that you can continue to ask for feedback as the months roll along. No one fixes their blind spots instantly; it takes self-awareness, acceptance, tenacity, and practice.

And if you want to be healthy, you have to know—and be working on—your blind spots. Healthy people know themselves well. They gain self-knowledge not through a high IQ, but through a desire and determination to become unswervingly authentic. They step back from their experience with a nonjudgmental and inquisitive attitude to accurately understand themselves. In other words, they know themselves well because they *choose* to.

# 7

## HARNESSING YOUR WILD SIDE

*The happiness of a man in this life*
*does not consist in the absence*
*but in the mastery of his passions.*

ALFRED, LORD TENNYSON

*T*he motion picture *Unfaithful,* starring Richard Gere and Diane Lane, features a typical, young American family whose relationships are shattered by uncontrolled anger and unrestrained sexual urges.

The main characters, Connie and Edward Sumner, appear happy together after eleven years of marriage. They are deeply in love and totally committed to their eight-year-old son. But Connie gets caught up in a torrid affair with a handsome stranger, even though she fights hard to resist her relentless desires.

At one point Connie tells her lover, "I think this was a mistake."

"There is no such thing as a mistake," he responds. "There are things you do and don't do."

Despite that equivocation, Connie discovers that actions do indeed have consequences. Her recklessness sets in motion a frightening and horrible set of events. Discovering his wife's indiscretions, Edward is stunned and enraged. Like his wife, he tries to tame his destructive impulses, to no avail. The result is total devastation for every person involved. It's a sad, torturous, awful story about unbridled sex and anger.

Painful as this film is to watch, it points to a universal truth about human beings: Every living, breathing person on earth has impulses that, if poorly managed, create chaos in their lives. But there is good news to go along with the bad—if these same impulses are managed wisely, they produce magnificent personal gains.

The goal of this chapter is to help you take your strongest, wildest impulses and use them for dramatic growth—growth that can exponentially increase and expand the boundaries of emotional and mental health in your life.

> **It is with our passions as it is with fire and water. They are good servants but bad masters.**
>
> *Aesop*

Learning to be in command of your strongest, wildest impulses is vitally important. Although you may be experiencing other wild horses in your life—such as a constant craving for food even though the scales indicate that you need to put on the brakes, or a much-too-often inner push to buy more things even though your finances are yelling out for an easing up in your spending, or a daily need to work more hours and expend more energy in the pursuit of your career goals even though your spouse and your family are crying out for more of your time and attention—most psychological theorists agree that the two most powerful emotions we have are our anger and sex drives. That's why we've dedicated this chapter to talking solely about these two "wild horses."

If these familiar and ferocious forces strike terror in your heart, you are not alone. You may know how these forces can overwhelm you, drive you to act irrationally, and leave you feeling guilty and helpless. Or perhaps you've been on the receiving end of anger or sexual abuse and you have the physical or emotional scars to show for it.

Indeed, there is little doubt that the mismanagement of sexual and angry feelings has wreaked havoc on our society. Consider these shocking facts:

• Some 10 million children are likely abused every year by their parents and relatives. Most of these are *loving* parents who simply lose control. Two-thirds of these kids are under the age of three.

- Estimates range from 960,000 incidents of violence against a current or former spouse, boyfriend, or girlfriend per year to 3 million women who are physically abused by their husband or boyfriend per year. While anger is obviously involved, sexual impulses frequently contribute to the devastation.
- Although sexual assaults remain the most underreported cases in the criminal-justice system, we know that every hour sixteen women confront rapists, and a woman is actually raped every six minutes. A total of over 96,000 forcible rapes are committed in this country each year.
- A murder occurs in the United States every thirty-four minutes, and a violent crime is committed every twenty-two seconds.
- Violence and out-of-control anger in schools have become a matter of extreme national importance. Far from being an isolated event, the Columbine High School massacre in Littleton, Colorado—which took the lives of fifteen people in April 1999—was just one of eight multiple killings by students within a two-year period.
- Road rage is a similar kind of escalating problem. A growing number of men, women, and children suffer injury or death at the hands of wildly angry drivers using bats, golf clubs, knives, and even cars themselves as weapons. Even national celebrity Jack Nicholson became upset with the driver of a Mercedes-Benz that cut him off. Nicholson got out of his car at a red light and repeatedly struck the roof and windshield of his enemy.

> **A fool gives full vent to his anger, but a wise man keeps himself under control.**
> *Proverbs 29:11*

But let's get beyond all these "extreme" cases and talk about the way ordinary, well-intentioned people like *you* manage intense feelings. Have you developed healthy and effective ways to deal with your anger? And when you get sexually "turned on," do you typically act with wisdom and good judgment?

Take this self-test to find out.

✦  ✦  ✦

## WHAT'S YOUR WILD SIDE?

Many people struggle mightily with the appropriate time and way to express anger and sexual feelings.

Read the following list of situations. In the space provided, estimate the degree to which each incident would ordinarily anger or provoke you. Use this rating scale.

0 = You would feel very angry.
1 = You would feel quite angry.
2 = You would feel moderately upset.
3 = You would feel a little irritated.
4 = You would feel very little or no annoyance.

1. You are teased in front of your friends.
2. You are hounded by a salesperson from the moment you walk into a store.
3. You are wearing a new pair of pants, and a waiter spills salad dressing on them.
4. You discover someone you trusted has broken your confidence.
5. You are overcharged by a repairman who has you over a barrel.
6. You are working at your computer, and a family member accidentally kicks the plug out. You lose a document you are working on.
7. Your colleague is more than fifteen minutes late for a lunch meeting.
8. You are cut off in traffic by a reckless driver.
9. You lend someone an important book, and it's never returned.
10. Your battery for your cell phone goes out in the middle of an important conversation.

Now, read the following list of statements. In the space provided, estimate the degree to which you agree or disagree with each one. Use this rating scale.

0 = I disagree very much with this.
1 = I disagree somewhat with this.
2 = I neither agree nor disagree with this.
3 = I agree somewhat with this.
4 = I wholeheartedly agree with this.

1. I almost always keep my sexual urges under control.
2. Sexual feelings are a normal and healthy part of life.
3. I've made conscious safeguards to keep me from making bad decisions involving my sex life.
4. Sexual urges can motivate me to engage in constructive behaviors.
5. The only problem with sexual feelings and urges occurs when they are not properly managed.
6. My sexual feelings rarely get me into trouble.
7. I can't remember a time when my sexual feelings caused me to do something I regretted.
8. I almost always make wise decisions when it comes to my sexual impulses.
9. Sex is a gift from God to be celebrated.
10. I have very little shame regarding my sexual choices.

## SCORING

There are 40 possible points on each of these subscales. If you scored 30 or higher on the first scale, you are doing quite well at managing your anger. If you scored 30 or higher on the second scale, this indicates that you have learned to manage your sexuality relatively well and that you tend to have a healthy perspective on sex. If your score on either one of these is lower than 30, you will benefit greatly from the principles and exercise you'll find in the remainder of this chapter.

✦    ✦    ✦

Many people, of course, struggle mightily with the appropriate time and way to express anger and sexual feelings. It's a struggle that has been around since the very beginning. Soon after the Bible's account of Creation, the story is told of unbridled anger leading one brother to kill another. And we can see the ricochet effects of that same angry force through every generation since.

The results of three decades of "sexual revolution" have left us with major problems of every sort. For instance, a million teenage girls find themselves pregnant every year, and the percentage of births to unwed mothers continues to rise. In some American cities, 85 to 90 percent of all teenagers who give birth are unwed mothers.

Then there's the high rate of divorce and marital dissatisfaction. Researchers point to poor mate selection as a primary cause of these problems, and the inability to manage sexual impulses frequently plays a crucial role since early sexual involvement impairs objective decision making.

The bottom line is clear: Millions of Americans have developed ineffective ways to handle sexual urges and anger, and this has resulted in significant heartache and chaos.

## FOCUSING ENERGY IN THE RIGHT DIRECTION

It's tempting to talk about anger and sexual impulses only in dark and foreboding terms—to emphasize the negative aspects of these emotions. But hear us clearly: These emotions can be managed so successfully that they become positive contributors to a person's (even a society's) emotional health. It is our strong conviction that emotional, physical, and spiritual health require the harnessing of these nuclear-powered inner drives. And it is undeniable that without harnessing these forces, a person cannot become unswervingly authentic.

> **Perfection of moral virtue does not wholly take away the passions, but regulates them.**
> *Thomas Aquinas*

The fact is, everyone has a body that automatically responds to important life events—and, therefore, everyone has anger and sexual impulses. That's the way we're wired. So if you sometimes feel "turbocharged" with these feelings, congratulations—you're human. There is nothing unusual about you.

Even though these two feelings operate in much the same way within us, they are obviously triggered quite differently. We typically get mad when we encounter primary pain, which is nearly always related to hurt, frustration, and fear. When we encounter these feelings, our body automatically makes energy available to us, enabling us to deal effectively with whatever is causing pain. Anger, then, is absolutely necessary in our effort to manage distress and discomfort. It is simply physiological preparedness, and we can learn to harness this energy so that our pain is minimized.

Sexual feelings are also a natural part of our biological inheritance. If our memory were inclusive enough, we could recall having sexual feelings in some rudimentary form almost from the beginning of our lives. There is absolutely nothing wrong with these feelings. Sacred writings such as the Song of Solomon celebrate the pure and sensuous love of a man and a woman. Sexual urges motivate us to engage in all sorts of constructive behaviors, produce a wide range of creative responses, and focus our attention on a person with whom we can form a long-term, meaningful partnership. But the trouble begins when these urges are not harnessed and managed within the bounds for which they were created.

Whatever we don't know about anger and sexual impulses, one thing is certain: They are unbelievably powerful! You can do wonderful, even miraculous, things when you are motivated by them. For example, athletes who control their angry feelings and marshal them in the service of their goals often pull off spectacular performances. John McEnroe was a tennis player who frequently became angry, and careful research shows that he almost always played more victoriously after he acknowledged and expressed his anger. Businessmen who can manage their anger often recognize its contributions to their successes. Lee Iacocca of Chrysler fame concluded, "I've come to believe that there isn't a problem in America today that we couldn't solve if we could become angry enough about it."

> **Control thy passions, lest they take vengeance on thee.**
>
> *Epictetus*

But just as often, you can create mayhem in your life by managing these forces irrationally.

Consider an example of how the positive application of anger can make changes for the better. After sixteen homicides in only six days in Los Angeles, the new police chief, William J. Bratton, called on the citizens of Los Angeles to get mad. He issued a challenge for the city to become so provoked that they fight back and stop the violence.

"I'm very disturbed and angry," Bratton said in an interview. "I need the city angry about gangbangers shaping the perception of Los Angeles."

Even though Bratton's challenge to the city is too recent for a careful analysis of long-term trends, there is evidence that the number of homicides in Los Angeles has already begun to decline. Bratton actually seems to have incited the city to take a stronger stand against violence in its streets, and there is evidence that his challenge is producing quantifiable results.

**When angry, count to ten before you speak; if very angry, a hundred.**
*Thomas Jefferson*

Chief Bratton recognized that intense emotions, properly channeled, can do a mountain of good in stopping horribly destructive behavior. Carefully managed anger, ironically enough, can be used as a corrective for mismanaged anger. When wisely directed, it can produce order and peace instead of chaos.

Millions of persons have utilized their anger to achieve personal goals. The theologian and religious reformer Martin Luther was known for his ability to manage his anger effectively. He said: "When I am angry, I can write, pray, and preach well, for then my whole temperament is quickened, my understanding sharpened, and all mundane vexations and temptations gone." Centuries later, another reformer with a similar name, Martin Luther King Jr., used his anger over racial discrimination to foment sweeping social changes.

Yet another compelling story about the power of anger appeared several years ago in the *Los Angeles Times*. The account featured an older woman named Deborah Larbalestrier, who lived in a high-crime section of Los Angeles. She had felt helpless and afraid because of the widespread robberies and other crimes on her street. One day she saw three teenage boys trying to steal her neighbor's car in broad daylight . . . and with her looking right at them.

Outraged, Ms. Larbalestrier decided it was time to act. She described the events to reporter Andy Furillo: "I went out there with a stick and I told them, 'How dare you insult me that way, robbing this car right in my face as if I didn't exist.' "

The teenagers ran off, but Larbalestrier wanted to make sure they didn't return. So she called a meeting of everybody on her block and told them: "We've become prisoners in our own homes. . . . We have to take our neighborhood back."

Then Larbalestrier went to the Los Angeles Police Department's Wilshire Division station to organize a Neighborhood Watch club for her street.

> Be still when you have nothing to say; when genuine passion moves you, say what you've got to say, and say it hot.
>
> *D. H. Lawrence*

At the time the article was written, there hadn't been a single crime on that block for a year and a half. This is the way anger can be turned from powerless rage into a tool for constructive change—and all of us have the ability to do just that.

## THE SECRET TO MANAGING ALL THIS POWER

To put it bluntly, if your anger and sexual impulses control *you,* your life will become a living hell. In their natural state, these feelings are totally undisciplined, frighteningly unpredictable, and arrogantly demanding. They can make you a miserable, selfish, impossible person.

But if you tame them, bring them under strict discipline, they can transport you to your fondest goals with the speed of a rocket.

*If you tame them!*

To do so, you must stay in control, channel all that potent energy, and remain confident about the end results you're pursuing. Psychologically, you must stay in command with your cognitive or *thinking* powers. When these urges build up steam, you need to think rationally, remaining aware that how you handle the situation will be crucial to your happiness or your sense of failure.

Here's a word picture to help you envision this process. Imagine yourself on a stagecoach moving across the dusty plains from Kansas City to Los Angeles. You have a team of eight horses in front of you, and you hold the reins. These young and spirited horses are raring to run, and their strength seems unlimited. The trail stretches out before you—hilly, narrow, and treacherous—but the prize of reaching Los Angeles will be well worth the journey.

If you let go of the reins, these mighty horses will run way too fast. They will inevitably choose the wrong fork in the road, run too close to the edge of the hill, and ultimately wreck the wagon, destroy the mission, and jeopardize your life. But if you steadily and wisely guide these energized animals, they'll power you right to Los Angeles—and fast!

## THE POTENTIAL FOR TRIUMPH OR TRAGEDY

This point is so critical for your own health and for your journey to unswerving authenticity and balanced relationships that we'll say it again: Intense anger or sexual feelings can propel you like a missile toward success or failure, victory or defeat. When you experience these strong emotions, you will inevitably act either brilliantly or destructively. Therefore, how you *manage* your anger and sexual urges will largely determine your quality of life.

Consider your sexual feelings for a moment. Let's assume that you're a man who's been married for fifteen years to a woman you met in college. The two of you love each other and are committed to spending the rest of your lives together. Periodically, though, your sexual needs are stronger than you are able to express and satisfy in your marriage. Sex is constantly on your mind, and your fantasies are unrelenting. Sometimes you feel like you can hardly control your urges.

> **Only as you do know yourself can your brain serve you as a sharp and efficient tool. Know your own failings, passions, and prejudices so you can separate them from what you see.**
>
> *Bernard M. Baruch*

If this is you, you'd better pay attention! You may try to stay na-ive and innocent, but you need desperately to grab hold of those reins. You must know precisely how you want to direct those raring horses. This is especially true when a work colleague—a bright, pretty, divorced woman—suddenly begins showing up at your desk "just to chat." Before long, you notice how she stands closer to you than she needs to and happens to arrive at the coffee machine at the same time you do. Then when she suggests you meet over dinner to discuss an upcoming presentation, her intentions are unmistakable.

Now is not the time for your horses to run free! They need clear, authoritative guidance. Staying strong and alert in the driver's seat, carefully supervising the expression of your desires, and ending up precisely where you want to be are the primary goals of a healthy life. The rewards can be astonishing.

How can you handle your sexual longings and your coworker's advances in a positive way? It wouldn't do any good to deny your needs. They are real and legitimate. We were created with an innate longing for connection. But the facts are in: You have a much better chance of getting those sexual longings satisfied to the fullest when you stay aware of them and when you contain them within a committed lifelong relationship.

> **The highest level of sexual excitement is in a monogamous relationship.**
> *Warren Beatty*

Lynn Harris, a *Glamour* magazine writer, re-cently interviewed numerous women, single and married, in her report on how women felt about their sexual experiences. To her surprise, she discovered that the woman who was the happiest said that her sexual experiences had been with one man. This at-tractive blonde, a thirty-year-old lawyer who has been married twelve years, had practiced abstinence as a single and now reported happily, "I've had more sex than most of my single friends, and I've been with only one person." The truth is, all the sexual conquests outside of marriage—how-ever tempting at times—can never measure up to the commitment of a marriage relationship.

So the last thing you want to do is to let your impulses control you. They will press you to seek *immediate* gratification, and they will try to convince you to forget about any repercussions. If you let go of the reins, you will inevitably endanger your marriage—or any potential dating relationship, if you are single—undermine your values, and trade away long-term happiness for short-term satisfaction.

> There is no such thing as casual sex, no matter how casual people are about it. After intercourse, a couple's relationship is somehow not what it was before.
>
> *Lewis Smedes*

But what a boon to your marriage if you turn the power of your sexual needs into a masterful plan for fostering intimacy with your wife. *She* is the woman you've chosen to be with for the rest of your days. So why not become a *genius* in solving this dilemma? Try the following:

- Talk about your needs. Ask your spouse about hers.
- Seek to understand each other better through active listening (rather than listening with your own agenda in mind).
- Be vulnerable. Share with your spouse what a struggle it is to have unfulfilled desires. Tell her you are committed to your relationship and your wedding vows, and want to find a path that's mutually satisfying.
- Ask how *you* could be a better lover—and be ready to listen without judging or criticizing your spouse's responses.
- Seek out a marriage-support group, or go to counseling together.
- Find ways to improve the quality of your sexual relationship.

As you seek healthy solutions to your sexual urges, each of you stands to benefit for as long as you both shall live. And such honesty will help you feel not only profoundly significant to each other but will also allow you to be unswervingly authentic, with nothing hidden from your spouse.

The stronger your sexual drives, the more opportunity there

will be for the destructiveness of your behavior—*or* the enhancement of your life. That's why emotionally healthy persons are *never* out of control for long when it comes to their wild side. The consequences are too enormous.

## ANGER HAS THE SAME POTENTIAL TO BE HELPFUL OR HARMFUL

If you are angry, it's a sure sign that something needs attention in your life. Something is askew, and it must be set right. Anger is like a red light flashing on the dashboard of your car. Overlook it at your own peril!

> **The sexual embrace, worthily understood, can only be compared with music and with prayer.**
>
> *James Hilton*

Let's say you discovered that four of your closest friends got together for lunch and nine holes of golf last Saturday. You like all four of them, and you assumed you were equally well liked by them. Moreover, you love to play golf every chance you get. But you weren't invited, and you are shocked. Worse, you feel hurt and rejected. The more you let yourself brood, the more enraged you become.

How would you respond? Try the "What Would You Do?" exercise now.

As your anger swells, you have five alternatives. Four will likely bring destruction; one might bring relational growth.

——————————— WHAT WOULD YOU DO? ———————————

If you were in a situation where your friends left you out of an activity, how would *you* respond? Would you

~ Let your friends have it full-force verbally?
~ Pretend nothing happened (but be inwardly passive-aggressive)?
~ Blame yourself?
~ Obsess over the rejection?
~ Quietly ask a friend what happened?

1. *You can explode.* You can call each of your friends and shout, "I heard what you did, you jerk! You purposely left me out. We're through." Chances are, this response will not foster the resolution and reconciliation you crave.

> It is easy to fly into a passion—anybody can do that—but to be angry with the right person and to the right extent and at the right time and with the right object and in the right way—that is not easy, and it is not everyone who can do it.
>
> *Aristotle*

2. *You can handle your anger underhandedly—avoid your four friends, say almost nothing when you do see them, and generally pout and sulk your way to interpersonal destruction.* Of course, your friends will probably have no idea why you're acting so sullen and remote.

3. *You can blame yourself and assume you were the cause of the rejection.* You might think, *They would've included me if I were funnier, outgoing, more interesting, or a better golfer.* The only result here is damage to your self-worth.

4. *You can obsess over your disappointment, do nothing about it, and continue to replay the hurtful event in your mind.* If you keep those toxic emotions churning, keep pouring acid into your stomach, and keep your muscles clenched, you'll inflict physical and psychological harm on yourself.

5. *You can do something positive, something that will likely lead to progress.* You can privately invite one or two of your friends to lunch. Go with the two you trust most, the two most likely to help you resolve the issue. Sitting at lunch with them, you can pick the appropriate time to share your disappointment and hurt. You can pad your statements with understanding: "I know how these things happen, and I shouldn't be so sensitive." Or, "I realize I may be misinterpreting this."

But then ask your friends if they can help you think it through. Tell them that if you are the problem, you sincerely want to change. You simply want to face the truth and get this matter behind you. This kind of "anger management" almost always leads to stronger relationships and clearer understanding about yourself.

Perhaps you're thinking that being excluded from lunch and a golf game is trivial. What if it were a huge problem, one that caused your anger to bubble up like volcanic lava? All right, let's assume you just found out your spouse or longtime dating partner has recently been involved emotionally and sexually with someone else. Your hurt is enormous, your frustration is beyond words, and your sense of threat is off the charts. What should you do?

*Keep the reins firmly in your hands!* Don't let the horses run wild. Take much more time to act on your feelings than you instinctively want to. When your energy is bursting within you, that's not the time to act impulsively. Strive hard to be patient.

When your anger or sexual energy is running high, you have a gigantic power reservoir available. You are capable of doing something terribly destructive, but you can *elect* to do something with lasting positive consequences. There are few times in life

> **Hot heads and cold hearts never solved anything.**
> *Billy Graham*

when you are in such a pivotal position to influence the quality of your future existence. If you stay solidly in the driver's seat and think clearly and wisely, you can make a brilliant decision that will bring tremendous growth to your life.

## THE SEVEN SECRETS OF HIGHLY EFFECTIVE STAGECOACH DRIVERS

On the basis of our combined five decades of counseling experience, we want to share the seven crucial secrets for turning anger and sexual energy into a force for personal gain—into a force that will help shape you into someone who is unswervingly authentic, who can face yourself, life situations, and relationships with confidence.

1. *Realize that you are the driver.* How this team of powerful horses behaves in the next few seconds, or the next few hours, is totally up to you. You hold the reins in your hands. You are the one in control. If you become convinced that your emotions are really in charge— that you're just along for the ride—you're headed for big trouble.

Being the driver means that you regulate the speed by letting loose or pulling up on the reins. The horses will turn left or right, according to your direction. You are free to guide them as you think best, and this freedom cannot be compromised by anyone else.

2. *Convince yourself that you have the power to make wise decisions.* The skillfulness of your driving will be determined by the thoroughness and accuracy of your thinking. The more proficient you become as a decision maker, the better your driving will be.

**Clarity of mind means clarity of passion, too; this is why a great and clear mind loves ardently and sees distinctly what it loves.**
*Blaise Pascal*

Your best choices will follow good decision-making rules. First, you will pay attention to what you think and feel. Then you will consider what the respected people in your life think and feel. Finally, you will pay attention to the teaching of the ages—the time-tested principles of truth that offer wisdom and guidance—and ask God for direction.

Marshaling these three sources of data, your challenge is to sift through all of it and make the wisest decision you can.

3. *Operate out of confidence.* As we discussed in earlier chapters, your sense of profound worth was established long ago by God, and you already know what a significant human being you are. That means you're not making decisions just to feel good about yourself. With your questions of personal significance solved, you're totally confident about your invulnerability to other people's evaluation and judgment.

You are handling your angry or sexual impulses as wisely as you can for one reason: You want your own life to be unswervingly authentic. And you want the lives of those closest to you to benefit from the optimal expression of your feelings in the proper, God-given context.

4. *Regulate the pace.* Life was not meant to be lived at breakneck speeds. You can't make good choices when you're charging

forward as swiftly as possible. Slow your horses down, and keep them under full control.

When your brain is throbbing and your heart is pounding from anger or sexual feelings, one of the best things you can do is *take your time*. Give yourself ample opportunity to think through all aspects of your decision.

5. *Train your horses when they are calm and composed.* The time to work on managing your anger or sexual impulses is when you are *not* aggressively or sexually revved up. Your cognitive machinery doesn't function well when adrenaline is blasting through your body.

> Be angry but do not sin; do not let the sun go down on your anger.
>
> *The apostle Paul, in Ephesians 4:26, NRSV*

Learning to handle drives and desires is something virtually anyone can master. But it isn't an *easy* skill to learn. It takes time and hard work. But we have watched hundreds of healthy people learn to use their most intense feelings for the benefit of their personal and relational growth. This skill is best learned when their drives are dormant.

6. *Take good care of your horses.* Once you learn how to direct your sexual and angry impulses for the betterment of your life, don't allow any of these powerful feelings to get stale, lose their vitality, or die early deaths.

In relation to anger, don't try to minimize it or repress it. Rather, work to remain hypersensitive to injustice and hurt—in your life and the lives of others. Moreover, stay idealistic about your life goals; dare to dream big dreams and pursue large visions. Clearly, your pursuit of these goals and dreams will set you up for all kinds of frustration, and this frustration will produce anger for you. Terrific! You now know exactly how to manage the energy from this anger to your advantage.

The same is true of your sexual feelings. We know of people who still enjoy sexual vitality at ninety years of age, and that's fantastic. Any person who has sexual impulses can utilize the accompanying power to achieve their fondest goals.

7. *When you become skilled, take on apprentice drivers.* We have noted that great managers of strong inner impulses become even more proficient when they teach their secrets to "younger and less experienced drivers." In the very act of helping others master this set of skills, the rules for maximizing your own abilities will become even clearer and more achievable.

> **Never lose your temper, except intentionally.**
>
> *Dwight Eisenhower*

## HEALTHY PEOPLE ARE WILD—AND IN CONTROL

You have plenty of angry and sexual feelings. God himself blessed you with these. However much you may try to hide these feelings, you are probably quite aware of them deep within your heart and mind. If you think you're not very angry or very sexual, you are likely just fooling yourself and engaging in unnecessary denial.

To the degree that you use all this powerful energy for good, your life will turn from ordinary to extraordinary, dull to dynamic. You will be able to do exciting and magnificent things—far beyond anything you may have dreamed.

It will all come down to how well you learn to manage those young, wild, spirited horses in you.

As we said at the outset, authenticity is one of the three secrets to health because it makes no room for imitation or fakery. And it is our belief that the two most important tools you have for becoming unswervingly authentic are your ability to discover your blind spots (increase your self-awareness) and to harness your wild side (manage your anger and sexuality). In our experience, the most authentic and genuine among us have maximized the usefulness of these two tools. But there's more. The fruit of authenticity is a track record of good decisions.

The person who is becoming unswervingly authentic, who is walking the walk, brings their newfound self-awareness and the productive energy they've gleaned from their "wild side" into the daily experience of making consistently good decisions. This is what authenticity is about and why it defines health and wholeness. Why? Because the decisions you make, big and small, impact the remainder of your life. They open and close doors. "Every great decision creates ripples—like a huge boulder dropped in a lake," said Benjamin Disraeli. "The ripples merge, rebound off the banks in unforseeable ways."

## MAXIMIZING YOUR AUTHENTICITY

If you are ever to feel good—deep down in your soul—it will be because you've learned to make good decisions that keep you true to yourself. It will be because you make decisions that maximize your authenticity. Healthy people work out their authenticity more and more skillfully over time. Unhealthy people regularly violate their authenticity and decide to do whatever is easiest, whatever will give them the greatest immediate reward, or whatever will please the important people in their life. (Of course, there is nothing wrong with pleasing the important people in your life, unless this is the sole source of data on which you base your decision.) When your decisions are based on pleasing others, for example, you bury any evidence of authenticity in your life. Dietrich Bonhoeffer said it succinctly, "The weak are always forced to decide between alternatives they have not chosen themselves."

It is in the moments of decision that your life is shaped. So before we leave this section, we are compelled to share with you an important decision-making principle that will help you more effectively maximize your authenticity. It's the principle we call your "Control Booth."

Imagine for a moment a relatively small room just behind your eyes, your Control Booth. It looks a little like the CBS or NBC booths at the Republican or Democratic conventions—with walls four or five feet high and a foot of glass above those walls. The booth has two doors—doors that can be locked. Inside the booth is all kinds of equipment to connect you with the outside world—telephones, fax machines, and television sets.

When you need to make a decision—about a large or a little matter—imagine going into your Control Booth, closing and locking the doors, and getting ready to gather all the data you need to make a wise decision. There are three sources of data to gather for most decisions you make:

- what you think and feel about the matter
- what the important people in your life think and feel
- what the values and guiding principles of the ages are

Once you have gathered these facts, your task is to stand in the middle of all this information and make the very best decision you can.

## BEING TRUE TO YOU

The purpose of entering your Control Booth and locking the doors is so that *you* are the one who gets to make this decision. After a certain age, you don't need your father or mother in the booth with you. You don't need your pastor or priest, your peer group, or your employer. You are a free person, and the healthier you are emotionally, the more you will experience and act on that freedom.

It isn't as though you don't listen to what others have to say about your decision. You listen carefully to their ideas. But here's the difference: After you hear them out, you consider their opinions *along with* your own thoughts and feelings and the clearest teaching of the timeless codes in which you believe. Then, standing in the middle of all this information, you make a *free* decision about what you will do.

Imagine, for instance, that you're considering a major matter, such as a career change that would require you to move from Chicago to New York. You have been offered a new position with a significant salary increase, considerably more responsibility, more time at home with your young family, but it will require a move away from your family of origin and the city you love. Your spouse is positive about the new position. Your family of origin doesn't like it at all. Your kids, without much real sense of what might be involved, are excited to move. Your present employer wants desperately to keep you and feels you would be abandoning him. Worse, your potential new employer has informed you that the company needs your decision by tomorrow at 8 A.M.

So you go to your Control Booth, lock the doors, and prepare to make your decision. You pray passionately for perceptive clarity, wisdom, and courage. And then you begin the exciting and frightening process of standing in the middle of all your data and making the best decision you can—one that represents deep sensitivity to your own thoughts and feelings, the thoughts and feelings of these important people, and your understanding from Scripture and creeds what your calling is as a person of faith in the twenty-first century.

Your decision, while it is just one of many you will make, will contribute a major piece of the puzzle that is you. If you make this decision wisely, you will have taken a giant step in the direction of authenticity.

## MAKING THE MOST OF YOUR MOMENTS

After discovering your blind spots and harnessing your wild side, you are primed to make the very best decisions possible. You see, authenticity is all about making moment-by-moment decisions about who you are and who you wish to be in this moment. The degree of authenticity you experience will depend on how skillful you become as a decision maker in these critical moments. Fundamentally, the decisions you make reflect the clarity of your self-knowledge, the value you place on the opinions and feelings of others, your awareness of the current situation (and any like it you've experienced in the past), and your belief in "overriding values."

These decisions will vary from small to very large. For instance, you always have a decision to make about when you will get out of bed. It may seem like a small one, but it will affect a lot about your life . . . at least *that* day. It needs to be the best decision you can make in that moment.

You will inevitably be faced with other choices that affect large areas of your existence. If you are considering moving from one part of the country to another, changing from one career to another, marrying someone, or working on your marriage rather than leaving it, your sense of being authentic may depend for a long time on how you make these decisions.

We'll say it again. Healthy people make decisions that maximize their authenticity. Unhealthy people regularly violate their authenticity with big and small decisions alike.

We would be remiss if we sidestepped a powerful element too often taken for granted when it comes to making authentic decisions—the source of your profound significance. Your relationship with a God who knows far more about you than you know about yourself is vital to good decision making. A God who is "familiar with all [your] ways," shows you compassion when you take the wrong path, and continually reveals his unfailing love. If you want to learn more about how to hone this skill, we urge you to read appendix B: "Charting Your Destiny," where we help you explore your God-given destiny in some of the most important decisions of your life (career, marriage, etc.).

*If thou wishest to be loved, love.*   SENECA 4 B.C.

SECRET #3

TO FEELING GOOD—DEEP DOWN IN YOUR SOUL

<>

*Self-Giving Love*

In 1883 Professor Henry Drummond began his famous lecture "The Greatest Thing in the World" by asking his college students a disarmingly simple question: "You have life before you. Once only can you live it. What is the noblest object of desire, the supreme gift to covet?"

The rhetorical question required no reply. Everyone knew the answer: *Love.* Self-giving love is the ultimate good. It lifts us outside ourselves. It helps us see beyond the normal range of human vision—and over walls of resentment and barriers of betrayal. Love rises above the petty demands and conflicts of life and inspires our spirit to give without getting. As the famous "love chapter" of the Bible says: "[Love] always protects, always trusts, always hopes, always perseveres. Love never fails."

When you set out on a consciously chosen course of action that accents the good of others, a deep change occurs in your soul. Pretentious egoism fades and your days are punctuated with spontaneous breathings of compassion and generosity, kindness and nurturance. Once you have laid claim to your profound significance and schooled yourself in the art of authenticity, your life is given to the *summum bonum*—the supreme good. The noblest of human qualities become your new compass on this "most excellent way." No question about it.

Sound sappy? Science doesn't think so. Recent studies found that the ability to practice appreciation and love is the *defining* mark of the most happy of human beings. When people engage in self-giving love by doing something extraordinarily positive, they use higher level brain functions and set off a series of neurochemical reactions that shower their system in positive emotions.

Perhaps you are wondering if this kind of happiness is triggered just as readily by having fun as it is by an act of self-giving love. Martin Seligman of the University of Pennsylvania wondered the same thing. He gave his students an assignment: to engage in one pleasurable activity and one philanthropic activity and then to write about both. Turns out, the "pleasurable" activity of hanging out with friends, watching a movie, or eating a delicious dessert paled in comparison with the effects of the loving action. Seligman states that "when our philanthropic acts were spontaneous . . . the whole day went better." He goes on to say that self-giving love is not accompanied by a separable stream of positive emotion; rather, "it consists in total engagement and in the loss of self-consciousness." Time stops when we lend a helping hand, nurture a hurting soul, or offer a listening ear.

A six-year-old Tanzanian boy named Abdallah Mtulu taught moviegoing audiences and the Hollywood elite this lesson with his film debut in *About Schmidt*. Abdallah, known as Ndugu in the film, can't read or write, doesn't speak English, and has never seen a movie. That didn't matter to the filmmakers. They were looking for realism—"a real child with a real, reputable organization." That's how they came to Childreach and to Abdallah, who lives in a village with a per capita family income of one dollar a day.

In the film, actor Jack Nicholson plays a retired insurance actuary who sponsors Ndugu and writes rambling letters to his "foster son," sending them off with a financial contribution. It is this loving act that ultimately brings Nicholson's character to a level of joy he has never known before. And the joy is apparently contagious. Since Abdallah had his picture-and-crayon drawing featured in the movie, donations to real-life relief agencies that help care for children like him have soared.

If there is anything better than to be loved, it is loving—and healthy people know it. But as they aspire to the greatness of self-giving love, they do so with keen awareness and personal acknowledgment of their human limits. In the process of developing unswerving authenticity, they have realized that they have needs, drives, rights, and goals that do not easily harmonize with selfless love.

But does that mean they give up those needs, drives, rights, and goals? We want to be clear: Love is not necessarily about self-denial. We have seen many well-intentioned people set out to "love" others by denying their own needs—as if performing a sacrifice was the goal. Not so. Healthy people know that self-giving love is not about doing without. As the greatest of love poems makes clear, we can give our body to be burned and still not be loving. Self-giving love does not demand a titanic sacrifice. Small things, done with great love, most often characterize the actions of a person who is healthy and whole.

Love is the result of hundreds of small decisions, each and every day. Do I hurry to my next appointment or check in with a coworker who's hurting? Do I put my phone calls on hold to play with my five-year-old or stick to my tasks to reduce my to-do list? Do I make the effort to warmly greet a visitor at church or rush to get to my normal seat? How we answer such small decisions determines how greatly we love. It determines how much we transcend our self to love without reward.

One of the most inspirational stories of self-giving love we have ever read is Mary Ann Bird's autobiographical "The Whisper Test." It's the story of a little girl who was different . . . and hated it. She was born with a cleft palate, and when she started school her classmates made it clear to her how she looked: "a little girl with a misshapen lip, crooked nose, lopsided teeth, and garbled speech."

She was convinced that no one outside her family could love her. When her classmates asked, "What happened to your lip?" she'd tell them she'd fallen and cut it on a piece of glass. "Somehow," she writes, "it seemed more acceptable to have suffered an accident than to have been born different."

There was, however, a teacher in the second grade whom all the students adored. Mrs. Leonard was short, round, and happy— "a sparkling lady." Annually, she administered a hearing test to everyone in the class. Finally it was Mary Ann's turn.

I knew from past years that as we stood against the door and covered one ear, the teacher sitting at her desk would whisper something, and we would have to repeat it back—things like, "The sky is blue," or "Do you have new shoes?" I waited there for those words that God must have put into her mouth, those seven words that changed my life. Mrs. Leonard said, in her whisper, "I wish you were my little girl."

Mrs. Leonard had a lock on love. You can be confident that she, like other healthy people, enjoyed the highest successes in living and the deepest levels of emotional satisfaction. Her tender care clearly embodied this hallmark of health—the *summum bonum*, the supreme good, the most excellent way.

And self-giving love is what this section of the book is all about. Truthfully, we have been eager for you to get to this point. For once you have experienced profound significance, really learned to cultivate and nurture your significance in the moments that make up each of your days, and once you have learned the secret of unswerving authenticity, really mastered your ability to sync your thoughts and feelings, you are primed to know the inexpressible joy of self-giving love. Significance and authenticity are the double doors to a wonderful world of truly loving the life you live.

In chapter 8, we give you the primary tool for loving others by teaching you to "read" your social barometer. This ability eases every social situation, increases your interpersonal competencies, and builds a connection to others that helps them feel completely cared for. Healthy people thrive on this. They are experts at reading the cues and hints in conversations and tuning in to another person's emotional needs. Without the ability to read your social barometer, you will never truly find "the most excellent way."

In chapter 9, we pull out all the stops to show you how to love other people to the very best of your ability. We hope it is our most inspiring chapter of the book because it represents the crown jewel of the person who is healthy and whole. Genuinely loving others, from a platform of significance and authenticity, is the defining mark of a life well lived. So we show you exactly how to set aside any hint of pride or anything else that might cause you to stumble on your way to loving as if your life depended upon it—because it does.

Every connection you have with another person—whether it be a friend, family member, or total stranger—is an opportunity to enjoy the pleasure of self-giving love. Every moment of every day that you are with another person is a chance to provide encouragement, support, and care. Self-giving love is a myriad of big and small acts of kindness and compassion, generosity and concern. When you begin living out these qualities, when they emanate from your core, you'll love the life you live like you never have before. This section will show you how.

# 8

## READING YOUR SOCIAL BAROMETER

*You can make more friends in two months*
*by becoming interested in other people*
*than you can in two years by trying*
*to get other people interested in you.*

DALE CARNEGIE

*T*he "close talker."

If you were a fan of the 1990s television phenomenon called *Seinfeld,* you immediately understand that phrase. The episode centered around a character who had little awareness of personal space. Upon inviting you to join him for a cup of coffee, he would stand within a couple of inches of you, putting his face embarrassingly close to yours. The character later spawned episodes involving a "soft talker," who was barely discernible in conversation, and a "high talker," who said everything very loudly. Even if you weren't a fan of the show, chances are you still get the idea. Some people are just socially "off"—oblivious to their social mores.

Much of psychological health is internal. It has to do with your thoughts and feelings, your character and spirit. But there is a significant component of your well-being that is "others-focused." It has to do with your relationships and how you read other people's faces, understand their emotions, join them in conversation, and interpret their actions. It has to do with reading your "social barometer."

What do we mean by that? In 1643 an Italian scientist in

Florence, Evangelista Torricelli, used a column of water in a thirty-four-foot tube to take the first-ever reading of barometric pressure. The column, soon replaced by mercury and reduced to a manageable size, has been used around the globe ever since by anyone wanting to forecast local weather. In the same way this device can predict climate conditions, your social barometer can become a reliable predictor of social conditions.

Reading your social barometer attunes you to others. It creates a smooth interpersonal exchange that puts others at ease. It increases your social competencies, making you more adept at creating meaningful and enjoyable connections. Healthy people thrive in intimate relationships because they read their social barometer. They develop a talent for rapport, building a web of social connection that enriches their lives. Healthy people rarely lack friends.

Also, the healthier you are as an individual, the more adroit you become socially. By learning to read your social barometer, you lower your risk for coming off as arrogant, insensitive, or uninterested. Your social barometer will tell you when and how to enter a conversation midstream and when to lie low. It will tell you when to keep talking and when to clam up. It will prevent you from being oblivious to cues and hints that the conversation is shifting gears. And it will tune you in to attempts by others to refocus on another topic.

Without the ability to read your social barometer, you would be like a meteorologist trying to forecast weather conditions—without knowing the barometric pressure. You would be at a loss, playing a social guessing game that's likely to miss the mark at any moment. For this reason we dedicate this chapter to helping you mature, grow, and flourish in the world of interpersonal relationships. Consider this area another critical part of the foundation for personal health. Without it, your relationships not only founder but so do you. Why? Because at the core of our existence as human beings lies a powerful drive to be with others. The absence of human contact, research has clearly shown, leads to more mental and physical sickness and stress.

In this chapter we'll begin by giving you directions for finding and reading your social barometer. Next we'll explore what science has to say about why some of us feel so socially insecure. Then we'll point you to the single most important social skill we know of—and take you to a deeper level for cultivating meaningful connections that few enjoy. Finally, we'll explore the payoff of social competence and self-giving love by examining the benefits of healthy relationships in general.

> **The deepest principle in human nature is the craving for appreciation.**
>
> *William James*

Contrary to what some think, great relationships—whether friendships or romances—don't fall out of the heavens on a favored few. A large body of research in the social sciences over the past twenty years has established that what was once thought to be fate is now solidly our own doing—or undoing. We determine the quality of our relationships because we can choose to read our social barometer . . . or not. The first key, of course, is knowing where to find it.

## FINDING YOUR SOCIAL BAROMETER

We are about to ask you a simple question. Before we do, however, we want you to know that how you answer this question will reveal whether or not you are already reading your social barometer. So take a contemplative moment to consider it. And be honest with yourself. Here's the question: *What thought races through your head when you walk into a roomful of people?*

While there are countless responses to this question, all of them are likely to fall into one of two basic camps. These two fundamental responses, in our experience, come in the form of two quiet questions:

- How am I doing?
- How are they doing?

Any social setting fundamentally elicits one of these two positions. When you walk into a room full of other people, either you are concerned with yourself and the impression you are about to make, or you are focused on them and what is taking place.

Whenever your approach falls into the category of *How are they doing?* you have found your social barometer.

Alternatively, when your basic social approach is to ask, *How am I doing?* you are relating without valuable interpersonal information that only your social barometer can give.

Relating to others without reading your social barometer is like wearing mirrored sunglasses with the lenses flipped around. You look out at the world and all you see is a reflection of yourself, your own needs, your own desires. Your self-focus prevents you from accurately recognizing other people's needs and desires as well as their motives and emotions. The point is this: Without your social barometer you are destined to be consumed by self-conscious behavior that will riddle your relationships with social insecurity.

> **You're blessed when you care. At the moment of being "care-full," you find yourselves cared for.**
>
> *Matthew 5:7, The Message*

All of us realize that there are moments when we are emotionally strong and steady, tuned in to our social environment, accurately reading the faces around us. And then there are other moments, in the very same day, where we are out of sync, self-conscious, and unsure. It's only human. But here's the difference. If you are indeed healthy, your interpersonal experiences of reading your social barometer accurately far outweigh the times you don't pay attention to your barometer. That means you have disciplined yourself to enter a room and quietly say to yourself, *How are these people doing?*

Without this kind of awareness of your social barometer, you will never be able to experience the height and the depth of self-giving love.

✦  ✦  ✦

## HOW WELL DO YOU READ PEOPLE?

Those of us who are adept at reading the faces of our friends and family increase our ability to build healthier relationships and lead happier lives. What's more, you can *learn* this skill if you are currently lacking it. Complete our self-test below to determine how well you read people. Record your answers at right by selecting either **Y** (yes), **S/M** (sometimes/maybe), or **N** (no) for each question.

## Your Work Life

1. Do you know there are certain days of the week that are best to approach your boss with a new idea or to ask a favor?  **Y   S/M   N**

2. Have you had run-ins or difficulties getting along with the bosses you have worked for over the years? \*\*\*   **Y   S/M   N**

3. In a meeting with several people from the office, have you ever thought you would get the ear of your boss by doing or saying something he/she would like, but then your boss barely notices? \*\*\*   **Y   S/M   N**

4. When you are having problems with a colleague at work and are tempted to talk to your boss about it, do you already know the kind of response he/she will give you?   **Y   S/M   N**

## Your Love Life

1. When your spouse retreats to a part of the house (e.g., the garage or sewing room) without telling you what he/she is up to, do you know when to let him/her unwind alone and when to ask questions?   **Y   S/M   N**

2. When you are enjoying a little romantic moment with sweet kisses, are you able to quickly tell if your spouse has something more in mind than just kissing?   **Y   S/M   N**

3. When you ask your spouse if he/she likes what you are wearing and he/she says he/she does, are you ever surprised to later learn that he/she really doesn't like the outfit but didn't want to hurt your feelings? \*\*\*   **Y   S/M   N**

4. Do you and your partner have a way of communicating non-verbally at a party when you can't use words in front of other people?   **Y   S/M   N**

## Your Social Life

1. When a friend asks for advice on something that's troubling him/her, are you quick to give him/her several suggestions to make the situation better? \*\*\*   **Y   S/M   N**

2. One of your closest friends is doodling on a paper napkin while the two of you are discussing his/her relationship with his/her sweetheart. Do you immediately know what the doodling is about?   **Y   S/M   N**

3. You leave a message for your friend to call you on your cell phone as soon as he/she can. You carry it with you all day and never get the call. Do you assume he/she is either especially busy or that your message slipped his/her mind?   **Y   S/M   N**

4. In a discussion, your friend keeps glancing up and to the right while he/she is thinking of a response to your questions. Do you know what this means?   **Y   S/M   N**

### Your Family Life

1. You are planning a holiday celebration with extended family and send out a couple of dozen invitations. Do you know before the invitations are even mailed who will come and who won't—and who will accept but show up late?   **Y   S/M   N**

2. Do most of your family members think of you as being sensitive to their needs?   **Y   S/M   N**

3. When you see a particular family member withdrawn from the rest of the family, do you tell that person to quit moping and join the party?***   **Y   S/M   N**

4. Imagine you are about to arrive at a family reunion. Do you know the roles most of the members will be playing? In other words, do you know who will be "the comedian," "the black sheep," "the mediator," and so on?   **Y   S/M   N**

### SCORING

Add up your scores according to the directions below, then read the exercises to learn how you can improve your ability to read others. If the question is marked with this symbol (***), the scoring is as follows: **Y** = 4, **S/M** = 2, **N** = 0. If the question isn't marked, the scoring is as follows: **Y** = 0, **S/M** = 2, **N** = 4.

## Your Work Life

Any score under 8 in this section means you read your boss well, but could probably benefit from a brief brushup on the strategies that insure you have an edge.

*What you can do*

❑ Learn your boss's body language. For example, when your boss leans forward to talk, it shows a letting down of her guard. When, for instance, she clasps her hands behind her back, it reveals frustration. When her palms are open, so is she. When she sits with her hands clasped behind her head, it means "you better impress me."

❑ Know when your boss is nervous. Here's what to look for: clearing the throat, running tongue along front teeth, twiddling thumbs, fidgeting with a watch or bracelet, tight-lipped grin, and darting eyes. Any or all of these will be present when your boss is feeling put on the spot or otherwise anxious. Once you know these signs, you can then help rescue your boss from a nervous moment and make his day.

❑ Read your boss's silence. If you're making a proposal and asking for an extra vacation day and your boss shows little reaction, he may be distracted or annoyed. But if he is making eye contact with you and leaning forward, your message is getting through—so you may want to ask for two days off instead of one!

## Your Love Life

Any score under 8 in this section means you understand your partner well, but could benefit from a few pointers to keep you reading him/her at your best.

*What you can do*

❑ Focus on your spouse's face. More than anyone in your life, your sweetheart's moods are revealed in subtle facial expressions. The raising of one eyebrow means he has questions. An upturned corner of one side of her mouth says she's frustrated or cynical. Biting his bottom lip means he is sincere. And blinking more than usual means she may not be telling the truth.

❏ Pinpoint your spouse's big needs. A key to reading anyone in a romantic relationship is to know a person's top ten needs and how they are expressed. If solitude is one of his big needs, for example, he may fold his arms and look to the floor when he is needing time alone. If she needs affirmation, her eyes will widen. If he needs recreation and activity, he may bounce his leg while sitting in a chair to signal boredom. So explore his big needs to read his little cues.

❏ Look for solutions when you get stumped. If you are continually getting mixed signals from your partner's body language, don't blame him/her. Work to understand what is really going on and be creative in finding avenues to better understand each other. He/she may have some very unique body language quirks you can only understand after you know what they mean.

## Your Social Life

Any score under 8 in this section means you have smooth sailing with your kindred spirits, but could boost your compatibility quotient with a few reminders and tips.

*What you can do*

❏ Know when your friend is frustrated. Everyone has certain issues, certain areas in their life, that cause more irritation than others. Your friend will reveal her frustration when she crosses her arms and legs, glances sideways, touches her nose, or rubs her eyes. Pay careful attention to these signals. They will save you from pushing your friend's buttons and causing needless annoyance.

❏ Get a read on your friend's anxiety level. She may say she's made a decision she feels good about, but if she is chewing a pen, biting her fingernails, or pinching her flesh you can bet she's not feeling confident. If she was self-assured, she'd be sitting up straight in her chair. She'd have her hands comfortably folded in her lap or together in a "steepled" position with her elbows on the chair's arms.

❏ Call on other friends for help. If you are feeling continually confused by a friend's body language, invite another kindred spirit in to give you some objectivity. Ask him how he reads your mutual friend. Explore his take on certain behaviors that seem to be inexplicable to you. A mutual friend can often shed light on the confusion.

**Your Family Life**
Any score under 8 in this section means you maintain fairly stable family relationships, but could probably benefit from keeping a few suggestions in mind for making your family all it was meant to be.

*What you can do*
❏ Survey the frustration level. A lot of needless pain can be avoided when you note signs of family frustration that aren't expressed outright. They are seen when your dad clenches his hands or makes a fistlike gesture. They are seen when your mom wrings her hands or runs her hand through her hair, or when your brother rubs the back of his neck or sighs deeply. All of these are signs of mounting frustration.

❏ Know when it's time to ask favors, and when it's not. If a family member has his hands in his coat pockets with his thumbs sticking out, he is feeling comfortable and confident—a good time to ask for the lift to the airport you need. If he is tugging one of his ears, fidgeting with his Palm Pilot, or jiggling his keys in his pocket, you better take a cab or wait before asking.

❏ When in doubt, honor your elders. You know they expect it, and they probably deserve it, so give your parents their due. If you are getting mixed signals from different family members, this is the right path. The more you show Mom and Dad that their opinion matters more than others' in the family, the more likely you are to end up on the same wavelength.

✦  ✦  ✦

## READING YOUR SOCIAL BAROMETER

A friend told us the story of Ron, a man in his forties, who was hired by an environmental institute that is dedicated to preserving an endangered species of bighorn sheep that live in the mountains just southwest of Palm Springs, California. Development of neighboring land was disturbing the sheep and interrupting their breeding activity, and the institute wanted to do something about it.

When Ron visited the institute, the director took him outside, pointed to the massive, rocky hills that rolled up behind the offices, and said softly, "There are a lot of them out today." Ron squinted up at the brown hills, trying to hide his amazement—not at the beauty of the bighorn sheep, but at his inability to see even one of them. Obviously accustomed to this reaction, the director tactfully called his attention to a sheep just below a triangular rock, and another on the crest of a hill to the left, and then another and another. Ron soon began to see dozens.

The director's eyesight was no better than Ron's. But he had learned to see the sheep. He knew how their shape broke the subtle patterns of the hills. He could detect the slight difference between their color and that of the rock. What was virtually automatic to him was foreign to Ron, until he, too, learned to see the sheep.

In much the same way, people who have experience reading their social barometer see interpersonal cues that the untrained eye repeatedly misses. They scan the social scene for important details to guide their actions. Not only do they listen to the *words* being spoken, they observe the person's nonverbals. They pay attention to voice tone, facial expressions, and eye contact. They recognize a nervous fidget. When they shake someone's hand, they take note of the feel of the handshake. They recognize an uncomfortable shift of weight in a chair. They are tuned in to unspoken feelings and are sensitive to signals that convey a person's interest.

How important is it to read your social barometer accurately? Researchers believe that about 90 percent of emotional communication is nonverbal. And studies like Robert Rosenthal's back up this estimate. Rosenthal, a psychologist, developed an assessment of people's ability to read emotional cues. It's called Profile of Nonverbal Sensitivity (PONS). He shows subjects a film of a young woman expressing feelings such as anger, jealousy, love, and gratitude. Unbeknownst to the viewer, one or another nonverbal cue has been edited out. In some instances, the face is visible but not the body. Or the woman's eyes are hidden, so the viewers have to judge the feeling by subtle cues. Interestingly enough, people with higher PONS scores, even if their IQs are quite average, tend to be more well-liked and more successful in their work and relationships.

Reading one's social barometer is not only about recognizing the cues that others are sending, however. It's also about seeing signs in oneself. To infer correctly what others are feeling, the socially skilled are able to identify and label their own experience accurately. Healthy people, while others-focused in social settings, pay close attention to their own internal psychological experiences as a means to improving relational connections. They are aware of even subtle feelings as they have them.

To avoid any confusion on this point, look at it this way. People asking, *How am I doing?* are looking for external validation. This validation is an end in itself. They mistakenly believe that if somebody is affirming them in some way, if they win someone's approval, then they are now more worthwhile. Self-respect and

> No one can make you feel inferior without your consent.
>
> *Eleanor Roosevelt*

significance, as we have said already, can never be grounded in external validation like this. So don't confuse this internal focus of reading one's social barometer with such a self-deceptive approach. No. Healthy people are tuned in to their own experience with others, not to find validation, but as a means to more effective relating.

## WHY WE BECOME SOCIALLY INSECURE

"I never feel at ease, whether it's on the job or at a family reunion. I'm always anxiety-ridden and worried that someone is looking at me, and I don't measure up. Whenever I have to make a team report at work, I get a lump in my throat and my mouth gets dry. Whenever I'm in a social setting, I feel self-conscious and insecure."

Ever felt that way? Do you know someone who does? Millions and millions of good-hearted people are in the grip of social insecurity. While it may not paralyze their relationships, it certainly suffocates their efforts. They may want to join a conversation but withdraw out of fear. Or, conversely, they may boldly enter in and then wish they hadn't. Their social insecurity makes relating to others often nerve-racking and sometimes painful.

> Loneliness and the feeling of being uncared for and unwanted are the greatest poverty.
>
> *Mother Teresa*

Why do so many people suffer socially? Those in the know point to several predictable pitfalls. So before we delve into the ins and outs of becoming more socially competent, let's take a look at each of these pitfalls.

### Pitfall #1: Comparing ourselves to others

"There is something not entirely displeasing in the misfortune of our close friends." The seventeenth-century French essayist who wrote these words must certainly have suffered from social insecurity. All decent human beings feel sorry when something bad happens to someone we care for, but for the insecure, another's misfortune is a means of feeling better about themselves.

What insecure people do not realize is that their very compulsion to measure their status against others is what is feeding their insecurity. With each comparison they diminish their potential to become intrinsically stronger and more stable on their own.

Now let's be honest: Everyone, no matter how healthy, occasionally pulls out the proverbial yardstick to compare their performance and their achievements to others'. It's only natural. But people entrenched in social insecurity are forever comparing themselves. It is their main means to feeling worthwhile—and that's why they rarely do. Social comparison inevitably leads to feelings of bitterness. There will always be someone who has more than you, makes more than you, does better than you, and feels better than you. Always. Still, some choose to torture themselves by comparing themselves to others, and the result is hollow vanity at best but most likely feelings of inferiority.

## Pitfall #2: Shyness

It is a nearly universal human trait. Most everyone has bouts of shyness and half of all people describe themselves as shy. Perhaps because it is so widespread and it conveys a sense of vulnerability, shyness can be viewed as endearing. Princess Diana, for example, garnered countless admirers with her "Shy Di" manner. There is nothing inherently wrong with shyness—not until a person feels imprisoned by it. Once shyness engenders excessive self-consciousness, to the point of preventing connections, it crosses a dangerous line.

Harvard researcher Jerome Kagan has shown that by eight weeks of age, babies display innate shyness or boldness. Yet, many shy babies become gregarious ten-year-olds and some outgoing babies become shy adults. This tells us that while a genetic predisposition plays a role in our timidity, shyness need not cripple our relationships. There are many steps the shy can take to develop satisfying relationships without violating their basic nature (many of which we point out later in this chapter), but when people categorically dismiss the possibility of social competence because of their shyness, they are making a big mistake. This will inevitably lead to a level of shyness that borders on social phobia where they will barely utter a sentence without obsessing over the impression they are making.

> **You're blessed when you're content with just who you are—no more, no less.**
>
> *Matthew 5:5, The Message*

## Pitfall #3: Sensitivity to criticism

No matter how hard you work, how great your ideas, or how wonderful your talent, you will be the object of criticism. Even the perfect motives of Jesus were often misunderstood, resulting in malicious criticism. No one is exempt. And how you respond to criticism will play a major role in your sense of security.

Consider Walt Disney. He was bankrupt when he went around Hollywood with his little "Steamboat Willie" cartoon idea. Can you imagine Disney trying to sell a talking mouse with a falsetto voice in the days of silent movies? Disney's dreams were big, and he had plenty of critics. People closest to him, however, believe Disney thrived on criticism. He was said to have asked ten people what they thought of a new idea, and if they were unanimous in their rejection of it, he would begin work on it immediately.

**To laugh often and much; to win the respect of intelligent people and the affection of children; to earn the appreciation of honest critics and endure the betrayal of false friends; to appreciate beauty, to find the best in others; to leave the world a little better.**

*Ralph Waldo Emerson*

A single critical comment, for many, is enough to shut down all sources of creativity. Few among us actually thrive on it like Walt did. But on the other end of the continuum are those whose sensitivity to criticism creates a social stalemate. They stymie all progress for fear of someone saying something critical. Sir Isaac Newton is said to have been so sensitive to criticism that he withheld the publication of a paper on optics for fifteen years, until his main critic died.

Pulitzer prize–winning journalist Henry Bayard Swope once noted: "I cannot give you the formula for success, but I can give you the formula for failure: Try to please everybody." The people who are overly sensitive to criticism are trying to do just that. No wonder they feel socially insecure.

Are *you* socially insecure? Try the "Do You Suffer Socially?" exercise on the next page to find out.

## DO YOU SUFFER SOCIALLY?

As you consider the pitfalls that lead to social suffering, take a moment to rate yourself on a scale of 1–10, with 1 being "never" and 10 being "all the time." How often do you find yourself

~ Comparing yourself to others?
~ Finding your own shyness to be a barrier in relationships?
~ Being sensitive to criticism?

Give an example or a situation that demonstrates why you rated yourself the way you did . . . and how that pitfall has affected you recently.

---

## THE FUNDAMENTAL SOCIAL SKILL

If you have avoided the common pitfalls of social insecurity and are becoming more tuned in to reading your social barometer, you are primed to focus on a single skill that the socially competent continually master. This single skill may be the most important thing you can do for making meaningful connections and for understanding and carrying out the principles of self-giving love. Its simplicity, if not studied, causes it to go unnoticed. But once you recognize its power, you will never approach a relationship without it. The skill? Asking a string of quality questions.

In 1937 the grandfather of all people-skills books was published. It was an overnight hit, eventually selling 15 million copies. And today that book, *How to Win Friends and Influence People* by Dale Carnegie, is just as useful as it was when it was first published. Why? Because Dale Carnegie had an understanding of human nature that will never be outdated and he knew how to ask quality questions. The skills he teaches in this classic book are undergirded by a pervasive principle: People crave to be known and appreciated.

Quality questions are intentionally designed to open up a person's spirit. They aren't throwaway questions, like, "How about those Red Sox?" or "Can you believe this weather?" though those types of questions certainly have their place.

**The applause of a single human being is of great consequence.**
*Samuel Johnson*

Quality questions invite vulnerability, but are not invasive. They are personal, but respect privacy. They are asked out of genuine interest, but are never blunt. A quality question conveys kindness, warmth, concern, and interest. It is couched in affirmation and appreciation.

Here's an example. Not long ago, the two of us were in Dallas together to speak at a conference. The host assigned to pick us up at the airport was waiting outside security with our names on a placard. "Howdy, my name is J. T.," he said as he reached to carry a suitcase or two. We hopped into his vehicle and were on our way—until we hit rush-hour traffic. We were at a near standstill for nearly two hours, and that gave us plenty of time to talk.

"Tell us about your hobbies, J. T. What do you do for fun?" we asked.

He became animated as he told us about playing racquetball.

"Sounds like you really enjoy it," one of us followed up, "and I bet you get plenty of exercise."

"Oh yes," he replied, and then he went into describing the competition he entered last year and how he fared.

"You really love it, don't you?" we said.

"It's not only fun; you're exactly right about it keeping me in shape." J. T. then told us about his father's triple-bypass surgery two years ago.

As the traffic crawled, we asked J. T. about his work.

"I love computer programming," he told us.

"I bet there's a story behind you getting into that field," we said.

J. T. told us about a high-school teacher who mentored him and how his father loved to tinker with electronics. J. T. then described several of his projects.

With plenty of time on our hands, we were able to ask J. T.

questions about his family. Questions about his church. Questions about his upbringing. We asked literally dozens of questions.

And you know what? When we finally pulled up to our hotel and began unloading our bags, J. T. asked each of us for our business cards and said, "You boys sure are interesting. It was great getting to know you." And with that he climbed into his SUV and sped away.

**Man was formed for society.**

Sir William Blackstone

We looked at each other and smiled.

Truth be told, J. T. didn't get to know us at all. In two hours of conversation, he did not ask a single question with the exception of the obligatory "How was your flight?" It's not an uncommon experience. Many people who have never found their social barometer don't know how to put the spotlight on the person they are with. They've never consciously considered how to pull a person out and make them feel known.

The only reason J. T. thought we were interesting is because we showed genuine interest in him. And we affirmed him on top of it. For nearly two hours, he was on center stage with two strangers who supplied him with a string of quality questions about himself. That kind of genuine interest had succeeded in making him feel good about himself as he sped off.

Perhaps you are already well aware of the power of this simple strategy. Maybe you have been doing it for years. Then congratulations! We are sure you don't lack for friends.

But if you are unsure about your social barometer, it's time to take action if you want to become the kind of person who radiates self-giving love. If you sometimes endure too many conversational lulls or feel socially awkward too frequently, or if you suffer from shyness, why not give this a try?

Take a colleague to lunch and begin a line of quality questions. We're convinced you will sense a new level of social confidence almost immediately. As you think in terms of *How are they doing?* and choose to be genuinely interested, you will witness how quickly this person feels understood and appreciated. But be prepared. If the person is socially unskilled, like J. T., the questions will be one-sided. You will be doing most (or all) of the question asking; the other person will be doing most of the talking.

**Lonely people talking to each other can make each other lonelier.**
*Lillian Hellman*

If, on the other hand, they are reading their own social barometer, they will eventually turn the tables. And you will witness the social law of reciprocity that states, "Vulnerability begets vulnerability." Once they reveal information about their career aspirations, for example, they will be genuinely interested in yours. And when this kind of give-and-take occurs on nearly any subject, you will find yourself in the midst of a terrific conversation. You are enjoying emotional rapport and social synchrony.

## THE ART OF EMPATHY

Angela teetered as she walked across a medical conference room, thighs chafing, sweat glands sweating. She tried to squeeze into a regular-size chair, but her lumpy hips snagged on the arms. She moved to an extrawide armless chair, but then she couldn't cross her plumped-out legs.

A dietitian helped her climb aboard a stationary bicycle that had been fitted with an oversize seat. But when Angela tried to pedal, thick, doughy rolls of abdominal tissue pressed against her fleshy thighs, impeding movement.

"Every move I made was an effort," Angela, thirty-five, later admitted. By then, however, she was slimmed down to her actual weight: 110 pounds.

Angela had been zipped into a bulky beige "empathy suit," designed to help medical personnel better understand the plight of their obese patients. The suit weighs only thirty pounds, but it feels heavier and effectively blimps out small, low-fat people like Angela. Its sheer heft and bulk is intended to give them a new, deepened understanding of the workaday world of the obese.

Does it work? You bet. Angela saw firsthand that even a simple movement such as walking may be challenging for the obese. Having worn the suit "makes me feel more respectful, more aware of their feelings," she says.

That's the power of self-giving love—putting oneself in the skin of another. Take any profession . . . teaching second graders, for example. You can improve a teacher's effectiveness by having her walk through her classroom on her knees. As she sees that space from a second grader's perspective, she will be better equipped to teach them. Or how about serving fast food? The major chains spend bundles of money sending "fake customers" into their stores to see it as they do. Advertising firms on Madison Avenue make their living by putting themselves in the consumer's shoes. Growing churches are growing because they study the experience of a first-time visitor, and the pastor imagines what it is like to sit in the pew. Disney World's "cast members" know that guests will average sixty contact opportunities in a single day at their theme park, and they want to make each of them a magic moment; so they continually work at empathizing with families. And, of course, a counselor wouldn't last a day without practicing empathy. How well we know!

The point is that empathy—the ability to accurately see the world through another's eyes—is at the heart of true understanding and the ability to extend self-giving love. Whether it be in medicine, business, education, or entertainment, empathy is a major determiner of success. More importantly, when it comes to our most important relationships, empathy is essential. Without empathy, healthy relationships are impossible. Self-giving love is null and void.

> **No act of kindness, however small, is ever wasted.**
>
> *Aesop*

Consider your contentment when another person senses what you are feeling without you having to say so. This is the essence of empathy. While we can have interesting conversations and smooth social exchanges without it, we will never enter the inner chambers of a person's heart without empathy. It is the key to unlocking a person's spirit at the most intimate and vulnerable levels.

If asking a string of quality questions is the equivalent of a B.A. in relationships, empathy will earn you your Ph.D. in the social arts. Empathy is evidence of relational brilliance.

In 1990 Yale psychologist Peter Salovey and the University of New Hampshire's John Mayer coined the phrase "emotional intelligence" to describe qualities that bring human interactions to their peak of performance. Harvard psychologist and *New York Times* science writer Daniel Goleman brought the phrase into the national conversation with his groundbreaking book on the subject. He calls empathy our "social radar" and believes it operates at different levels. At the very least, empathy enables us to read another's emotions. At a higher level, it entails sensing a person's unspoken concerns. And at the highest levels, empathy is understanding the concerns that lie behind the person's feelings.

The key to identifying and understanding another person's emotional terrain, experts agree, is an intimate familiarity with one's own. Goleman cites the research of Robert Levenson at the University of California at Berkeley as a prime example. Levenson brings married couples into his physiology lab for two discussions: a neutral talk about their day and a second fifteen-minute emotionally charged discussion concerning a disagreement. Levenson records the husband's and wife's heart rate, muscle tension, changes in facial expressions, and so on. After the disagreement, one partner leaves. A replay of the talk is then narrated by the other partner, noting feelings on their end that were not expressed. Then the roles are reversed and that partner leaves, allowing the other person to narrate the same scene from their partner's perspective.

> **Self-pity is our worst enemy and if we yield to it, we can never do anything good in the world.**
>
> *Helen Keller*

This is where researchers found something extraordinary. Partners adept at empathizing were seen to mimic their partner's body while they empathize. If the heart rate of the partner in the videotape went up, so did the heart rate of the partner who was empathizing; if the heart rate slowed down, so did that of the empathic spouse. This phenomenon, called *entrainment,* demands we put aside our own emotional agendas for the time being to clearly receive the other person's signals. For, as Goleman says, "When we are caught up in our own strong emotions, we are off on a different physiological vector, impervious to the more subtle cues that allow rapport."

Putting aside our own emotional agenda for empathy's sake brings us back to the question we posed earlier: What races through your head when you walk into a roomful of people? If you are not quietly asking yourself, *How are these people doing?* you will never provide the psychological space for empathy to do its work. But when you do, you will begin to enjoy relational connections at a depth you never knew was possible.

## THE FRUIT OF A HEALTHY RELATIONSHIP

With an understanding of how to find and read your social barometer, an exploration of social competency, and a study of the fine art of empathy, we want to leave you in this chapter with a bit of inspiration. We believe that inspiration goes a long way in helping you use your social barometer to engender self-giving love.

You'll remember that we've said who you are is more important than what you do. This is particularly true in your relationships. Tips and techniques can be helpful, but a relationship ultimately rests on the psychological health of two people. In fact, your relationships can only be as healthy as the least healthy person in them. So we will say it again: If you want a healthy relationship, the most important thing you can do is get yourself healthy. And we know, because you are reading this book, that's exactly what you are doing. So with that in mind, we want to highlight the payoff for your efforts. By recounting these payoffs to yourself on occasion, you will increase the likelihood of a more self-giving lifestyle.

> **Every time you smile at someone, it is an action of love, a gift to that person, a beautiful thing.**
>
> *Mother Teresa*

When two healthy people (both tuned in to their social barometer) get together, it's like drinking lemonade in the desert. They breathe a collective sigh. They relax. They can be who they are, and they know that just being together will restore their spirits. Why? Because some things—what we call the fruit of a healthy relationship—are certain. In a healthy relationship, you can count on, at the very least, these four qualities: confidentiality, honesty, personal space (when needed), and almost always a good laugh.

### Fruit #1: Confidentiality

A Jewish publication ran an advertisement dominated by a drawing of a very stern-looking, bearded rabbi of the nineteenth century, the Chofetz Chaim, who wrote a book about gossip called *Guard Your Tongue*. At the bottom of the page was a "hot-line" number to call anonymously if you have information about someone's potential marriage, business dealings, or whatever. A rabbi at the other end will tell you whether your gossip is important enough to pass along. If not, you are counseled to guard your tongue.

Interesting, isn't it? The advertisement reveals as much about the state of our relationships as it does about our propensity for gossip. Who among us hasn't been hurt by a broken confidence? It usually begins when your friend says to someone: "You have to promise you won't tell Brenda I told you this because she made me swear not to tell anyone. . . ." It sounds very confidential. But then why are they telling you the secret? They appear to be keeping a secret but aren't. Jesus understood this when he said, "Therefore whatever you have spoken in the dark will be heard in the light, and what you have spoken in the ear in inner rooms will be proclaimed on the housetops."

We've all shared private and personal information with a trusted friend, only to learn later that our friend has blabbed it to the world. But does this mean we can't expect *anyone* to keep their mouth closed? No. Not if they're healthy. We *need* to tell our secrets. It helps us explore what's troubling us and sometimes leads to helpful feedback. Sharing our secrets lets us test the reaction to what we've been holding in our heart. Not only that, it's a relief not to be the only person who has experienced a certain temptation or tragedy. It makes us feel less alone when we unburden our soul and a friend says "me too" or "I understand." Sharing a secret can bring us closer together and deepen our relationship—but only if the relationship is healthy. Healthy people consider it a privilege to hear what's on our mind, and they leave it at that. When it comes to keeping a confidence, healthy people are a human vault.

## Fruit #2: Honesty

"Genuine relationships cannot exist where one of the parties is unwilling to hear the truth," said Cicero, "and the other is equally indisposed to speak it." As painful as the truth might be, a healthy relationship cannot survive without it. As the well-known proverb says, "A friend loves at all times, and a brother is born for adversity." Now this does not mean that honesty gives license to be insulting, offensive, or badgering. Healthy relationships call for speaking the truth in love and respect. Without these ingredients, honesty is a lethal weapon. Perhaps that's what caused Cicero to add, "Remove respect from friendship and you have taken away the most splendid ornament it possesses." People deserve the respect of knowing the truth. They deserve to know if they are hurting someone's feelings, being too aggressive, too lazy, too anything. And healthy people know they can't live without this kind of feedback. For without it, they cannot achieve unswerving authenticity, as we discussed in the Secret #2 section of this book, or understand themselves well enough to be able to empathize with others and extend self-giving love freely, without conditions or restraints.

> The best portion of a good man's life—his little, nameless, unremembered acts of kindness and love.
>
> *William Wordsworth*

Some time ago I (Les) was counseling a twenty-something student named Lisa who came to my office in hopes of resolving a problem with a close friend. Lisa wasted no time in telling me the problem concerned her friend's stinginess.

"Jenny is so tight, she squeaks when she walks," Lisa confessed.

"Is this a new problem?" I asked.

"Oh no, it's been going on for years. But it's really wearing thin, and I find myself wanting to avoid being with Jenny whenever money is involved."

Lisa went on to tell me how meticulous Jenny can be when trying to figure out a shared bill at a restaurant. She told me about the time it took an extra ten minutes to pay for parking at a downtown garage because she wanted to make change for splitting the bill.

"How does Jenny respond when you talk to her about being so stingy?"

"Talk to her?!" she exclaimed. "I've never brought the subject up. I don't want to hurt her feelings."

Lisa and I spent the next several minutes exploring how much she valued her relationship with Jenny. Turns out, they were "best friends." But here she was, on the brink of tossing away an eight-year friendship because she didn't want to hurt Jenny's feelings. In other words, the one friendship she cared more about than any other was about to go under because she couldn't speak the truth.

Fortunately, with a little advice and coaching, Lisa mustered up the courage to confront Jenny on this annoying habit and the problem began slowly to reverse itself. The point to be learned here is that friends who do not care enough to confront may save themselves a little awkwardness in the present, but they will end up losing their friendships in the future. A healthy relationship is built on honesty.

Healthy people aren't afraid to be honest, and they aren't afraid to be themselves. They follow Emerson's advice: "Better be a nettle in the side of your friend than his echo." Translation: Speak the truth, because if you are afraid of making enemies, you'll never have good friends.

### Fruit #3: Personal space

Emotionally needy people don't understand the meaning of space. They mother and smother us with their very presence. Their constant connecting becomes oppressive—if not possessive. This kind of person has no appreciation for what C. S. Lewis meant when he said: "In each of my friends there is something that only some other friend can fully bring out." In other words, Lewis recognized the need for space in a healthy relationship. He saw the need for multifaceted relationships that help us shine where another friend, even a close one, simply is not able. This is one of the marks of a space-giving relationship: Each person relinquishes a possessive hold to enable the cultivation of other relationships.

Along this same line, a healthy relationship respects serenity. It recognizes the value of a thoughtful silence and a private retreat. Philosopher and author Henry David Thoreau once said, "I never found the companion that was so companionable as solitude." Let's face it: There are times in everyone's life when we need to be alone—times when we need to gather our wits and allow our soul to catch up. Healthy people understand this. Part of self-giving love means that we provide space, when needed, for the companion of solitude to enter a relationship. Of course, we also know when to return, when to break the silence and rejoin the other person's journey.

All of us need space for the companion of solitude but, even more, we need to be in relationship. After all, it is this very space and separation provided by a healthy relationship that draws us back to a full appreciation of the relationship.

> So long as we serve; so long as we are loved by others, I would almost say that we are indispensable; and no man is useless while he has a friend.
>
> *Robert Louis Stevenson*

### Fruit #4: Humor

Humor is always risky. What is appealing to some is appalling to others. In a survey of over fourteen thousand *Psychology Today* readers who rated thirty jokes, the findings were unequivocal. "Every single joke," it was reported, "had a substantial number of fans who rated it 'very funny,' while another group dismissed it as 'not at all funny.'" Apparently, our funny bones are located in different places. Some laugh uproariously at the slapstick of Larry,

Moe, and Curly, while others enjoy the more cerebral humor of Woody Allen.

Despite its risk, healthy people are willing to take it. Humor is like a litmus test for mutual understanding between two people. Sometimes it fails miserably, but it can also reveal the possibility of a deeper connection. Perhaps more importantly, laughter is the fuel that keeps healthy relationships going once they are born. It's what enables friends to help each other cope in the midst of crisis. After all, where would we be without someone who could make us laugh?

Viktor Frankl is a profound example of how humor can empower a person to contend with horrendous circumstances. In his classic book, *Man's Search for Meaning,* Frankl speaks of using humor to survive imprisonment during World War II. Frankl and another inmate would invent at least one amusing story daily to help them cope with their horrors.

"If you can find humor in anything," according to comedian Bill Cosby, "you can survive it." Researchers agree. Studies reveal that individuals who have a strong sense of humor—who can laugh easily with at least one other person—are less likely to experience depression and other forms of mood disturbance. Scientists hypothesize that humor helps us cope because it offers a fresh perspective. When the naturalist William Beebe used to visit his friend President Theodore Roosevelt at Sagamore Hill, both would take an evening stroll after dinner. Then one or the other would go through a customary ritual. He would look up at the stars and say, "That is the spiral galaxy of Andromeda. It is as large as our Milky Way. It is one of a hundred million galaxies. It is 750,000 light-years away. It consists of 100 billion suns, each larger than our sun." Then silence would follow. Finally, one of them would say, "Now I think our problems seem small enough."

Every healthy relationship knows that humor lends a fresh eye to our troubles and gives us a new perspective.

How healthy are *your* relationships? Try the "Relationship Check" exercise now.

## RELATIONSHIP CHECK

1. Think of the three people most important to you with whom you have regular contact.

   ~

   ~

   ~

2. Evaluate your relationship with each of these people. Do you see in those relationships a mutual respect and adherence to the following qualities? If so, in what ways? If not, why not? Consider these qualities for each of the three people you listed:

   ~ Confidentiality
   ~ Honesty
   ~ Personal space (when needed)
   ~ Humor
   ~ Self-giving love

---

In this chapter we hope you've come to understand more about your own social barometer—and how to read it. We've explained why the healthier you are, the healthier your relationships become. Which brings us back to the question we started this chapter with: Are you a "close talker"? Are you emotionally tone deaf to others? Are you ever accused of talking too much or being too reserved? The good news, as you have just seen, is that social competence can be learned. More importantly, as you become psychologically healthier, the social skills of tuning in to others begins to come more naturally and you eventually focus, not on the skills it requires, but on the needs and concerns of those around you. In other words, you are focused, in time, on self-giving love—and as a result, your relationships will never be the same.

# 9

## LOVING LIKE YOUR LIFE DEPENDED ON IT

*You will find as you look back upon your life*
*that the moments when you have really lived*
*are the moments when you have done things*
*in the spirit of love.*

HENRY DRUMMOND

*I*'ll never forget the time I (Neil) took my friend Harold Graham to play golf. Though he was an outstanding athlete at our college, he made no pretense about being a golfer. In fact, he'd never set foot on a golf course before that day.

On the first tee we were joined by two older men who were seasoned golfers. They were dressed immaculately, and their golf equipment was expensive and stylish. When they both hit their drives far out on that first hole, Harold gave me a wary look. He rummaged through his old bag and fished out three or four balls. They were all driving-range balls with a bright orange band around them. As the other gentlemen exchanged glances, I hurried over to lend Harold one of my new balls . . . which he proceeded to hit into a nearby bush. After five minutes of searching for the ball, we gave up. I helped him tee up another ball . . . which he dribbled about twenty feet.

And that's the way it went for eighteen holes. My entire focus that day was on helping Harold do what he needed to do to avoid embarrassment and enjoy himself. I gently offered some pointers, lent him my clubs, gave him lots of encouragement, and kept the mood light so he could laugh at his struggles rather than feel miserable.

To my amazement, when the scores were tallied at the end of the round, I had the best score I'd ever achieved on the course. I had been so absorbed in helping my friend that I'd been freed from the worry and anxiety that would have diminished my own performance. Serving and assisting Harold enabled my own ability to reach new heights.

It's a fundamental psychological law: When you help other people, you immediately receive a payoff yourself. George Burton Adams, an American educator and historian, said it nicely: "Note how good you feel after you have encouraged someone else. No other argument is necessary to suggest that you should never miss the opportunity to give encouragement." Ralph Waldo Emerson put it this way: "You cannot sincerely help another without helping yourself." And he could not have been more right. When we serve, we grow. Each act of kindness, each act of self-giving love, expands our life.

> **What a grand thing, to be loved! What a grander thing still, to love!**
>
> *Victor Hugo*

You are sitting alone, for example, lost in self-doubt or wallowing in self-pity. The phone rings. It's a friend who's really in need. Without conscious thought, you break out of your isolation. You listen. You give words of assurance. You serve. When you put the receiver back in its cradle, who feels better? Your friend does, you hope. But you do, too!

A benevolent spirit is the trademark of a person who is becoming healthy and whole. Once you have rooted your life in profound significance and once you have cultivated unswerving authenticity, your life is all about the business of loving others.

No human experience can compare to being loved by a person who is not needy and is genuinely interested in you. This is why significance and authenticity are prerequisites to healthy love.

If you try to love others in the absence of profound significance, you end up trying to earn a sense of worth by acting worthy.

Your actions are hollow, and loving becomes a duty rather than an opportunity. And even if you have a relatively secure sense of significance but you are short on authenticity, your love will repeatedly fall short, for it will become a manipulative tool, cajoling people into your will. True love, the kind we all long for, is only given when significance and authenticity are secure.

Consider a simple illustration of a regulation baseball. The center of the ball is made of the finest grade cork. It represents profound significance—the core of every healthy person. This core of the baseball is reinforced by a distinct rubber shell, representing unswerving authenticity—it insures that the ball does not lose its spherical shape. The next part of the construction of a baseball, the biggest part, is the wrapping of over two hundred yards of wool. This represents the strands of love in which we encircle our life. Each time we do good we wrap our life with another strand of self-giving love that immediately bolsters our significance and authenticity and more clearly defines our identity.

> **Love is, above all, the gift of oneself.**
> *Jean Anouilh*

So we dedicate this chapter to helping you love fully. We want to help you wrap your life with countless strands of love. We begin with a quick definition and an exploration of why self-giving love matters so much—why it is so crucial to personal fulfillment and meaning . . . why it is the first fruits of a life well lived. And we paint a picture of what it can do in your own life and in the lives of those you encounter. Next, we delve into the act of kindness itself, exposing its secret ingredient. We'll show you exactly what sparks any act of self-giving love and why our human pride so often blocks it. From there we take a good look at what can go wrong when we are trying to be loving. We'll examine love's counterfeits and school you in the fine art of detecting the real deal. Finally, through several examples, we'll show you just how contagious kindness can be; how it multiplies as we "pay it forward."

+ + +

## HOW LOVED DO YOU MAKE OTHERS FEEL?

So how do you measure up when it comes to loving others? Do you make those around you feel loved? Take this quiz and find out. Record your answers below, then add up your score.

1. The word that most aptly describes you is
   a. Compassionate
   b. Kind
   c. Generous

2. If your sweetheart brings home news of a major disappointment from their workplace, you are likely to say:
   a. "I know how I'd feel if that happened to me, but how are you feeling?"
   b. "I'm so sorry, but you have so many other good things going for you."
   c. "You must feel devastated; I can't imagine how hurt you feel."

3. When I'm choosing a birthday gift for a friend, I
   a. Try to make it as personal and meaningful as possible
   b. Try to make it as fun and exciting as possible
   c. Try to make it as useful and economical as possible

4. Which of the three statements below do you believe is the most accurate?
   a. Doing loving things is more important than *being* loving
   b. Being loving is more important than *doing* loving things
   c. Either you're loving or you aren't

5. When I'm having a disagreement with a person I love, I
   a. Try to understand their position before trying to get them to understand mine
   b. Try to resolve it by giving in to their side even if I know I'm right
   c. Try to get my perspective heard clearly, regardless of the outcome

6. One of my biggest hurdles to being a loving person is
    a. Self-focus
    b. A judgmental attitude
    c. Apathy

7. Which statement do you hear most often from the people you love?
    a. "You always know just how I feel and just what to say."
    b. "You're sometimes so eager to meet my needs, you meet needs I don't have."
    c. "I know you love me, but sometimes I have to remind myself."

8. Everyone walks the first mile in a relationship—just to be a decent person. How often do you walk the extra mile for a person?
    a. Often
    b. Sometimes
    c. Rarely

9. It's been said that the heart of a loving relationship is putting yourself in the other person's shoes. Do you agree?
    a. Yes—even if it means you might get a few blisters now and then
    b. Most of the time—but that doesn't mean I give up my own shoes
    c. Only when the person's shoes are the same size as mine

10. One of the things I'm likely to do to let my sweetheart know I love them is
    a. Treat them to a special back rub or something else they enjoy
    b. Let them golf or shop with friends without making them feel guilty
    c. Cook a favorite meal

11. If someone needs me to pick up their prescription at the
drugstore, even when I'm especially busy, I typically
a. Run the errand without much complaining
b. Try to do it, but let them know how difficult it will be
c. Tell them it simply will not work with my schedule

## ANSWER KEY

Circle your responses. Then add up the number of ●'s, ■'s and ◆'s
you have, per the chart below.

| Question | 1 | 2 | 3 | 4 | 5 | 6 | 7 | 8 | 9 | 10 | 11 |
|---|---|---|---|---|---|---|---|---|---|---|---|
| A | ● | ● | ● | ■ | ● | ● | ● | ● | ● | ● | ● |
| B | ■ | ◆ | ■ | ● | ■ | ■ | ■ | ■ | ■ | ◆ | ■ |
| C | ◆ | ■ | ◆ | ◆ | ◆ | ◆ | ◆ | ◆ | ◆ | ■ | ◆ |

## What Your Answers Mean

*Mostly ●'s*

You not only *do* loving things, you *are* a loving person and the
people around you know it. Nobody mistakes you for a phony,
wanna-be lover. You are the real deal. You know how to make
people feel warm and at ease. They open up to you more than they
do with others. You have developed a special gift that will bring
blessing to most everyone you encounter.

*What to Do*

❏ Do something just for you. When was the last time you
enjoyed a leisurely latte while reading a good book? Or how
about taking a long bubble bath in the middle of the day?
Because you are so good at meeting other people's needs,
you may never indulge yourself.

❏ Allow others to serve you. Your spouse surprises you with
breakfast in bed. How do you feel? Does a twinge of guilt run
through your body? Relax. You need to receive the love of
others as well as you give your love to them.

❏ Keep doing what you're doing. Your friends are drawn to you because they like the way you make them feel. Wherever you are is the safest place on earth for your family members. Protect your loving ways by recharging your batteries and relishing the gift you are to those around you.

*Mostly ■'s*
You are a loving person who works hard to make people feel loved—even when you don't feel like it. The problem you run into sometimes is that you do the right thing for the wrong reasons. You may give a friend a birthday gift, for example, only to have it checked off your to-do list, not really to celebrate your friend. And sometimes your friend knows it. On the whole, your concern for people is evident, but in your struggle to be the loving person you want to be, you can benefit from a few pointers.

*What you can do*
❏ Focus on your most loving qualities. Maybe you're an especially good listener. Perhaps you know how to choose the perfect gift. Or maybe you have a knack for noticing when someone is feeling lonely. This loving ability you have will become your trademark. Don't neglect it.
❏ Celebrate others' successes. Most people find it easy to care for a friend who just lost a job or received some disappointing news. But a truly loving person also celebrates a friend's accomplishments. Take notice when people around you do well. It may be one of the most loving things you ever do.
❏ Keep your motivation in check. The next time you do something loving for your spouse, ask yourself why you're doing it. If it's out of guilt, for example, you'll need to realign your motivation. After all, everyone has a built-in radar detector for insincere motivations. And nobody likes a guilt gift.

*Mostly ◆'s*

You want to be a loving person, but you sometimes struggle to do the loving things you know to do. There are a myriad of stumbling blocks on your path to good intentions. From time to time, you may be tired, cranky, self-absorbed, or even oblivious. Whatever the reason, you are going to need to ramp up your efforts to cultivate the behaviors that make the people around you feel loved. Here are a few more suggestions to add to the pointers we give later in this chapter.

*What you can do*

❏ Generate gratitude. The more thankful you are, the more loving you become. Make a list of things you appreciate about the people in your life. Make a specific list for each person. When you are with a particular person, try to recall what you have on that list and let them know what you appreciate.

❏ Center yourself. Loving people are fully present in their relationships, not distracted. They make you feel like you are the only person on the planet when you are with them. The more at peace you are with yourself, the better you will be at this important quality. So the next time you're in a conversation, relax. Set aside your to-do list, and focus on the person you're with.

❏ Practice empathy. Studies have shown that this quality, more than any other, is at the heart of loving others. The more you can see the world as your teenage son or aging mother sees it, the more accurately you will understand their needs and the more loving you will become.

✦ ✦ ✦

## WHAT IS SELF-GIVING LOVE?

Here's an easy definition to remember. Self-giving love is "selfishness in reverse." It is not concerned with benefits, and it expects nothing in return. Whether it is offering directions to someone who appears lost, giving an especially generous tip to a server who seems needy, or encouraging a friend who didn't get an expected promotion, self-giving love is done out of care, compassion, and kindness—expecting neither repayment or appreciation.

There is hardly a more famous story of self-giving love than the parable of the Good Samaritan. The very phrase "Good Samaritan" has been enshrined in our culture by its use in the names of hospitals and care centers worldwide. It's a story that's told and re-told in houses of worship every week. It is one of those Gospel passages, like the Christmas and Easter stories, that probably wears out professional preachers because its point seems obvious: It is better to be kind, to take care of a person in need, than to pass by and let him bleed. Enough said. We're done. Anybody not heard that before? So why not finish up early, and get to the coffee hour?

Because, of course, its point is not so obvious. We struggle to love without expecting something in return. We wrestle with doing the right thing when no one's watching. And when we do, pride and arrogance seem to enter into our efforts without invitation. Not that there is anything wrong in wanting to be noticed, wanting people to applaud you. But there is something wrong with boasting. We boast to promote an image of ourselves we want others to buy. In short, we boast about our self-giving love because we lack significance (more about that in a moment). The point is, self-giving love entails a purity that is easily tainted. We humans seldom act with clear-cut single motives. So, for this reason, if no other, we continually need to be reminded and inspired by the Good Samaritan, the person filled with compassion, voluntarily giving time, energy, and money to even a total stranger—expecting nothing in return.

> **It is better to take the risk of giving to the undeserving than to take the risk of neglecting the deserving.**
>
> *Clement of Alexandria*

## WHY SELF-GIVING LOVE MATTERS

One day a student asked anthropologist Margaret Mead for the earliest sign of civilization in a given culture. He expected the answer to be a clay pot or perhaps a fishhook or grinding stone. Her answer was "a healed femur." Mead explained that no healed femurs are found where the law of the jungle, survival of the fittest, reigns. A healed femur shows that someone cared. Someone had to do that injured person's hunting and gathering until the leg healed. The evidence of compassion, said Mead, is the first sign of civilization.

And it's also the first sign that a person is truly on the pathway of fulfillment, wholeness, and spiritual health. No one has ever developed into a well-rounded personality, or has lived an effective life, unless he has learned to love others without selfish gain. This single skill is the very hinge upon which happy living hangs. Without a generous spirit, a benevolent attitude, a civilized mind-set, a person's life remains in the dark ages.

Let's say it straight: Until you wrap your life in love, you will never be genuinely happy. Fulfillment forever eludes us if we do not honor the law of self-giving love. History is filled with examples of people, even heads of state, who counted themselves failures although they had accumulated untold riches and incalculable power. The truly successful, the most fulfilled, have never counted on longevity or wealth or honors or power. Benjamin Franklin understood this when he said he owed his happiness to the philosophy he had formulated early on in his life: "The most acceptable service to God is doing good to man."

**Do everything in love.**

*1 Corinthians 16:14*

Strangely, generosity of spirit can be scarce even in abundance. You may recall that we opened this book with a story of Michelangelo in Florence, Italy. We described his four partially finished sculptures, "Captives," now on display at the Galleria dell'Accademia. What few do not know about the great Renaissance master Michelangelo is that while he lavished time and energy on his work, he apparently did not lavish love on others—particularly with his finances. That is the conclusion of the recent book, *The Wealth of Michelangelo*. It reveals a surprising financial profile of unacknowledged wealth and unwarranted thrift. Although Michelangelo has often been cast as somewhat poor, he died in 1564 with the modern equivalent of tens of millions of dollars. That money was not some late-in-life windfall. Research shows that for most of Michelangelo's years, he was phenomenally rich. But he declined to show it or share it. He routinely warded off requests for help by bemoaning his lot. Michelangelo's tenderness came through in his art, but not many of his relationships.

It's a tragedy, really. One that is retold countless times. A person's passion for adulation, wealth, fame, or any other form of "success" can push other people's needs aside in an illusive quest for contentment. Consider Carre Otis. She was among the world's top supermodels for seventeen years, beginning her career at the age of fourteen.

To prepare for each photo shoot, Carre routinely binged and purged, took laxatives and diet pills, and exercised intensely. Being extremely thin made possible a modeling career that earned her twenty thousand dollars a day. Cocaine helped her to diet, and she used heroin later on in her career. She married actor Mickey Rourke, but they soon divorced. This destructive lifestyle led to a mental and emotional breakdown.

After emerging from treatment at a mental institution, she became committed to changing her life. She began eating normally and abstaining from all drugs and alcohol. She gained thirty pounds, went from a size 2 to a size 12, and is now successful as a "plus size" model.

Recently, on her thirty-second birthday, a friend invited her on a humanitarian mission to distribute clothes and toys to kids living in orphanages in Nepal. For the first time she saw what starvation really was. Looking back on her experience, she explained to reporter Cynthia McFadden on a television newsmagazine program: "If somebody asked me, 'When did you feel the most beautiful?' I would say, when I was traveling through the Himalayas in dirty

> A man of a right spirit is not a man of narrow and private views, but is greatly interested and concerned for the good of the community to which he belongs, and particularly of the city or village in which he resides, and for the true welfare of the society of which he is a member.
>
> *Jonathan Edwards*

clothes, dirty hair, hadn't had a shower in a week, and was giving kids clothes. That's when I felt like the most beautiful woman, and the woman I've always aspired to be."

That's why self-giving love is so crucial. It brings us to the place where we discover our destiny; the place where we are most benevolent; the place God always intended that we live.

## THE POWER OF SELF-GIVING LOVE

We've already noted that self-giving love has a way of helping the giver do his best—just as it did for Neil when he was golfing with Harold. But we would be remiss if we did not note how powerfully self-giving love helps others do their best, too.

Successful film director Frank Darabont saw this firsthand with actor Tom Hanks. When Frank was asked what he would remember about directing the award-winning film *The Green Mile,* he replied, "Fifteen, twenty years from now, what will I remember? There was one thing—and I'll never forget this: When Tom was playing a scene with Michael Duncan. As we're shooting, the camera is on Michael first, and I'm realizing that I'm getting distracted by Hanks." Darabont goes on to say that Hanks was delivering an Academy Award–winning performance, off-camera, for Michael Duncan—"to give him every possible thing he needs or can use to deliver the best possible performance."

> **Love your neighbor as yourself.**
> *Matthew 19:19*

Tom Hanks made a selfless commitment to helping rising actor Michael Duncan achieve his best. "He wanted Michael to do so well. He wanted him to look so good. I'll never forget that," said the director. You may recall that in 1999 Michael Clarke Duncan was nominated for an Academy Award in the Best Actor in a Supporting Role category.

You don't have to be a movie star to help others do their best. Sometimes all it takes is an encouraging word. Scott Adams, creator of the popular "Dilbert" cartoon, tells this story about his beginnings as a cartoonist: "When I was trying to become a syndicated cartoonist, I sent my portfolio to one cartoon editor after another—and received one rejection after another." He goes on to say that one editor even called and suggested he take art classes. "Then Sarah Gillespie, an editor at United Media and one of the real experts in the field, called to offer me a contract. At first, I didn't believe her. I asked if I'd have to change my style, get a partner—or learn how to draw. But she believed I was already good enough to be a nationally syndicated cartoonist."

Scott then reveals this dramatic turning point in his professional life. "Her confidence in me completely changed my frame of reference and altered how I thought about my own abilities. This may sound bizarre, but from the minute I got off the phone with her, I could draw better. You can see a marked improvement in the quality of the cartoons I drew after that conversation."

Roberta Guaspari-Tzavaras is another example. The daughter of a factory worker, she would have never picked up a violin had it not been for a public-school program that offered musical education. So she wanted to give back what others had given to her. She took her talents to Harlem, where few—even the parents—believed that their kids would have enough discipline to learn such a demanding instrument. But Roberta believed in them. She was undaunted. She began teaching in the public schools, demanding that her students practice every day. When budget cuts eliminated her job, she found private funds to keep the program alive.

One night in Harlem, 130 youngsters walked onstage with their violins. They silently studied their teacher's face, bows in hand, awaiting her cue. Then came the music, filling the room with palpable energy. Tears streamed down parents' faces. It seemed like a miracle.

Virtuoso Isaac Stern was in the audience for the event, which would have never taken place without Roberta's benevolence. "This is not a concert," Stern stated. "This is a way to make these kids proud of themselves. It is an act of living."

> Do all the good you can, by all the means you can, in all the ways you can, in all the places you can, at all the times you can, to all the people you can, as long as ever you can.
>
> *John Wesley*

Amazing, isn't it? One simple boost in a person's life can make all the difference. When we set out on a quest of self-giving love we begin a ripple effect of positive change in people's lives that we may never even know about. The question is how. How can we encourage, care for, and love like this? What's the secret? Perhaps there are many. But in our experience, it hinges upon just one.

## THE SECRET OF SELF-GIVING LOVE

The Jewish poet and storyteller Noah ben Shea tells a parable that serves as a valuable reminder of the roles we play in life.

After a meal, some children turned to their father, Jacob, and asked if he would tell them a story. "A story about what?" asked Jacob.

"About a giant," said the children, squealing.

Jacob smiled, leaned against the warm stones at the side of the fireplace, and his voice turned softly inward. "Once there was a boy who asked his father to take him to see the great parade that passed through the village. The father, remembering the parade from when he was a boy, quickly agreed, and the next morning the boy and his father set out together. As they approached the parade route, people started to push in from all sides, and the crowd grew thick. When the people along the way became almost a wall, the father lifted his son and placed him on his shoulders."

"What happened next?" a little boy asked Jacob.

"Soon the parade began. And as it passed, the boy kept telling his father how wonderful it was and how spectacular were the colors and images. The boy, in fact, grew so prideful of what he saw that he mocked those who saw less, saying, even to his father, 'If only you could see what I see.' "

"But," said Jacob, staring straight into the faces of the children, "what the boy did not look at was why he could see. What the boy forgot was that once his father, too, could see."

Then, as if he had finished the story, Jacob stopped speaking.

"Is that it?" said a disappointed girl. "We thought you were going to tell us a story about a giant."

"But I did," said Jacob. "I told you a story about a boy who could have been a giant."

"How?" asked the children.

"A giant," said Jacob, "is anyone who remembers we are all sitting on someone else's shoulders."

"And what does it make us if we don't remember?" asked the boy.

"A burden," answered Jacob.

This is the secret to self-giving love: *Remembering that we are sitting on someone else's shoulders.* The moment we begin to think that we have gotten to where we are solely by our own efforts we stomp out humility. Arrogance enters the picture. And know this: Arrogance always breeds conceit and callousness. Any act of charity done from a callous heart is done for show. It is void of authenticity. It may be the right thing, but it is done for all the wrong reasons.

A kind and compassionate heart is found in the person who may be well accomplished, wildly successful, immensely powerful, but who is also humble. We'll say it again: Humility is the secret to self-giving love. It opens the door and makes a way for every act of kindness. Or, as William Grunall says, "Humility is the necessary veil to all other graces."

> **Goodness consists not in the outward things we do but in the inward things we are.**
> *Edwin Hubbel Chapin*

Allow us to drive this point further with another simple story. This one is told of a nine-year-old boy who is sitting at his desk in school when all of a sudden there is a puddle between his feet, and the front of his pants are wet. He thinks his heart is going to stop, because he knows when the boys find out, he'll never hear the end of it. And when the girls find out, they'll never speak to him again.

The boy puts his head down and prays silently, *Dear God, this is an emergency! I need help now.* He looks up from his prayer to see the teacher with a look in her eyes that says he's been discovered.

As the teacher is coming to snatch him up, a classmate named Susie is carrying a goldfish bowl filled with water. She stumbles and dumps the goldfish bowl in his lap. He pretends to be angry but prays, *Thank you, God! Thank you!*

Now, rather than being the object of ridicule, this kid is the object of sympathy. The teacher rushes him downstairs and gives him gym shorts to put on while his pants dry out. When he comes back to class, all the kids are on their hands and knees cleaning up around his desk.

But as life would have it, the ridicule that should have been his has been transferred to Susie. She tries to help, but they tell her to get out: "You've done enough damage."

At the end of the day, students are waiting at the bus stop. The boy walks over to Susie and whispers, "Susie, you did that on purpose, didn't you?"

Susie whispers back, "I wet my pants once too."

How do you nurture humility? By remembering that you have been there, too. And if you haven't, it is only by the grace of God. You hear about parents whose teenage son has been arrested for drinking and driving, for example, and without humility you are likely to stand on your platform of self-righteousness and say, "Well, we would never allow our son to do that." Or you can say, "But for the grace of God, go I." You learn that a person you know from church has been caught in an ugly situation of betraying his spouse. Without humility, you are likely to pass judgment on everything about him: "I never did trust that guy." But if you come down from your superiority stance, you can say, "But for the grace of God, go I."

> **If you judge people, you have no time to love them.**
> *Mother Teresa*

Humility. It is the secret, the catalyst, for self-giving love. So never forget whose shoulders you sit on and, if a few circumstances were different, how you could very well be in the same position as the person you are tempted to judge.

## LOVE'S COUNTERFEITS

At the top of this chapter, we noted that self-giving love done without profound significance becomes hollow. And love without unswerving authenticity becomes manipulative. These two pitfalls are so significant, so detrimental, that we want to take a closer look at exactly how they dismantle even our best efforts.

## Counterfeit #1: Love without significance

"To me, it's more important to be loved than to love," says author Brennan Manning. "When I have not had the experience of being loved by God, just as I am and not as I should be, then loving others becomes a duty, a responsibility, a chore. But if I let myself be loved as I am, . . . then I can reach out to others in a more effortless way."

A more "effortless way." Manning has tapped into a very important point here. While self-giving love requires effort much of the time, it becomes more effortless when we know we are loved.

So, to paraphrase Shakespeare: To love or be loved, that is *not* the question. It's not the question at all. For being loved propels us to love others. It is not a question of either/or but both/and.

Love without significance inevitably leads to the "disease to please." You know the symptoms: low self-esteem, fear of conflict, denial of one's own needs, and an overfunctioning conscience. The disease to please compels a person to seek significance from others by attempting to give them what they want. So these people say yes not because they agree, but because they think it will make other people like them. To be blunt, they lie—to themselves and everyone else—as a means of compensating for their lack of significance.

Mahatma Gandhi said, "A 'No' uttered from deepest conviction is better and greater than a 'Yes' merely uttered to please, or what is worse, to avoid trouble." Without significance, people are likely to dole out yeses to avoid making waves. They rarely say, "My feelings got hurt when you . . ." or "I think we need to resolve this problem you and I are having." Conflict is avoided at all costs because they are eager to please. Sooner or later, however, they will be cornered and forced into con-

> The supreme happiness in life is the conviction that we are loved—for ourselves, or rather, in spite of ourselves.
>
> *Victor Hugo*

flict. At this point they either give in ("I'm the one to blame, it's my fault"), or they explode. In either case, the disease to please mocks love with a mere imitation of what it could be.

The only thing worse, perhaps, is "love" that comes from a heart of mixed motives.

### Counterfeit #2: Love without authenticity

The rarest medal in the Olympics wasn't created from gold, but from a bolt.

The story begins on a cold, winter afternoon in Innsbruck, Austria, at the 1964 Olympic two-man bobsled competition. A British team driven by Tony Nash had just completed its first run, which had put them in second place. Then they made a most disheartening discovery. They had broken a bolt on the rear axle of their sled, which would put them out of the competition.

> After the verb "to love," "to help" is the most beautiful verb in the world.
>
> *Bertha von Suttner*

At the bottom of the hill, the great Italian bobsled driver Eugenio Monti, who was in first place, heard of their plight. Without hesitation, Monti removed the bolt from the rear axle of his own sled and sent it to the top of the hill. The British team affixed it to their sled and then completed their run down the mountain, winning the gold medal. Monti's Italian team took the bronze.

When asked about his act of sportsmanship, Eugenio Monti deflected any praise, saying, "Tony Nash did not win because I gave him a bolt. Tony Nash won because he was the best driver."

The story of Monti's selfless act spread. And because of it he was given the first De Coubertin Medal for sportsmanship. The award, named after the founder of the modern Olympics, is one of the noblest honors that can be bestowed upon an Olympic athlete; in other words, the most precious hardware any Olympian can own.

Why? Because it is recognition of pure altruism. Authentic goodwill. Genuine benevolence. Real self-giving love. And that, of course, is the best kind. When kindness gets entangled with mixed motives, its value drops like lead. Love that comes from an authentic heart, on the other hand, is a love of immeasurable value.

Unswerving authenticity insures that we do the right thing for the right reasons. It aligns our head with our heart and keeps us congruent. No guilt motivation. No martyr mentality. No ulterior motives. It's about as rare as the De Coubertin Medal in the Olympics and it's prized like no other gift. When one receives an authentic act of benevolence, it is treasured.

How do—or can—you show self-giving love? Try "The Self-Giving Game" exercise to find out.

---

## THE SELF-GIVING GAME

Take a few minutes to reflect practically on your life and the people who surround you. As you "walk through your day," in what ways can you show self-giving love?

Make a quick list. It could be anything from helping a spouse do laundry or dishes to giving a mom of young kids a "night off" to staying a few minutes late to assist a new coworker with a project. . . .

~

~

~

Once you've made your list, ask yourself, *What one thing could I do today to show self-giving love?* And then carry it out. As you show self-giving love, you'll be amazed at the benefits not only to others, but to yourself . . . and you'll want to give more.

---

## THE INFECTIOUS POWER OF GOODWILL

Kindness begets kindness. It's a principle ingeniously depicted in the film *Pay It Forward*, about a seventh grader's plan to make a difference in the world. On the first day of school, Trevor

McKinney and his classmates are challenged by their social studies teacher, Mr. Simonet (played by Kevin Spacey), to change the world. Written on the blackboard, the challenge reads: "Think of an idea to change our world—and put it into action." While most children disinterestedly slouch in their desks, Trevor is mesmerized by the possibility of changing the world.

As Trevor rides his dirt bike back to the modest home in which he and his struggling, alcoholic mom live, he detours to a place where the homeless gather. An unkempt, unshaven man devouring a chocolate cookie catches Trevor's eye. Motivated by his teacher's challenge, Trevor invites the man to come and sleep in his garage. Trevor's mother (played by Helen Hunt) is unaware of this arrangement until she awakens one evening to find the homeless man working on her broken-down pickup. Holding the man at gunpoint, she asks him to explain himself. He starts the truck to show her that he has successfully repaired it and tells her about Trevor's kindness. He says, "Somebody comes along like your son and gives me a leg up, I'll take it. I can't mess up again, or I'll be dead. I'm just paying it forward." Quizzically, Trevor's mom asks, "What's paying it forward?"

> If you do a good job for others, you heal yourself at the same time, because a dose of joy is a spiritual cure.
> *Dietrich Bonhoeffer*

The next day Trevor explains to his class his amazing plan of paying it forward. Mr. Simonet and Trevor's classmates are enthralled by Trevor's idea. To explain his plan, he draws a circle and says, "That's me." Underneath it, he draws three other circles, saying, "That's three other people. I'm going to help them, but it has to be something really big—something they can't do for themselves. So I do it for them, and they do it for three people. That's nine people." And nine lives turn into twenty-seven. As the movie proceeds, "paying it forward" changes the lives of the rich, the poor, the homeless, and a prisoner.

*That's just a movie,* you may say. And you're right. We've never encountered a real-life plan that's so structured and intentional. But we've seen this dramatic principle at work many times in our own lives and many others.

I (Les) grew up in Boston. One day, when I was riding on a crowded subway train, something happened. And it's a scene that has stayed with me, even decades later. Every few seconds someone in the car of the train shouted unintelligible words. I craned my neck to see that the outbursts were coming from a disheveled man who was most certainly mentally challenged. Sitting fairly close to him was a woman reading a newspaper. As I watched, he reached out, touched her shoulder, and quickly brought his hand back. She ignored his touch. He did it again a few seconds later. It seemed like a game a small child might play. Each time his face showed that he was pretending not to have touched her. No one said anything, but those sitting near him exchanged nervous glances and began to inch away.

What happened next surprised me, if not everyone observing this. The woman put down her paper and touched him on the shoulder but kept looking at the man. He smiled and so did she. Instead of rebuking him, she politely engaged the man in conversation. "Do you know where your stop is?"

He nodded that he did.

"Do you need any help getting to where you are going?"

He shook his head no.

I don't know what motivated this woman to treat an embarrassing stranger on the subway with such kindness. But the way she asked these questions showed that she was genuinely concerned for his welfare. She talked to him as a real person with real needs, not just as an annoyance on her commute.

I'll never forget that. I've replayed the scene in my head many times, mostly when I run into a person who is mentally challenged. The woman would never guess that what she did that day on the subway is still paying off. I'm not sure why it made such a lasting impression. Perhaps it's because I was at the tender age of twelve when I saw it. Or

> **We make a living by what we get.**
> **We make a life by what we give.**
> *Winston Churchill*

maybe it was because her kindness was so pure. Whatever the reason, I can tell you that it continues to inspire me, decades later.

Kindness is contagious. The owner of a drive-through coffee business in southwest Portland, Oregon, is an eyewitness to this fact. She was surprised one morning to have one of her customers not only pay for her own mocha but also for the mocha of the person in the car behind her. It put a smile on the owner's face to tell the next customer her drink had already been paid for. The second customer was so pleased that someone else had purchased her coffee that she bought coffee for the next customer. This string of kindnesses—one stranger paying for the mocha of the next customer—continued for two hours and twenty-seven customers.

That's often the consequence of kindness. It begets more kindness. And it's enough to make most anyone happy. Literally.

## SERIOUSLY HAPPY

We leave you in this chapter with one final story. A true story.

A recent *USA Today* announced that they had found the "Happiest Man in America." He wasn't a millionaire and didn't possess the looks of a male model. His twenty-three-hundred-square-foot home is no mansion. By no means was he a celebrity enjoying the perks of fame. Nope. J. P. "Gus" Godsey, forty-five, is an ordinary guy who comes off as "10 gallons of happiness in a 5-gallon bag." A married dad who lives in Virginia Beach, Virginia, Gus is a stockbroker who has savored some good moments of professional success. But that success is only a fraction of what sent his scores off the charts on every objective measurement of happiness. At the core of his personality was a generous attitude and a spirit that propels him toward acts of kindness like few others.

> Love is not a single act, but a climate in which we live, a lifetime venture in which we are always learning, discovering, growing.
>
> *Ardis Whitman*

In a word, "giving" describes Gus best. "This is my passion," he says, "something I devote so much of my energies to." His char-

itable efforts are geared mostly toward helping the needy, shelter-
ing the homeless, and improving literacy among at-risk kids. "My
favorite quote is from William James," says Gus, "who said, 'The
greatest use of life is to spend it for something that will outlast it.'
I want to leave a lasting endowment that will continue to help
people long after I'm gone."

Knowing that Gus Godsey has a tremendously giving heart did
not surprise us. All the research on happiness and fulfillment in life
points to this important attribute. People who reach the pinnacle of
health, happiness, and wholeness exude a spirit of self-giving love.

Once you have a secure lock on profound significance, where
you know deep down that you are worthwhile, and once you cultivate unswerving authenticity, where who you are and what you do
is congruent, self-giving love begins to take root and is sure to blos-
som into a kind of happiness that many only dream of.

We've done our best in this section to show you that self-giving love is the third secret to loving the life you live. It's the third leg on our tripod of health and wholeness. And it's our belief that the two most important tools you have for experiencing self-giving love are reading your social barometer (attuning yourself to those around you) and loving like your life depended on it (treating kindness and encouragement of others as if it were oxygen for your lungs). In our experience, the most self-giving among us have maximized the usefulness of these two tools. Of course, this kind of love is not an accomplishment that can be checked off your to-do list. It's an unending experience and process.

In short, self-giving love is the lifework of every healthy human being. So with that in mind, we want to relay a couple of stories to you of ordinary people, one young and one old, who demonstrated self-giving love in extraordinary ways.

## LIFE-DEFINING LOVE

Recently, I (Les) attended a dinner engagement and was seated next to the evening's speaker, Lisa Beamer. On September 11, 2001, Lisa's husband, Todd, was on that fateful flight that was hijacked by terrorists and wrestled to the ground in Pennsylvania. That night I heard firsthand about the heroic act started with the two words that have since become emblazoned on everything from Air Force jets to city fire trucks: *Let's roll.*

Perhaps no other incident of our time exemplifies an act of self-giving love more powerfully than what Todd and the others did on United Flight 93 that morning. After hearing the summary of his 9-1-1 phone call to a GTE supervisor, Lisa says:

> The information confirmed to me that Todd was "who he was" right to the very end of his life. It was a tremendous

comfort to know that in his last moments, his faith in God remained strong, and his love for us, his family, was at the forefront of his thoughts. I was glad to know that Todd felt he had some control of his destiny, that he might be able to effect change even to the end.

We didn't know Todd Beamer personally. But from everything we've learned about him, Todd was confident of his profound significance. He was unswervingly authentic. And his last actions were ones of self-giving love. On September 13 a company e-mail was sent to all the employees of the Oracle Corporation, where Todd worked: "It is unquestionable that Todd's brave actions, and [those] of his fellow passengers, saved countless lives on the ground."

Because Todd was always "who he was" and was ready to meet his Creator, he was freed to focus on the task at hand. And the results are written in history: On September 11, 2001, United Flight 93 was the only terrorist-guided plane that didn't hit its intended target. Instead, the flight crashed into a field in Shanksville, Pennsylvania. Although all onboard were killed, no one on the ground was hurt.

## THE PROFITS OF LOVE
What about you? Do you think the stories of self-giving we've shared in this chapter are "out of range" for someone as "common" as you? Or that you have to have a crisis to show a magnanimous spirit of self-giving love? Then let us tell you another story. Oseola McCarty, at age eighty-seven, surely understands the beauty of authentic giving. She did one thing all her life: laundry. Now she's famous for it—or at least for what she did with her profits.

For decades, Miss McCarty earned fifty cents per load doing laundry for the well-to-do families of Hattiesburg, Mississippi. She even preferred a washboard over an electric washing machine. Every week she put a little bit in a savings account. When she finally retired, she asked her banker how much money she had socked away.

"Two hundred fifty thousand dollars," was his reply. She was in shock.

"I had more than I could use in the bank," she explained. "I can't carry anything away from here with me, so I thought it was best to give it to some child to get an education."

This shy, never-married laundry woman gave $150,000 to nearby University of Southern Mississippi to help African-American young people attend college. "It's more blessed to give than to receive," she told reporters. "I've tried it." Oseola didn't give to get her name in the paper. She didn't want a scholarship named in her honor. She truly wanted to help. And she did.

Self-giving love comes in countless forms. But when you meet people who embody it in any fashion, you can be sure of one thing: They feel good—deep down in their soul—and they *love* the life they live.

◇

*The Life of Your Dreams*

# 10

## LOVE THE LIFE YOU LIVE

*The only limit to our realization of tomorrow*
*will be our doubts of today. Let us*
*move forward with strong and active faith.*

FRANKLIN D. ROOSEVELT

*H*ere's great news: *You* can daily experience the life of your dreams, a life you will thoroughly love living, and you can begin *immediately!* The three secrets we've revealed to you in this book, if used consistently, will propel you like a rocket toward this life of emotional and spiritual abundance.

We're not saying that *maybe* it can happen for you. We're talking about a guarantee. These ideas are time-tested, and they have worked for millions of men and women. You are no exception. If you subscribe to these prescriptions and live them out from morning to night, you will be changed beyond your belief. For all the world, it will seem like a miracle. And it will be! From the inside of you to the outside of you, from your thoughts to your feelings and your actions, from your self-conception to the way you perceive your family and friends—even strangers—you can be miraculously changed, made new, transformed, given a fresh beginning, reborn!

### IT DOESN'T MATTER WHERE YOUR LIFE IS RIGHT NOW
Wherever you are on life's journey, the guarantee applies specifically to you. If everything about your life is already pretty good, we guar-

antee that it can become even better. If you are currently dragging through life with a dark cloud over your head, the sun can shine again, consistently, on your days and even on your nights. If your most important relationships are hit-or-miss, sometimes pretty good but sometimes miserable, you can turn them around 180 degrees.

We've watched these profound truths change people of every age and station. Some of them were brilliant, but most were not. Some were quite rich, but most were of average means. People in every age group have found these three secrets to be profoundly life changing. Even if you feel desperate in your present circumstances, we strongly encourage you to get started on the path we have written about. We're convinced that your experience will be as meaningful as it has been for millions of others.

### How does this kind of dramatic change take place?

You may be wondering how it can be that you have worked so hard for so many years, and yet your life is so far below what you want it to be. And now, we come along with three *ancient* ideas, and we're telling you that your adoption of these ideas can revolutionize your life! Where do we get off making such claims?

We admit that these three ideas are as old as the hills. There's little that is new about any of this material. But here's the truth: We are two veteran psychologists who have worked intimately with thousands of people. We've tried all kinds of approaches in our efforts to help men and women like you discover the life of their dreams. Most of these approaches were *new* and *sophisticated,* seemingly full of promise. But many years ago, we became deeply convinced that the new and sophisticated didn't work nearly as well—at least not over time—as the old and proven. We eventually saw the light and migrated back to these three ancient principles because we are convinced they are the only ones that can rekindle the fire in your life, reestablish the peace at the center of your soul, and restore the profound purpose for living that maybe you once glimpsed at a high point in your life. They are the only ones that can replace superficial values, like grubbing for money, with values that really work—like recognizing the necessity of God in your life and treating your neighbor as a cherished friend.

More specifically, this kind of dramatic change takes place because it logically links you to the three important centers in your life. Let us state again how this works.

### #1: You must start with getting properly linked with God

There are, perhaps, a thousand paths to follow in pursuing a sense of profound significance in your life. The two most obvious are to earn it or to recognize it.

Most men and women in our society have been taught to earn it. And they try desperately hard! They work long hours in their frantic desire to feel good about themselves. They're positive that the money they eventually make—or the promotions they achieve—will establish their inner sense of being valuable. Most of the time, they don't *like* the work they do, but they are powerfully motivated to *get ahead,* deeply believing that this will result in what they most desire—an inner sense of profound significance.

This never works, of course. They almost never reach a level that makes them feel, even for a day, that they are intrinsically valuable, let alone *profoundly significant.* It's a fascinating fact, however, that their repeated failures never convince them of the futility of their strategy. Like an animal that persistently tries to escape a cage by struggling with steel bars on the front of the enclosure, instead of turning around and noting a wide-open escape route at the back, these persons keep frantically trying their worthless strategy of earning their way to significance. As long as they focus all their energy and attention in this direction, of course, they are doomed to failure.

The most powerful point of this book is that a sense of profound significance is the *only* foundation for a truly healthy life, and there is only one way to experience it. This *way* is so simple that it is typically overlooked. It centers in the act of simply receiving, through faith, that there is a God, that he created you as a person of profound significance. This fact of your significance has forever been true about you, and it forever will be true. But until you accept this life-changing fact, your days will likely be filled with a series of frantic efforts that end each time in another heart-breaking failure.

But once you get your significance well-established on the grounds of your faith, you will be well on your way to a deeply healthy life. This is all possible because you get into a right relationship with God. And once you get into a right relationship with the one true God, you will be totally freed from your slavery to false gods. You won't be dominated by your addiction to work or to making a good impression on others, or by any of your other unsuccessful strategies designed to help you finally feel good about yourself. You will simply be a free person—clear to your very roots and forevermore.

### #2: Then you get properly linked with yourself

Our second point, of course, is all about your getting correctly linked with yourself. On the basis of the profound significance you experience, you are then free to focus on being your best self.

There is only one way to get linked to this *best self* in a healthy fashion, and that is for you to be unswervingly authentic. This means that you try with all your heart to be that person God created you to be.

No one can determine who this "authentic you" is but you. The path to discovering your true self is to make careful decisions— one small or large decision at a time—and then to operate your life on the basis of these decisions. The making of each of these decisions involves the same basic process. You go down to the center of yourself, stand alone in your Control Booth, collect all the important data at every choice point of your life, and then with courage and determination, you live out each of these decisions.

As you live authentically on a moment-by-moment basis, you will become deeply linked to the true you. And it is the living out of this true you that puts you totally in sync with your best self. In this very act, you optimize your chances for an abundant life, and you automatically experience the joy of being the only self you truly are.

### #3: Finally, you get deeply linked to all the people in your life

It doesn't matter if these are relatives, friends, acquaintances, strangers, or even enemies. Once we gain a deep sense of our own significance and are unswervingly authentic, our healthiness will move us inevitably in the direction of giving ourselves away to others—what we have called, in this book, self-giving love.

It is in the very moment that we are most authentic that we will be most giving of ourselves. And when this moment becomes habitual for us, we can know beyond the shadow of any doubt that we have radically changed at the center of our souls. The change that always releases us to be both authentic and deeply loving is the sharp and pervasive recognition of our own profound significance.

The point is, there is no such thing as a healthy life that does not spill over with love and service for others. The kind of health that we know to be genuine is the kind that leads to self-giving love. And it is right in the middle of this kind of love that healthy people receive their deepest joy and meaning.

## CAN THIS KIND OF HEALTHY LIFE ACTUALLY BE YOURS?

As we reach the end of this book about health, we wonder if you are still questioning whether you want to "jump in." We passionately hope you will. Nothing in life can compare with the riches of emotional and spiritual health that permeates every pore of your being. If you are stuck, we want to help you get free. If you have become snagged at any point in the process, we don't want to let go of you until you have become unsnagged.

Don't forget: It all begins with getting yourself into a right relationship with God. And then you can begin to live out this life that has been given only to you. You can be authentic. And if you will be unswervingly authentic, you will be surprised by the excitement it will create for you. There is no excitement in this world that compares with each person being totally the person they were created to be.

And then the absolute joy begins. You get to watch yourself giving freely of yourself—your love—in every relationship you experience.

We have watched thousands of persons get themselves healthy like this, and we know with a confidence that is beyond measure that it can happen for *you*.

## CAN YOU UNDERSTAND HOW HARD IT IS TO LET YOU GO?

Both of us have experienced such a partnership with our readers in this project. You have been on our minds in every chapter—sometimes in every paragraph. We totally believe in these three secrets. We know they can bring health to your life. And we passionately want you to experience a wonderful newness at the center of your soul and in all your relationships.

We cannot begin to tell you how much we appreciate your reading this book. This is literally the best we have to give, and the fact that you have listened to our voices fills us with gratitude.

Here's what we wish for you: We want you to encounter a deeper level of understanding of your own significance than you have ever known. We want you to give every last ounce of energy in being the unique person you are, because we know this will give you all the excitement for which you have always yearned. And we cannot wait to hear how all this freeing up of your heart and your soul results in the growth of every single relationship you have.

We wish all of this for you, and we will pull for you every step of the way.

APPENDIX A

*𝒪ptimizing Your Spirit*

*We must not allow the clock and the calendar to blind us to the fact*

*that each moment of life is a miracle and mystery.*

H. G. WELLS

Optimizing your own spirit, we're convinced, is vital to becoming a supremely healthy person. Why? Our research indicates that you cannot maximize your emotional health without maximizing your spiritual life, because your soul is your most important connection to a caring and loving God—a God who loves you as if you were the only person in the world to love.

Your soul—or your "spirit," in other words—is the seat of your significance. If you neglect this crucial area, you will never truly enjoy abiding worth. And you are sure to miss out on the full experience of ultimate love if you neglect the vitality of a soulful connection with your Creator.

In the pages that follow, we want to help you cultivate and develop your spirit. First we'll define what your spirit really is and where it dwells. Then we'll talk about how your soul is connected with God, our Creator—and the difference between being simply "spiritual" and truly "religious." We'll show how scientific research is backing up what we of faith have known all along—that a growing, personal relationship with God is the most important step you can take to infuse your entire existence with meaning and satisfaction.

## WHERE YOUR SPIRIT DWELLS

Since the words *soul, spirit, spiritual life,* and other derivations are thrown around willy-nilly in our society, let us be clear about our context. Your *spirit* is internal—dwelling deep inside you. You can't see or quantify it. Perhaps that's why so many of us struggle with our spirit.

But perhaps the following explanation will help. Your spirit grows *invisibly* out of an *invisible* part of you that is central to your essence. Your *being* is virtually synonymous with your *spirit*. From this place all the questions that are most profound and vital emerge:

- Who am I—*really*—in the deepest parts of myself?
- What makes up the core of who I am, after all the externals are stripped away?
- Who is in charge of this world and the universe, and am I connected to this Supreme Being?
- What happens when I die?
- What is the purpose of my life?
- How am I related to all these people around me?

How often have you asked these questions of yourself—if ever? If you are not usually given to introspection and philosophizing and you do not already have a meaningful faith at your core, all of this may seem strange and foreign to you. As a matter of fact, it's not easy for any of us to get comfortable with spiritual pursuits. Our culture seems intent on distracting us from such issues. We are consistently told by the media and other sources that what matters in life is the tangible, visual things—what kind of car you drive, the size of the house you live in, the stylishness of your wardrobe, and so on. Since most American families have a television on seven hours a day, it's no wonder we don't focus much on something as ephemeral as our *spirit*.

But here's the crucial point: Your soul begins to be optimized when you focus on *spiritual matters*—when you acknowledge that there is far more to life than material things. The spirit within you becomes awakened and alive when you recognize that the mystery of life far transcends that which you can touch and see and taste. That there is, indeed, a longing within each of us to know our Creator more intimately. To know why we were created and where we are going, not only in life, but after we die. Until such issues are resolved within, you will never truly *know* your profound significance, understand the longing in your spirit, or have the lasting, personal relationship with God that brings calm and peace in today's tumultuous world.

What's more, instead of merely sitting back and waiting for God to zap you with spiritual change, your growth will gain momentum if you actively and positively participate. So we challenge you to look deep within yourself and explore that "subterranean" world where your most essential thoughts, feelings, and longings reside, while not losing or ignoring your connection to God, either.

## YOUR SPIRIT AND A SPIRITUAL GOD

The first prerequisite for a healthy soul is an organizing principle—a framework or context in which to understand this aspect of yourself. The Bible posits that the foundation upon which you craft your life is an all-knowing, all-powerful, never-changing God who has created all things and wishes to relate personally with every person on earth. The first words of Genesis establish the central figure in the unfolding drama: *In the beginning God created . . .*

Participating in the world of the spirit and believing that there is a spiritual God are huge leaps for many people. But the fact is that denying there is any world of the spirit, given all the available research, may require an even greater leap of faith. Some researchers are convinced that a person's spirit flourishes when the individual accesses in a positive way the spiritual world and *especially* when he or she encounters the Spirit of God. These investigators have come to believe that the human spirit is engineered to be at its best when we develop a constructive and intense faith in a spiritual reality and a personal and caring God.

Dr. Herbert Benson, professor at Harvard Medical School and the president and founder of the Mind/Body Medical Institute, has written two influential books on the power and biology of belief.

Working in the midst of a scientific community that tends to be skeptical about anything religious and spiritual, Benson freely admits his own belief in God: "My reasoning and personal experience lead me to believe that there is a God. And yes, a thoughtful design must have been at work in the universe in which such definite patterns emerge, in which incredible coincidences produced our world, and in which humans are wired to bear a physiologically healing faith."

Benson frequently refers to the "belief-inspired healing in many of my patients." He has carefully studied why people with a particular type of faith recover faster and stay well longer. He has concluded that these phenomena are not mere chance or happenstance. Summarizing nearly thirty years of intensive research, Benson says:

> I am astonished that my scientific studies have so conclusively shown that our bodies are wired to believe, that our bodies are nourished and healed by prayer and other exercises of belief. To me, this capability does not seem to be a fluke; our design does not seem haphazard. In the same way that physicists have found their scientific journeys inexorably leading to a conclusion of "deliberate supernatural design," my scientific studies have again and again returned to the potency of faith, so ingrained in the body we cannot find a time in history when man and woman did not worship gods, pray, and entertain fervent beliefs.

Moreover, Benson is being joined by a growing number of scientists, physicians, and researchers who acknowledge the interconnection between physiology and spirituality.

## SCIENCE INVESTIGATES . . .

For many decades the scientific community stayed far away from anything smacking of religion or spirituality. But during the last twenty years, this has changed. Now one of the hottest topics in physical- and mental-health research involves the consequences of spiritual belief.

This research involves questions like these: If a spiritually inclined person regularly engages in spiritual practices (prayer, meditation, reflection, and so on), does this change anything about his life? Does it make him a healthier person—physically and emotionally?

More than three hundred carefully designed and executed research studies indicate that spiritually actualized people live longer, experience less stress, require less medication, and develop significantly fewer emotional and physical maladies. Further, some thirty-five careful reviews of empirical research studies have systematically concluded that the healthiness of your spirit results in significant contributions to your mental, emotional, and physical health.

One study was conducted by Dr. Warren Berland, a veteran psychological researcher in New York City, who became fascinated by the astonishing survival of thirty-three men and women who had been diagnosed with cancer and given less than a 20 percent chance of surviving five years. Twenty-eight of the thirty-three had already lived longer than five years, some as many as fifteen years, and the other five who had been given a more recent diagnosis were still living, though none of their physicians had expected them to be. All thirty-three of them were moving vigorously into the future.

Berland wanted to know why these patients were still alive—and going strong—when their prognosis had been so bleak. So he decided to ask the patients themselves why *they* thought their lives had defied all expectations. The reason given by most patients: God. From their point of view, God was far more responsible for their survival than conventional or alternative medical treatments. Mind you, these men and women were not selected because of any religious orientation, but when they focused their attention on spiritual matters, their physical lives overcame the expected consequences of their cancer.

Numerous other studies have demonstrated the link between spirituality and health, but let us highlight just a few:

- A Duke University study of 577 men and women hospitalized for physical conditions demonstrated that depression was signifi-

cantly lower and quality of life higher for those who used positive coping strategies (e.g., having faith in God and praying).

- In another study from Duke University, postoperative patients
  who engaged in spiritual practices spent an average of eleven
  days in the hospital compared with nonreligious patients who
  spent an average of twenty-five days.
- A 1995 study at Dartmouth-Hitchcock Medical Center found
  that one of the best predictors of survival for 232 heart-surgery
  patients was the degree to which the patients reported drawing
  strength and comfort from religious faith.
- Dr. David Larson, a research psychiatrist at the National Institute for Healthcare Research, surveyed thirty years of studies
  about blood pressure. His findings showed that churchgoers
  have lower blood pressure than nonchurchgoers, even when
  adjusted to account for smoking and other risk factors.
- A careful review of four major epidemiological studies
  (involving 126,000 participants) concluded that "those
  frequently attending religious services had approximately
  29 percent fewer deaths from all causes (over a specified
  time period) when compared to those who were not religiously active."
- A 1996 review of several studies indicated that spirituality is
  associated with less alcohol and drug abuse, lower suicide
  rates, less criminal behavior, and higher marital satisfaction.

"Nobody knows what really happens in human beings when
they pray or when you pray for them in terms of the physiological
mechanisms involved," says Duke's Dr. Mitchell Krucoff. "But it's
not uncommon to be clueless about mechanisms." The article,
"Can Prayer Really Heal?" goes on to say:

> In studies at several medical centers, prayer and faith have
> been shown to speed recovery from depression, alcoholism,
> hip surgery, drug addiction, stroke, rheumatoid arthritis,

heart attacks and bypass surgery. . . . Some scientists speculate that prayer may foster a state of peace and calm that
could lead to beneficial changes in the cardiovascular and
immune system. . . . "I decided that not using prayer on
behalf of my patients was the equivalent of withholding a
needed medication or surgical procedure," says Dr. Larry
Dossey, a former internist who is the author of *Healing
Words* and *Prayer Is Good Medicine.* "I prayed for my
patients daily."

The point is clear: *prayer works.* And research is showing that
prayer, much like exercise and diet, has a connection with better
health. It leads to benefits such as decreased anxiety and an en-
hanced sense of well-being. But is it just prayer in general that will
bring long-term results in *all* areas of health? Or does the prayer
have to be focused on something or someone other than yourself?
Here's what we've concluded from our studies.

## OUR CONCLUSIONS

Between us, we have been clinical psychologists for more than fifty
years. Several thousand men and women have shared their most
intimate struggles and secrets with us. We have explored the human experience from virtually every angle and searched intensively
for a clearer understanding of how people develop their spiritual
lives—and what the consequences are when they succeed. As a result, we have come to several conclusions.

But before we share these with you, we want to acknowledge
that you may be reading this book from a different religious, cul-
tural, or career perspective. You may hold a set of core conclusions
about these matters that varies a little or a lot from ours. We
deeply respect your total freedom to maintain your beliefs. We
share our conclusions with you so that you will know exactly
where we stand as you read this book, and so that you can examine
these conclusions to determine if they have any value for you.

- Every person has a set of personal qualities that comprise their *spirit,* and individuals become known for this essential aspect of their identity. Their spirit may be self-centered, angry, defensive, and boring, or it may be generous, joyful, kind, and gentle.
- The degree to which a person optimizes his soul is the degree to which he will succeed in life. If his spirit is well-cultivated—if he becomes secure, unselfish, winsome, patient, kind, and generous—he will likely be successful in his relationships, career, and other endeavors. He will be more positive about his future, and less threatened about difficult circumstances and about death.
- A great spirit is almost always the consequence of learning how to nurture and nourish one's spiritual life. The entry path to the world of the spiritual is through relaxed but disciplined prayer and meditation.
- The essence of a healthy spiritual life is a personal relationship with a loving, positive, affirming God. To the degree that a person feels unconditionally loved by this God, deeply and fully forgiven for personal blunders, his spirit is likely to flourish.
- The specific character of the God in whom a person has faith will largely determine the quality and growth of his own spirit. The two of us come from a Christian perspective, and we believe that the God portrayed in Jesus' parable of the Prodigal Son is the one and only true God. And it is only through knowing him intimately that a person can most effectively develop a spirit characterized by generosity, timeless vision, unselfishness, and optimism.

## MORE POWER, MORE VIBRANCY?

When you optimize your spirit, do you have more power? What do you think? Is the link between vibrant spirituality and physical and emotional health mere coincidence, happenstance, chance? Or are there, in fact, specific rules that govern the impact of spiritual practice on healthfulness?

We believe that when you grow your spirit, you gain access to an astounding source of power. Moreover, we suspect that learning to operate within the spiritual realm makes available spiritual influence, or "leverage," far more extensive than anything that exists within the material world. The Bible notes that "the prayer of a righteous man is powerful and effective."

In the midst of our thinking and writing on these issues, we experienced a real-life test case. Les and his wife, Leslie, just had a new baby, Jackson Leslie Parrott. Because their first child, John, had such a perilous birth process (born at twenty-eight weeks, weighing only one pound and requiring a three-month hospital stay), there was considerable concern about Jack's birth.

Indeed, Leslie had a difficult pregnancy, and in the third trimester, Jack's growth slowed precipitously. So did his apparent movement in Leslie's womb. The doctors tried to wait as long as possible for the birth, reasoning that the longer Jack could stay in the womb, the stronger his lungs would become and the sooner he could go home.

Meanwhile, I (Neil) was in almost daily conversation with either Les or Leslie. I had a growing concern about Leslie, especially in relation to the stress of holding on "just a few more days" before giving birth. Every medical precaution was taken to protect her health, but there was no secret about her toxemia, breathing difficulties, and potential blood-pressure problems.

On the night before the doctors decided to induce labor, I had a long telephone conversation with both Les and Leslie, who were at the hospital. With all the news of Jack's slow growth and lack of movement, I hung up the phone full of emotion. My wife, Marylyn, and I prayed passionately for a miracle—for the baby to be born healthy and for Leslie to endure the process with no long-term complications.

Scores, maybe hundreds, of other friends and family members of the Parrotts were praying as well. When the news came the next morning that Jack had been born perfectly healthy, capable of breathing on his own and able to be taken home in two or three days, and that Leslie would have no long-term complications, my wife and I excitedly expressed our appreciation to God. We were convinced the highly successful birth and the passionate prayers were intimately related. This did not at all seem to be mere happenstance. To me, it was "the most meaningful miracle" I had experienced in a decade.

But are we kidding ourselves? Would Jack have been born just as healthy if we had never bothered to pray? Could it be that the telephone conversation, the encouraging and supportive words, did whatever good was necessary? Was it just a matter of psychosomatics—positive thoughts that manifest themselves in physical ways? Or is there spiritual power that works quite independently of psychological contact—power that is triggered when men and women pray to God?

We don't have to rely on intuition or blind faith to answer the question, "Does prayer work?" At least two carefully designed research studies provide compelling evidence. One of them, conducted by R. B. Byrd, involved two groups of patients recovering from acute myocardial infarction. A team of people was enlisted to pray for one group, while no one in the control group was prayed for. Neither patients nor doctors knew who was being prayed for and who wasn't.

The results were clear: Patients in the prayed-for group fared significantly better than the other patients on a number of health-related outcome categories. They required 7 percent fewer antibiotics at discharge, had 6 percent less pulmonary edema, 6 percent less congestive heart failure, and 5 percent less cardiopulmonary arrest. The intercessory prayer, objectively studied, had stunning positive effects.

Was this a fluke? Another group of researchers wanted to find out, so they attempted to replicate Byrd's findings. They studied intercessory prayer with 990 patients. Utilizing careful experimental controls, they again found that the prayed-for group in the coronary care unit had significantly better outcomes.

These findings have incredible significance. Scores of prior studies have demonstrated positive effects from prayer, but now on the basis of these intercessory-prayer studies, we catch a glimpse of the *independent* power of prayer. These are not results that could have been "psychologically transmitted"; positive results showed up even when the *persons who were praying* and the ones who were *prayed for* were totally unaware of each other.

This provides evidence of a spiritual world, a totally different reality that operates with consistency—with well-developed rules and massive power potential. It's clear that persons who have optimized spirits can access spiritual power on behalf of themselves and others. This greatly increases the importance of developing, or nurturing, an optimized spirit.

## NURTURING YOUR SPIRIT

In order to optimize your spirit and to participate fully in the powerful ways of the spiritual world, you must develop three distinctive qualities (we've discussed them earlier in the book, but here they are—all in one place):

1. First, you must come to a deep and confident appreciation of your own profound significance as a human being.
2. Then you need to be unswervingly authentic—congruent and whole—living your life with unified internal harmony.
3. Finally, you need to understand and practice self-giving love.

When you have fully developed these three aspects of basic psychological health, you are in a position of access to spiritual power.

Still, most of us have not attained anything like perfect scores on the dimensions of significance, authenticity, and self-giving love. Thus, our spirits languish. We are too often straining to defend ourselves, promote ourselves, and save ourselves. And frequently, we work against ourselves because we are not experiencing inner harmony. Finally, we often sense that we are passive recipients of life, unable to steer our course, simply accepting our lot in life.

So how do we move forward and effectively grow our spirits? From our perspective, the growth of our spirits will depend on what we believe is true about the major issues underlying our existence *as well as* what we spend our time and energy focusing on within ourselves. This is where we encounter both religion and spirituality.

Religious practices are separate from spiritual pursuits, but the two are intricately linked. Spiritual practices usually involve prayer, meditation, singing, and generally focusing at the deepest levels on our search for significance, our pursuit of wholeness, and our expression of gratitude.

But you cannot achieve psychological health until you get yourself synchronized with beliefs that promote health in a powerful way. This is what "true" religion is all about—beliefs that harmonize with principles that consistently contribute to the attainment of psychological significance, wholeness, and freedom. You need to be religiously healthy in order to attain psychological health.

What do we mean by this? For instance, the Judeo-Christian religion centers on a powerful, always-involved God. And the specific personal message of this God is that he created us for relationship with him. He grants us intrinsic worth, ultimate significance, and assures us that his love is unconditional, for all time, and reaches past all boundaries. And the Bible makes it clear that this attribution of worth will never be withdrawn. When fully accepted and integrated, this religious principle is fundamental to attaining a psychologically healthy life. It has been proven to change millions of lives across the centuries!

Similarly, this same God calls us to become the persons he has uniquely created us to be—persons with particular talents and quirky personalities who know, at their core, that they are profoundly significant because they belong to God. When we respond to this challenge, we are being *religiously responsive* to our cognitive beliefs.

Correct thinking in this *religious* area leads to psychological growth and an eventual optimization of our deepest, most sacred self—our spirit.

## ARE YOU SPIRITUAL . . . OR RELIGIOUS?

During the last twenty years, it has become fashionable for people to say, "I'm a spiritual person, but I'm not very religious." This usually suggests that a person subscribes to no formal religious beliefs, has no church affiliation, but does have an active interest in the big issues of life. They may also pray, meditate, or "visualize" in their own idiosyncratic ways.

As psychologists, it strikes us as highly unlikely that spirituality unguided by *correct* religious principles will lead to the consistent growth of a person's spirit. After all, the power of spirituality must be positioned and directed by correct beliefs about those matters that are essential for the development of psychological health. Otherwise there is no real lasting change in the person's spirit. It is only when people relate to the Creator of the universe—instead of focusing solely on their "inner self"—that life change can occur. Otherwise our self-consumption blocks any hope of experiencing profound significance from a Creator who knows us and loves us.

A major study by a team of prominent researchers that was published in 2002 revealed what, to them, was an unexpected finding. The subgroup from their sample that was both highly spiritual *and* highly religious turned out to be the healthiest of all groups. The researchers noted:

> They attended services, prayed, meditated, read the Bible, and had more daily spiritual experiences than the "spiritual only" group. They were less distressed and more trusting than the "religion only" group. They experienced substantial benefits from their balanced religious orientation.

Our own clinical experience, as well as our understanding of countless research studies, has shown that maximizing your spirit will depend on both the nature of your religious beliefs (i.e., who you believe controls the universe) and the vibrancy of your spiritual expression. We believe this crucial balance of what you believe and how you practice and express it is what your spirit really needs to grow.

## GOOD NEWS FOR CHURCHGOERS

A stunning body of empirical research indicates that people who consistently attend religious services experience incredible physical and emotional health benefits.

We found this a bit surprising—not just because the list of benefits is so broad and varied, but because we had not believed that simply attending religious services frequently would necessarily lead to any profound inner growth, any expansion of your spirit. We thought that the adequacy and accuracy of your personal beliefs and the vitality of your spiritual practices would determine the level of your emotional and physical health benefits. But something else is going on here.

When the National Institute of Healthcare Research explored the relationship between religious and spiritual experience on health, the result was the 1998 publication *Scientific Research on Spirituality and Health: A Consensus Report.* It reviewed a large group of studies showing that frequent religious service attendance, *all by itself,* had broad-range effects on physical and emotional health. These included significantly lower rates of coronary disease, emphysema, cirrhosis, and suicide; lower blood pressure; lower rates of myocardial infarction; and reduced levels of pain in cancer.

If indeed frequent attendance at religious services is singly related to these many health benefits, how do we explain such a dramatic phenomenon?

We speculate that every-week attendees may, over time, assimilate a set of beliefs that directly relates to the three fundamental factors of profound significance, unswerving authenticity, and self-giving love. As we grow more in our knowledge of who God is and how he interacts with humankind, we may also experience a gradually increasing set of positive feelings. For example, as we believe more strongly in our intrinsic value and worth, as people created by God and loved by God, we may more confidently seek to develop our spiritual life. And as we do, our spirit grows, and the benefits of this growth are the very benefits the researchers have uncovered: "love, joy, peace, patience, kindness, goodness, faithfulness, gentleness and self-control."

We become confident of our worth, are more secure in who we are, and consistently strive for a purposeful life. Our spirits are unfettered. We are ready to soar!

APPENDIX B

## *Charting Your Destiny*

*To realize one's destiny is a person's only obligation.*

PAULO COELHO

"It's your destiny." How many times have you heard that phrase? It's used in movies, in the media, and by people of all faiths.

But what exactly *is* destiny anyway? And how in the world do you discover *your* destiny? And what role does God play in directing your life?

*Merriam-Webster's Collegiate Dictionary* defines *destiny* as "something to which a person or thing is destined: fortune; a predetermined course of events often held to be an irresistible power or agency." But what does this long definition really mean? And especially to those of us who believe not only in God, but that he created us to have a personal relationship with him and free choice over our actions?

Most of us are born with aspects that "determine" certain basic things about ourselves—such as our personality type and the "speed" at which we like to move—things that we must take very seriously if we are to end up with the right mate, the right work, and the right community. In fact, more of these things are stored in our "organic" makeup than in our learning.

Does that mean that we don't have free choice? that we can't change these aspects? No. But it means that our choice to change those things can only go so far. We were created with unique personalities, minds, and bodies. Our Creator, more than anyone or anything in the universe, has given us profound significance and pulls for us to be unswervingly authentic. So common sense says that if you discover, and then live out, your God-given destiny, if you become more and more the person you were created to be, you will indeed be emotionally, mentally, and spiritually healthy.

There's an old fable that may shed light on the issue.

Once upon a time, the animals decided they should do something meaningful to meet the problems of the new world. So they organized a school.

They adopted an activity curriculum of running, climbing, swimming, and flying. To make it easier to administer the curriculum, all the animals took all the subjects.

The *duck* was excellent in swimming; in fact, he was better than his instructor. But he made only passing grades in flying, and was very poor in running. Since he was slow in running, he had to drop swimming and stay after school to practice running. This caused his web feet to be badly worn, so that he was only average in swimming. But average was quite acceptable, so nobody worried about that— except the duck.

The *rabbit* started at the top of his class in running, but developed a nervous twitch in his leg muscles because of so much make-up work in swimming.

The *squirrel* was excellent in climbing, but he encountered constant frustration in flying class because his teacher made him start from the ground up instead of from the tree-top down. He developed charley horses from overexertion, and so only got a C in climbing and a D in running.

The *eagle* was a problem child, and was severely disciplined for being a nonconformist. In climbing classes he beat all the others to the top of the tree, but insisted on using his own way to get there. . . .

The obvious moral of the story is a simple one—each creature has its own set of capabilities in which it will naturally excel—unless it is expected or forced to fill a mold that doesn't fit. When that happens, frustration, discouragement, and even guilt bring overall mediocrity or complete defeat. A duck is a duck—and *only* a duck. It is built to swim, not to run or fly and certainly not to climb. A squirrel is a squirrel—and *only* that. To move it out of its forte, climbing, and then expect it to swim or fly will drive a squirrel nuts. Eagles are beautiful creatures in the air but not in a footrace. The rabbit will win every time . . . unless, of course, the eagle gets hungry.

*You* have been given, by birth and experience, a well-defined set of attributes that is entirely unique to you. When you discover what they are and let them guide you in becoming a specific kind of person, you will become magnificently healthy and unswervingly authentic. You will then be freed to experience the next hallmark of health, self-giving love.

But if you try to be somebody you're not, if you resist being the person you truly are, frustration will be your constant companion. And failure will always be nipping at your heels.

This appendix is designed to help you clarify your God-given destiny. In a world that's eager to tell individuals what their destinies *should* be, it might not be easy for you to identify your own destiny—and then to act on it. But until you learn whether you're a climber, runner, flier, or swimmer, you may feel like a duck out of water or a rabbit off of land. Try as hard as you will, without careful attention to your destiny, you're certain to experience awkwardness and inefficiency. But if you discover your God-given calling, you will be well on your way not only to becoming unswervingly authentic, but having a life better than you could ever have imagined.

That's why it doesn't matter who you are or where in the world you live—if you're a human being, you need to search out your destiny. When you find it and have the freedom to pursue it, you will feel profoundly significant, deep down in your core, because you will know God created you for a special purpose and is leading you to fulfill that purpose.

As you become unswervingly confident of the God who has searched and known you, you will begin to understand more about who you are, how you respond, and why you respond the way you do. You will achieve maximum meaning in the little and large things of life and experience the excitement of reaching beyond yourself into the hearts and lives of others.

## DESTINY ISN'T JUST ABOUT A CAREER BUT ABOUT YOUR *LIFE*

While destiny *includes* what you do as a career, it's about a whole lot more. It's about the life you *choose* to live—how you distribute your time and energy, whom you choose to include in your intimate circle, what your interests are, how important family is to you, and what you do with your "inner," private thought time. It's about the role of money in your life, the place of children, the question of whether you remain single or get married, and how much of your time and energies you will choose to devote to developing your spiritual life . . . to understanding who God is, who you are, and how you interconnect.

So what is *your* destiny? How can you use your God-given personality and talents to love the life you live? So that no matter what you do, you become more and more authentic and aren't mistakenly swayed by the opinions or emotions of others around you? How do you maximize your enjoyment, minimize your stress, and feel good—deep down in your soul—that you have become *exactly* the person God created you to be? That means if you're a rabbit, you confidently act like a rabbit; if you're a duck you proudly act like a duck. (Frankly, we don't care if you're a rabbit or a duck, but if you *are* a rabbit, we certainly hope you're not spending any time trying to be a duck. All such actions will lead to is intense frustration.)

Take Benjamin Franklin for example. When he was seventeen years old, he was convinced that his destiny was to be a writer.

Hearing about his ambition, the people who knew him well ridiculed him. When he couldn't handle his father's criticism and his brother's constant abuse any longer, he decided to run away from home to pursue the dream he believed to be central to his life. Everything in him rejected the idea of the apprenticeship that his father thought best for him. Writing was what he most liked to do—as well as what he thought he did best. His father, convinced Ben was making a huge mistake and wasting his life, refused to support his son in the slightest, and the process of becoming a writer became incredibly difficult. Ben often had barely enough money to buy a loaf of bread. But his persistence clearly paid off, and he became one of America's greatest writers, inventors, and statesmen. In the process of realizing his destiny, he overcame all kinds of discouraging words and impossible odds. In fact, some say this is what drove him so passionately toward his destiny—that he so believed in his talents and dreams that he wasn't willing to give up. And this is exactly what it takes to achieve your destiny.

## DETERMINING YOUR CALLING, YOUR DESTINY

For thirty years David Alan Hubbard was the president of Fuller Theological Seminary. Both of us knew him well and greatly admired him. Dr. Hubbard liked to say that a person's calling, their destiny, revolves around three questions:

1. What is it that you thoroughly enjoy doing?
2. What is it that you are really good at doing?
3. And finally, what is it that, beyond enjoying it and being good at it, other people tell you has a positive impact on their lives?

Take a few minutes to answer the above questions yourself on a piece of paper.

Please note that *nothing* is your God-given calling—your destiny—if your positive response to any of these three questions is missing.

235

How can you find out, realistically, what your destiny—your life direction—is?

You have to start squarely at the center of yourself, and your self-evaluation needs to be thorough and thoughtful. Howard Figler is a nationally recognized expert on helping men and women select what he calls a *soul career*. He recommends that you take inventory of your personal convictions, beliefs, and values—that you make a list of the things you really care about in life. His goal for you: to help you feed your passions and personality. If you don't start at the center of yourself in your search for a destiny, he suggests, you will never end up with a plan for your life that will lead to your happiness and contentment.

Far too many of us chart our destinies in life on the basis of what will bring us money, status, popularity, or fame. We forget about these wise words: "Do not store up for yourselves treasures on earth, where moth and rust destroy, and where thieves break in and steal. . . . For where your treasure is, there your heart will be also."

So we sell our emotional health and happiness for fleeting satisfactions. Thus we choose a life path that leads us like a guided missile—fast and accurately—to a chronic experience of frustration and boredom. Some surveys indicate that as many as 80 percent of men and women are dissatisfied with their work—wishing every day that they didn't have to do what they once chose to do.

In the article, "Take Charge of Your Destiny by Drawing Up a Career Plan," Russ Jones—a career columnist for the *Wall Street Journal,* the premier newspaper in America focused on helping readers make money—sounds like a psychologist or a theologian. He argues against basing your choice of a destiny, or a career, on making money. "Examine who you are," he writes, "why you exist and what you believe, then make a commitment to aligning your work and your spirit." The secret to finding your destiny, Jones agrees, is to let it emerge out of your soul. But how do we know what our soul is saying?

## LISTENING TO YOUR SOUL

One of the most popular books in the world during the last few years was *The Alchemist* by Paulo Coelho. It's a riveting and charming fable about a young Andalusian shepherd boy named Santiago who travels from his homeland in Spain to the Egyptian desert in search of a treasure that he believes is buried in the pyramids. As he relentlessly pursues his dream to find worldly goods, he eventually uncovers the most profound secret of human existence—one that each of us must and can discover. It is when we begin to listen to our *hearts* that we can know our destinies, and it is only the living out of that destiny that allows us to discover abundant life. So compelling is Coelho's fable that millions of persons in 117 countries who speak forty-one different languages have identified Santiago's quest as their own.

*Nothing* about your life matters as much as uncovering your destiny—what Coelho calls your "Personal Legend." It is a prize of unfathomable value. "The closer you get to realizing your Personal Legend," Coelho says, "the more that Personal Legend becomes [your] true reason for being." For those of us who believe in a personal God, our faith becomes closely intertwined with that Personal Legend. For we know that our destiny is not simply of ourselves. Rather, it is with God that we "live and move and have our being." Without him, we have no future. No destiny. No abundant life on earth or forever after.

But even for those of us of faith, an individual destiny is not always simple to find. On your journey you may well be subjected to constant tests of your persistence and courage. In fact, Coelho says "courage is the quality most essential to understanding" who you really are.

Sometimes we are afraid to pursue our most important dreams. Coelho says our reasons boil down to fear—that we don't deserve them or that we will be unable to achieve them. Our deserving to discover who we truly are relates to whether we have allowed ourselves to receive a sense of profound significance. If the matter of significance is settled in our lives, our fear of not deserving will tend to vanish.

If you are confident in who you are—if you are unswervingly authentic—then you will be in tune with what God is saying to you in your head, deep down in your soul, and in your heart.

Realizing your Personal Legend—your *unswerving authenticity*—is consistently the result of your careful collection of the crucial data about every decision you need to make. You likely will never be a *perfect* decision maker. There has only been one perfect decision maker who walked this earth, and that was Jesus. Your data may not be accurately enough collected, or the decision you make as you stand in the middle of it may not be precise enough. So identifying your Personal Legend may require many attempts.

From moment to moment, as you try to identify the person God created you to be, it's crucial to maintain a high degree of patience. Matters of the heart take a lot of time and careful attention to detail. There is no need to be impulsive; impulsivity will frequently lead to painful mistakes in charting your destiny. That means we must pay attention to the signposts—experiences along the way that can provide additional data that can make the decision-making process consistently more accurate.

## GETTING IN SYNC WITH YOUR DESTINY

Dr. Gordon Kirk has been the senior pastor of Lake Avenue Church in Pasadena, California, for eleven years. Over six thousand men and women attend this city (almost "inner city") church every weekend. Almost exactly 25 percent of these attendees are Asian, 25 percent are African-American, 25 percent are Hispanic, and 25 percent are Caucasian. It's like a United Nations church.

Gordon Kirk has an uncanny ability to lead this old city church into a new way of worshiping and serving in a diverse community. But his leadership abilities weren't on my mind when I (Neil) interviewed him. I wanted to know about his heart—more precisely, his estimate of the extent to which he is living out his destiny. And so I asked him—about his career, his family, and his community.

"I feel like I am right in the center of the life I am supposed to live," he said in a quietly confident way. "I feel totally in harmony with my 'true self,' and if I could change the way my life is going, I can't think of anything to change."

It hasn't always been that way for Gordon. Discovering and living out his Personal Legend required a mountain of courage. He encountered resistance all along the way, and getting to where he is now took a clear vision and strong faith. He started out as an academician, and some of his older colleagues encouraged him to stay in academia. But he felt called to a local parish. Then he served a large suburban church with a vast majority of parishioners who were well-to-do, part of the majority, and less inclusive than he wished. Again, in order to discover his destiny, he had to resist the comfortable trappings of his suburbs. Finally he moved to his present city church, an old and well-established church in a community of rapid change. This church resisted changing, and Gordon worked for nearly ten years before the leadership began to catch his vision, his calling, which included ministry to vast segments of the poorest areas, worship services in various languages, and a leadership mix that was maximally inclusive.

But the rewards for people who patiently persist in their eagerness to live their own life, not someone else's life or a life designed to win some external prize, are well worth the effort. You can see it in the spontaneity of their laughter, the vitality of their spirit, the richness of their caring, and the creativity of their contributions.

But when you violate your true self, when the life you are living is not at all the life you were meant to live, you will experience chronic and painful resistance from within. Your days will be hounded by stress and boredom, your nights will be filled with steady feelings of regret and foreboding, and your future will seem lifeless and uninviting.

We have both seen a steady stream of men and women in psychotherapy who are feeling out of sync with their destinies, their Personal Legends, and are confused about how to get right with themselves. Sometimes these persons think the source of their misery is their marriage, but the real problem often turns out to be something else—like their career or their lack of meaningful community. Whatever the source of the problem, the result can make life seem dingy and unexciting.

Many have recognized that they are living their life as an impostor—not the true, fulfilled, and satisfying life God meant for them to have, but a fake life based on their own and others' expectations that leads them to despair. Some of these courageous persons have managed to transform their lives. Almost always, the secret of their transformation is in letting their destiny emerge from the center of their souls.

Katharine Graham was one of these persons. Born the fourth of five children in a very wealthy family, Kay's mother had high expectations for her children's lives and little interest in helping Kay identify and live out her destiny. Kay's family owned *The Washington Post* newspaper, certainly one of the two or three most powerful and influential newspapers in North America. But Kay was shy and passive; she felt like she never measured up. Even more so, she thought of herself as "dowdy" and lacking in self-assurance. She was a long way from feeling that she was at the center of the life she was born to live.

Then she was married—to a brilliant man, Phil Graham, who took over the family newspaper and was lauded as a genius. He dominated all the decisions in their family life. There was almost no opportunity for her to let her life speak. She was the dutiful follower, the implementer of his decisions, the one who patiently stood in the shadows. Her sense of destiny remained buried.

And then things went bad. Phil Graham suffered from bouts of heavy drinking. His terrible anger was a constant threat to their relationship. He became deeply involved with another woman, and he was locked in a struggle with manic depression. Eventually he committed suicide.

It was only after all these tragic events that Kay's destiny gradually became evident. She reluctantly took over the family business, and it wasn't long before she was blossoming. She became the talented and powerful publisher of *The Washington Post*. Her self-concept became clearer and more positive. She began to enjoy her work. She recognized that she was good at it, and people affirmed that destiny by telling her that her contribution was critical. Once she began to discover her destiny, her rise to prominence was meteoric. She became widely recognized as one of the top newspaper publishers in the world. In 1998 she even won a Pulitzer prize for her autobiography.

## IF YOU WANT TO LOVE THE LIFE YOU LIVE . . .

Perhaps you feel like Katharine Graham—your life purpose seems hidden deep in the shadows of your consciousness. If so, there's a productive process for getting back on the satisfying path. A person's *destiny* can most accurately be ascertained as you live out three major life choices. So next we'll take a look at each of these choices and how they affect your quest for unswerving authenticity.

### Choice #1: Which career?

The first choice has to do with career—the work you choose to do.

Show us a man or woman who is unhappy in their work and yet feels comfortable with the way they are living out their destiny, and we will show you a rare exception. What you do for work is simply too central to your life. And by "work," we mean everything from climbing the corporate ladder to diapering babies to teaching a class to weeding a garden. If you find the work you do frustrating, boring, repetitive, and unfulfilling, then your destiny most likely is hidden in some basement closet . . . a dusty, lifeless relic of your intended, but unrealized, history.

Renowned author Parker J. Palmer believes that your career choice is vital to the discovery and living out of your destiny. He maintains that your choice must emerge out of your *inner* self. His stimulating question triggers an avalanche of thoughts in his readers: "Is the life I am living the same as the life that is living in me?" He throws down the challenge: "Before you tell your life what you intend to do with it, listen to what it intends to do with you."

Palmer maintains that you can't determine your career simply on the basis of being willful. It doesn't matter how noble your career choice may be or how high and holy your intentions are. This choice has to emerge from your "true self," a self that has some definite limits and some admirable potentials. Matching your career choice with the person you truly are at the center of yourself—this is the recipe for discovering your destiny in the world of vocation.

What does this mean practically for you?

If your career is stressful and unsatisfying, it's never too late to modify, or totally alter, what you do every day. Start with an honest and hard-hitting self-evaluation.

Ask yourself the three critical questions involved in finding the right career:

a. *What do I really enjoy doing?* I (Neil) spent eight years of my life as an administrator. I was the dean of a graduate school of psychology, and I chafed under every administrative responsibility I carried. Managing the paperwork of my job was an endless and unrewarding task for me. I often had three tall stacks of memos and applications and complaints and questions on my desk, and my only enjoyment came from leafing through those stacks and finding things that had taken care of themselves through the days of my procrastination. All of my *true self* opposed that administrative job, and when your true self gets violated, it makes you pay.

It took a year off for me to gain the insight that this job—so seductively wrapped in status and honor—was not at all the place in which I could live out my destiny. During those quiet, reflective days, I began to look at what I really do enjoy doing. It was Parker Palmer who said: "The soul speaks its truth only under quiet, inviting, and trustworthy conditions." When you are inundated with work, stressed to overflowing with undesirable tasks, and chronically eager for just a little more vacation, your heart doesn't have a chance to speak.

So take some time away to let your inner self answer the critical question about what kind of work seems to harmonize with you. Pray, asking God for his help and guidance. Obviously, all of us are unique as human beings, and identifying our own specific preferences is a critical part of the career-choosing process.

b. *What am I really good at?* I (Neil) was a terrible administrator. But I was pretty good as a visionary, and I could inspire people to take action. I had good business judgment. I finally came to recognize these abilities that I was not only good at, but that brought meaning and help to others. And I really liked acting on these abilities. If careers are truly the "living out" of our God-given destiny, we must like what we do.

c. *What do I do well that brings meaning to others?* Friends, colleagues, and family members are often eager to tell you how your behavior positively affects them. If you are on a committee, ask your fellow committee members how you have functioned most positively within the committee structure— perhaps as a leader, a person who keeps the discussion focused, or a recorder of the minutes. If you are in a family structure, invite your family to give you feedback about what you do that is helpful to them. In other words, try not to miss a chance to collect data about the particular ways you positively impact the people around you.

And it is only through time, through experiencing what we are good at (and not good at) that we come to recognize this career. That's why both Les and I are strong believers in the need to choose a career gradually. It's unusual for a person to suddenly discover a life's work that answers all of these questions in a highly positive way. For both of us, finding our destinies in the area of career has been a step forward and half a step to the side, and then another step forward. But when you eventually find yourself doing every day what you thoroughly enjoy, what you're really good at, and what brings meaning to others, you will see your destiny, or life plan, begin to unfold in front of you.

Believe it's not possible? Then listen to this story. . . .

I (Neil) saw a man in therapy for eighteen months who moved from a "B" life to an "A+" life all because he got his destiny focused. And once he did, he was off to the races.

Robert (not his real name, of course) came to me when he was fifty-six and burned out with his life. He had been an attorney for thirty years and was recognized as one of the leading attorneys in his large city. However, although his career provided him and his wife, Nancy, a good living, everything about his existence bordered on boring. Robert and Nancy's three children were out of college, and two were married with children of their own. The grandchildren were wonderful, but Robert didn't see them that often, and even if he had, they couldn't provide what he was aching for.

"Maybe this was all my life was supposed to be," Robert said at our first session. He didn't know if it made any sense to see me once a week. He didn't feel good about his life, but he hoped—somehow—that he could make it at least a little better.

One morning I asked him: "Do you sense that you are living out your destiny?"

"What do you mean by destiny?" he asked.

I told Robert the fable of the animals, and then gave him several minutes' explanation of what you have already read in this appendix.

"Well," he said slowly, "I feel strongly that Nancy is the right woman for me. She always has been. And I think I have the right group of friends and the right faith. But let's face it. I have never really enjoyed being a lawyer. I've made good money, but it's a daily grind. I move from one case to the next because I have to."

And then there was a long silence. I waited for the other shoe to drop.

"But I don't really think I can do anything about it now."

Robert *didn't* do anything about it that day, or the next time we were together. But the seed had been planted, and his big, two-billion-megabyte-capacity brain had been alerted to the possibility of a veritable revolution in his life.

"What would you really *like* to do with your career?" I asked him at a later session. He thought for a long time and then listed three things he thought he might thoroughly enjoy. He wanted to start a business that might have a chance to change the world for good, a business that might involve one or more of his children and maybe his wife. We talked about what a business like that might be about.

"I want to get into the business of marital reconciliation," he said. "After thirty years of seeing countless marriages die, many of them unnecessarily, I want to set up a powerful Internet program designed to keep husbands and wives together. I have a hundred ideas about what I could get them to do, ways they could work through their issues and maintain their families and their lives together."

Let me cut to the chase: Robert *did* start that business—with his wife and one of his sons—and it has been a monumental success. Thousands of Americans have benefited from it. And because their earnings have been so plentiful, Robert and Nancy are about to start a foundation to help hurting couples and families.

When one person discovers his or her destiny, it starts an avalanche of positive social consequences with unbelievable potential benefits. It's one thing that Robert is a totally rejuvenated man today. But perhaps even more importantly, it's downright inspirational that he has helped so many people at the most painful and pivotal point of their lives.

That's why our challenge to you is to be true to who you are, at your inner core—that unique person God fashioned in the womb. An old Hasidic tale speaks to the importance of becoming the self you truly are. Toward the end of his life the character, Rabbi

Zusya, says, "In the coming world they will not ask me: 'Why were you not Moses?' They will ask me: 'Why were you not Zusya?' "

## Choice #2: To marry or not? And if to marry, whom? And what if you're already married?

If career choice is central to the discovery of your destiny, the decision you make in relation to marriage is significantly more critical. Especially if you believe in the biblical marriage model of "one man, one woman" for a lifetime—until death parts them. That means you don't change spouses like you change jobs. Once you marry, you've made a choice for a lifetime . . . and yet nearly half the families in America have been touched by divorce and infidelity.

That should lead all of us—whether currently married, single, engaged, or single again—to look at the institution of marriage with a more serious eye.

In the year 2000 there were 98 million singles in the United States. Some of them are not interested in marriage. They like being single, and they are convinced that the living out of their Personal Legend would be seriously compromised were they to marry.

Thirty-two-year-old Jeremy, for instance, has chosen to live out his Personal Legend passionately—as a medical assistant who travels with doctors to perform surgeries on children in third-world countries. The children, who wouldn't have a chance for survival without this kind of help, now have a chance not only at life, but a *significant* life. People told Jeremy he was foolish to give up a prominent intern position at a well-known hospital to go out "in the middle of nowhere and risk all kinds of germs." Besides, these detractors said, "How many children can you really help? It's just a drop in the bucket even if you save a few." But Jeremy was convinced of God's guidance in that area and he followed his heart. Today, three years later, he wouldn't dream of doing anything else. He is not only satisfied with his "single" life, but fulfilled in his personal, God-given destiny. He's rewarded by the smile of each child he has helped back to health and wholeness.

For those who do choose to pursue marriage, their choice of a partner is a major determiner of whether they discover their destiny (or not) and are able to live it out. Marriage involves so much togetherness, so much intimacy, and the degree to which you marry the *right* person is highly correlated with the amount of freedom you have to be authentic—the person *you* truly are.

For example, let's say you are dating someone you think is really terrific. The only problem is, that person feels almost "too good" for you. Is it *you*, or the other person, who's the problem? Or is it merely the place you intersect that's the problem? Perhaps he's from a wealthy home; you grew up scraping pennies. And you feel so uncomfortable every time you have to enter his parents' house and dare to sit on their Victorian furniture that you try to act more "hip" than you really are. Or your girl-friend is so much more attractive than you that you wonder why she could be interested in you . . .

Although these may seem like "small factors" when you're in love, they can become big problems that divide a marriage and keep each of you from becoming authentic.

If you are in a serious relationship, you need to know how crucial your choice of spouse really is. It must emanate from the deepest reaches of your Control Booth and be made carefully and prayerfully. While there are intuitive aspects of this choice, such as how a person looks and how you feel about them, the most fundamental considerations are more scientific. They can actually be measured and studied. For instance, research studies that my team and I (Neil) have completed indicate there are twenty-nine critical dimensions that need to be matched for mate selection to be successful. If you're interested in taking this test, go to eHarmony.com, complete the extensive inventory, and then read over the personality profile you will receive. This six-page profile will provide you with a flood of personal information about yourself.

When two people are well matched on these twenty-nine dimensions, the marriage is bound to be fulfilling. Even more important, both partners will be able to pursue their individual destinies while growing closer to each other and to God because their marital relationship will be healthy and supportive.

Both of us are nearly obsessed with the importance of building a good, strong marriage when a person does, in fact, elect to be married. (Just a quick look at the list of books we've written individually proves our claim to obsession on this topic.) We are convinced, through our own and others' experiences, that a great marriage makes the living out of a personal destiny, the achievement of a Personal Legend, so much more likely. In order to reach a high level of emotional and spiritual health, every person needs a lot of freedom, and a lot of encouragement and support.

That's exactly what you get in a great marriage partner: Someone who is so inwardly secure that he or she can be unselfishly supportive and encouraging—without demanding control, without reducing your freedom. If your freedom was seriously curtailed by your spouse, you wouldn't be able to listen to your own heart. You wouldn't feel comfortable being in your Control Booth alone. And you would soon begin to fall short of *unswerving* authenticity. Failing this, you would then automatically become less loving toward others (including your spouse), less able to share the final secret to feeling good—deep down in your soul (Secret #3: Self-Giving Love).

We cannot say enough about how overwhelmingly important it is to get married to the right person, if you do get married. Without making this choice wisely, you will never feel profoundly significant, you will not be able to be unswervingly authentic, and you cannot know the joy of unconditional love.

And yet we know the reality so many of you live with every day: It's really hard to discover and live out your Personal Legend in the area of marriage if either of two things is true:

• You are single but desperately want to be married.
• You are married to someone with whom you are seriously mismatched.

But when it comes to marriage, the secrets to achieving your Personal Legend can be stated simply: (1) To remain happily single if you wish to be single, (2) To marry your soul mate if, indeed, you wish to be married, (3) To get your marriage on a significant growth curve if it is not everything you want it to be.

We have written over a dozen books about these subjects, and you may wish to read one or more of these (most of them are clearly described in their titles or subtitles). For particular help in the areas discussed in this chapter, you may be interested in either one of our two most popular books: *Finding the Love of Your Life* (by Neil) and *Saving Your Marriage Before It Starts* (by Les).

### Choice #3: What community to establish?

The final choice concerns the community of family and friends you establish—and the amount of time and energy you distribute to these persons. Why is this so important? Because the community you choose will either facilitate or block your pursuit of unswerving authenticity and your individual destiny. If, for instance, you choose friends who impose their opinions on you as authoritative truth, your freedom to discover the real you may be severely curtailed. The same, of course, is true of family members with whom you spend your time. Let's say you have an inner longing to pursue art classes, and yet your father insists that you choose elementary education as a vocation. "At least you won't starve then," he says. But will you be fulfilling your God-given destiny? And, after all, you're twenty-six, so shouldn't you be deciding for yourself?

As soon as you become involved regularly in a church, you immediately "inherit" a community of friends. If this community asks questions of you such as, "Where are your areas of strength?" "How much of a time commitment can you afford?" rather than making demands on you for conformity ("Well, of course you'll attend all the Sunday night services anyway . . ."), you will have a far better chance of finding and living out your destiny.

The bottom line? Your destiny may or may not become apparent in the work you do, the marriage in which you engage, and the community you choose. If you make these choices poorly, your destiny may remain hidden from your view. All you will know is that you are unhappy, bored, frustrated, and not in harmony with the person God created you to be. You will have that "sinking feeling" that the person you are and the person you were meant to be are two very different persons.

But if you make these choices well, you will experience a growing sense that you are living out your destiny. Moreover, you will enjoy a greater amount of freedom to spend time listening to your heart, making wise choices within your Control Booth, and pursuing your Personal Legend.

If you trust your community so deeply and are confident they will not judge you, you will feel ready to respond to their questions and urgings. And as you respond, you will catch a clearer glimpse of your Personal Legend.

Longtime friends Dale and Kathy Bruner are master "question askers." When they came to our house for dinner the other night, I (Neil) experienced some insights I have never experienced before—and all because the Bruners first assess the quality of the relationship, making sure it is solid and capable of being tested, and then they come right after you. They're smart enough to impose almost nothing on you; rather, they seem intent on helping you figure out what you are all about. They're not a bit reluctant to ask about politics, religion, family dynamics, or anything that has to do with how you "tick."

In the same way, your community of intimate insiders will play a major role in helping you identify and live out your destiny. Far too often our destinies lurk in the corners of our inner selves. It's almost as though they are too threatened to make themselves apparent to others—or even to us. We need all the help we can get in teasing these parts of us to the surface. If our emotional health depends on our living out our destinies, it's certainly nice to choose people to surround us who have no agenda other than to help us figure out precisely who we were born to be.

## DREAMING BIG!

Once you clarify your destiny within the three life areas we just discussed, your hard work is largely complete. Now the fun begins! We have watched thousands of men and women decide on their destinies and seen the amazing results. As soon as they identified their God-given talents and understood the lives they were born to live, their growth accelerated. They began to love their lives, and they radiated with incredible energy and power. Like a golfer who swings naturally and slowly, yet hits the ball farther than ever, they began to experience joyfulness, winsomeness, and a level of interpersonal success they had never known before.

When you begin becoming the person you truly are, the heights you can reach will be far beyond anything you have imagined, and the depths you can realize will simply amaze you. You will be convinced of your profound significance to yourself, others, and God. You will be clear on your life purpose. You will be unswervingly authentic. Your relationships will be marked with a straightforwardness and honesty that may not have been there before. You will be drawn closer and closer toward the One who created you. And you won't be able to help yourself—you will feel genuine love for others.

When it comes to couples, dreaming is enormously helpful. But there must be plenty of opportunity for both individuals to dream separate dreams for their lives—along with an opportunity for them to dream a dream about their life together. Every person on earth has an obligation to discover and live out his or her own destiny, and it is simply not enough to live *through* your partner, even if you help them live out their Personal Legend. For your life to be truly healthy, you need your very own dream.

It is through those dreams that you multiply the size of your potential, and you access your most dynamic supply of energy to give yourself unbelievable power and speed. The role of dreaming a big dream is to provide direction for this nuclear-powered growth potential—and a road map you can follow.

So dream big! Dreams and visions stimulate the brain and mobilize the action centers. Whatever it is that you dream about with regularity, you will begin to hope for. Hope stimulates planning. Planning produces behavior that's designed to move you forward. This brings progress. It allows you to dramatically live out your destiny in a way that will bring abundance to your soul and meaning to every person you encounter.

And it all begins with a dream.

## SOURCES

*Throughout this book we endeavor to give credit as much as possible wherever our writing has been informed or inspired by someone else's writing. We also hope to tell readers who are interested how they can track down our references or get more information on a topic that interests them. This requires source notes. A majority of readers, however, find little numbers in the text distracting. It interrupts their reading. So for those who care, we provide information on our sources in this section.*

### Chapter One—Improving You, Your Life, and Your Relationships—Forever
p. 4: (All of us) A. Masten, "Ordinary Magic: Resilience Processes in Development," *American Psychologist* 56 (2001): 227–238.

p. 6 (A contemporary generation) Scholarly articles pertaining to "well-being," "happiness," and "life satisfaction" have mushroomed from a mere 150 articles at the beginning of the 1980s to thousands today. No longer is the science of psychology only speaking about suffering. Joy has entered the lexicon of serious scholars.

### Chapter Two—How to Get Healthy: A Deep and Simple Plan
p. 9 (The Bible says) The book of Psalms is filled with these life-affirming principles.
p. 12 ("What will it profit") Mark 8:36, NKJV

### SECRET #1: PROFOUND SIGNIFICANCE
#### Introduction to Profound Significance
p. 22 (Even if we agree) E. Diener et al., "Subjective Well-Being: Three Decades of Progress," *Psychological Bulletin* 125: 276–302.

p. 22 (Ultimately, we find) M. Argyle, "Causes and Correlates of Happiness," in *Well Being: The Foundations of Hedonic Psychology,* ed. Daniel Kahneman, Norbert Schwarz, and Edward Diener (New York: Russell Sage Foundation, 2003).

p. 22 ("Everything was meaningless") Ecclesiastes 2:11

p. 24 (However good) A. M. Isen, A. S. Rosenzweig, and M. J. Young, "The Influence of Positive Affect on Clinical Problem Solving," *Medical Decision Making* 11 (1991): 221–227.

p. 25 ("I've known you") See Psalm 139; Isaiah 43:1; Romans 8:35-39.

### Chapter Four—Tuning In to Your Self-Talk
p. 29 (Healthy persons) A. Morin and J. Everett, "Inner Speech As a Mediator of Self-Awareness, Self-Consciousness, and Self-Knowledge," *New Ideas in Psychology* 8 (1990): 337–356.

p. 31 (The brain is a circuitry) Barbara Hoberman Levine, *Your Body Believes Every Word You Say: The Language of the Body/Mind Connection* (Boulder Creek, Calif.: Aslan, 1991).

p. 31 (And, over time) Sandra Blakeslee, "Tracing the Brain's Pathways for Linking Emotion and Reason," *New York Times*, 6 December 1994, B1.

p. 33 (It is often composed) C. P. Neck and C. C. Manz, "Thought Self-Leadership: The Influence of Self-Talk and Mental Imagery on Performance," *Journal of Organizational Behavior* 13 (1992): 681–699.

pp. 37–38 (It all started) Howard Brody, *The Placebo Response* (New York: HarperCollins, 2000).

p. 38 (Abundant medical research) Howard M. Spiro, *The Power of Hope: A Doctor's Perspective* (New Haven, Conn.: Yale University Press, 1998).

pp. 38–39 (The impact of self-talk) Two seminal works that thoroughly document these studies can be found in *Reason and Emotion in Psychotherapy* (New York: Stuart, 1962) by Albert Ellis and *Cognitive Therapy of Depression: A Treatment Manual* (New York: Guilford, 1979) by A. T. Beck, A. J. Rush, B. F. Shaw, and G. Emery. In addition, Albert Bandura's article, "Self-Efficacy: Toward a Unifying Theory of Behavioral Change," *Psychological Review* 84: 191–215, greatly strengthened the foundation for this thinking.

p. 45 (Most often this) R. D. Grainger, "The Use and Abuse of Negative Thinking," *American Journal of Nursing* 91 (1991): 13–14.

p. 46 (And according to) Shad Helmstetter, *What to Say When You Talk to Yourself* (New York: Fine Communications, 1997).

p. 49 ("All the days") See Psalm 139:16

**Chapter Five—Moving Past Your Past**
p. 60 (It was not) E. F. Loftus and G. R. Loftus, "On the Permanence of Stored Information in the Human Brain," *American Psychologist* 35 (1980): 409–420.

p. 60 (So unwitting) J. W. Schooler, D. Gerhard and E. F. Loftus, "Qualities of the Unreal," *Journal of Experimental Psychology: Learning, Memory, and Cognition* 12 (1986): 171–181.

p. 60 (After retellings) H. L. Roediger III, M. A. Wheeler, and S. Rajaram, "Remembering, Knowing, and Reconstructing the Past," in *The Psychology of Learning and Motivation: Advances in Research and Theory*, vol. 30, ed. D. L. Medin (Orlando, Fla.: Academic Press, 1993).

p. 61 (Siblings who can't) J. M. Berger, "Whose Life Is It, Anyway?" *Internal Medicine News* 35 (2002): 3.

p. 64 (At the University of Kansas) Raymond L. Higgins, Rita J. Stucky, and C. R. Snyder, *Excuses: Masquerades in Search of Grace* (New York: Wiley-Interscience, 1983). See also M. L. Snyder et al., "Avoidance of the Handicapped: An Attributional Ambiguity Analysis," *Journal of Personality and Social Psychology* 37 (1979): 2297–2306.

pp. 68–69 (Consider the following) James W. Pennebaker, *Opening Up: The Healing Power of Expressing Emotions* (New York: Guildford Press, 1997).

p. 74 (Studies do not) The best review and synthesis of this literature of which we are aware is found in *Authentic Happiness* (New York: Free Press, 2002) by Martin Seligman. He has masterfully consolidated many studies in this area. Here is a sampling of those studies: R. Forehand, "Parental Divorce and Adolescent Maladjustment: Scientific Inquiry vs. Published Information," *Behavior Research and Therapy* 30 (1992): 319–328; G. Brown and T. Harris, *Social Origins of Depression* (London: Tavistock, 1978); R. Galbraith, "Sibling Spacing and Intellectual Development: A Closer Look at the Confluence Models," *Developmental Psychology* 18 (1982): 151–173; A. Clarke and A. D. Clarke, *Early Experience: Myth and Evidence* (New York: Free Press, 1976); M. Rutter, "The Long-Term Effects of Early Experience," *Developmental Medicine and Child Neurology* 22 (1980): 800–815.

p. 75 (Research suggests) See C. Kalb, "Pen, Paper, Power! Confessional Writing Can Be Good for You," *Newsweek*, 26 April 1999, 75. Stephen Lepore, an associate professor of psychology at Carnegie Mellon University, found that students who wrote expressively about their emotions before an exam had the same number of intrusive thoughts as those who wrote about superficial things. But they reported fewer symptoms of distress. Lepore believes their worries about the test simply became less disturbing.

p. 76 (It's difficult) S. Paul, "Letting Go of Emotional Baggage," Knight Ridder/Tribune News Service, 29 December 1998.

p. 79 ("having a strong") R. Larson, "Is Feeling 'In Control' Related to Happiness in Daily Life?" *Psychological Reports* 64 (1989): 775–784.

p. 79 (It's clear) See John 8:32

**A Few Closing Thoughts on Profound Significance**
pp. 82–83 (Lee Edward Travis) Donald F. Tweedie and Paul W. Clement, *Psychologist Pro Tem—In Honor of the 80th Birthday of Lee Edward Travis* (Los Angeles: University of Southern California Press, 1976).

p. 83 (Have you had) See Galatians 5:22-23

p. 84 ("Absurdities have given") Donald F. Tweedie and Paul W. Clement, *Psychologist Pro Tem—In Honor of the 80th Birthday of Lee Edward Travis* (Los Angeles: University of Southern California Press, 1976).

**SECRET #2: UNSWERVING AUTHENTICITY**
**Introduction to Unswerving Authenticity**
p. 89 ("Real isn't how") Margery Williams, *The Velveteen Rabbit* (New York: Holt, Rinehart and Winston, 1983), 4.

p. 90 (We're afraid) B. Fredrickson, "The Role of Positive Emotions in Positive Psychology: The Broaden-and-Build Theory of Positive Emotions," *American Psychologist* 56 (2001): 218–226.

p. 90 ("making one's own") Henri Nouwen, *The Wounded Healer* (New York: Doubleday, 1972).

### Chapter Six—Discovering Your Blind Spots

p. 94 (And research shows) Robert J. Sternberg, *Why Smart People Can Be So Stupid* (New Haven, Conn.: Yale University Press, 2002).

p. 95 (Dr. Steven Pinker) S. Pinker, *How the Mind Works* (New York: W.W. Norton and Company, 1997).

p. 100 ("he became aware") Marcus Buckingham and Donald Clifton, *Now, Discover Your Strengths* (New York: Free Press, 2001), 21.

p. 100 (Authors of) For more information on discovering your strengths, consult the book *Now, Discover Your Strengths,* by Marcus Buckingham and Donald O. Clifton (New York: The Free Press, 2001).

p. 101 (In a comparison) M. W. McCall and M. Lombardo, *Off the Track: Why and How Successful Executives Get Derailed,* Technical Report 21 (Greensboro, N.C.: Center for Creative Leadership, 1987).

p. 101 ("accuracy in self-assessment") R. Boyatzis, *The Competent Manager: A Model for Effective Performance* (New York: John Wiley and Sons, 1982); commentary and reference from Daniel Goleman, *Working With Emotional Intelligence* (New York: Bantam, 1998).

p. 102 (Their egoism) J. Krueger and R. A. Mueller, "Unskilled, Unaware, or Both? The Better-Than-Average Heuristic and Statistical Regression Predict Errors in Estimates of Own Performance," *Journal of Personality and Social Psychology* 82 (2002): 180–188.

p. 103 (Some people simply) P. J. Silvia and T. S. Dumval, "Predicting the Interpersonal Targets of Self-Serving Attributions," *Journal of Experimental Social Psychology* 37 (2001): 333–340.

p. 111(Those viewers) P. Salovey and J. D. Mayer, "Emotional Attention, Clarity and Repair: Exploring Emotional Intelligence Using the Trait Meta-Mood Scale," in *Emotion, Disclosure, and Health,* ed. James W. Pennebaker (Washington, D.C.: American Psychological Press, 1995).

p. 111 (Those who kept) Daniel Goleman, *Working with Emotional Intelligence* (New York: Bantam, 1998).

p. 112 (Being self-aware) Daniel Goleman, author of *Emotional Intelligence* (Bantam, 1995), provides dozens of studies conducted in a variety of settings that underscore the value of empathy in relationship to self-awareness.

p. 113 ("I wanted to connect") Oprah Winfrey, "What I Know for Sure," *O: The Oprah Magazine,* February 2002, 184.

p. 114 (A recent study) J. Butcher, "Self-Recognition Located in Right Hemisphere," *The Lancet* 357 (2001): 203.

p. 117 (You can arrange) P. J. Silvia and T. S. Duval, "Objective Self-Awareness Theory: Recent Progress and Enduring Problems," *Personality and Social Psychology Review* 5 (2001): 230–241.

p. 117 (It holds great) R. W. Robak, "Self-Definition in Psychotherapy: Is It Time to Revisit Self-Perception Theory?" *North American Journal of Psychology* 3 (2001): 529–534.

p. 119 ("Wounds from") Proverbs 27:6

### Chapter Seven—Harnessing Your Wild Side

p. 122 (Some 10 million) The primary sources of national statistics on child abuse and neglect are two studies sponsored by the U.S. Department of Health and Human Services: *Child Maltreatment: Reports from the States to the National Child Abuse and Neglect Data System (NCANDS)* and the *National Incidence Study (NIS).*

p. 123 (Estimates range) U.S. Department of Justice, *Violence by Intimates: Analysis of Data on Crimes by Current or Former Spouses, Boyfriends,* March 1998.

p. 123 (3 million women) The Commonwealth Fund, *Health Concerns Across a Woman's Lifespan: 1998 Survey of Women's Health,* May 1999.

p. 123 (Although sexual assaults) Federal Bureau of Investigation, *Uniform Crime Reports,* 1999. This report also states that the United States has a rape rate 13 times higher than Britain's, nearly 4 times higher than Germany's, and more than 20 times higher than Japan's.

Another report by the Centers for Disease Control and Prevention and the National Institute of Justice, *Extent, Nature, and Consequences of Intimate Partner Violence* (July 2000) states: "Nearly 25 percent of American women report being raped and/or physically assaulted by a current or former spouse, cohabiting partner, or date at some time in their lifetime," according to the *National Violence Against Women Survey,* conducted from November 1995 to May 1996.

p. 123 (A murder occurs) Federal Bureau of Investigation, *Uniform Crime Reports,* 1999.

p. 123 (Violence and) E. Aronson, "The Power of Self-Persuasion," *American Psychologist* 54 (1999): 875–886.

p. 123 (Road rage) M. Pepper, *Road Rage* (1997). Available on-line at <http://www.drivers.com/cgi-bin>.

p. 126 (In some American) Barbara Dafoe Whitehead, "The Failure of Sex Education," *Atlantic Monthly,* October 1995.

p. 127 ("I've come to believe") Neil Clark Warren, *Make Anger Your Ally* (Carol Stream, Ill.: Tyndale, 1990).

p. 128 (Consider an example) Marcia Garvey and Jessica Garrison, "Get Angry, Bratton Tells L.A.; Sixteen Homicides in Six Days Should Provoke Outrage and Move City Residents and Police to Action, the Chief Says of the Rash of Violence," *Los Angeles Times,* 21 November 2002.

pp. 128–129 (Yet another compelling) Andy Furillo, "Anger in the Service of Neighborhood Peace," *Los Angeles Times,* 2 December 1984.

p. 131 ("I've had more") Lynn Harris, "How Many Men Have You Slept With?" *Glamour,* December 2002, 196–199.

p. 133 (Four will likely) Anger management styles are fully discussed in *Make Anger Your Ally,* (Carol Stream, Ill: Tyndale, 1990) by Neil Clark Warren.

**A Few Closing Thoughts on Unswerving Authenticity**
p. 142 (Your relationship) See Psalm 139
p. 142 ("familiar with all") Psalm 139:3
p. 142 (his unfailing love) See Psalm 90:14

**SECRET #3: SELF-GIVING LOVE**
**Introduction to Self-Giving Love**
p. 145 ("[Love] always") 1 Corinthians 13:7-8
p. 145 (Perhaps you) J. Haidt, "The Emotional Dog and the Rational Tail: A Social Intuitionist Approach to Moral Judgment," *Psychological Review* 108 (2001): 814–834.

p. 146 ("when our philanthropic") Martin Seligman, *Authentic Happiness* (New York: Free Press, 2002), 9.

p. 146 (Since Abdallah) Scott Bowles, "Real Kid Touches 'Schmidt' Audience," *USA Today,* 23 January 2003, 1D.

p. 146 (In the process) The honest quandary about the tension of self-sacrifice and self-protection has captured many magnificent minds. Anders Nygren's classic book *Agape and Eros* contrasts "acquisitive desire" with "sacrificial giving." C. S. Lewis called *eros* "need-love" and *agape* "gift-love." Thousands of volumes have explored these dueling desires.

p. 147 (As the greatest) See 1 Corinthians 13:3

pp. 147–148 ("I knew from past") Mary Ann Bird, "The Whisper Test," quoted on-line as a stand-alone story.

**Chapter Eight—Reading Your Social Barometer**
p. 152 (Healthy people thrive) J. J. Campos and K. C. Barrett, "Toward a New Understanding of Emotions and Their Development," in *Emotions, Cognition, and Behavior,* ed. Carroll Izard, Jerome Kagan, and Robert Boleslaw Zajonc (New York: Cambridge University Press, 1988), 229–263.

p. 154 (Alternatively, when) V. Van Hasselt et al., "Social Skill Assessment and Training for Children: An Evaluative Review," *Behavior Research and Therapy* 17 (1979): 413–437.

p. 160 (In much the) C. J. Boyatzis and C. Satyaprasad, "Children's Facial and Gestural Decoding and Encoding: Relations between Skills and with Popularity," *Journal of Nonverbal Behavior* 18 (1994): 37–42.

p. 160 (They pay attention) Paul Ekman and Wallace Friesen, *Unmasking the Face* (Englewood Cliffs, N.J.: Prentice Hall, 1975).

p. 161 (It's called Profile) R. Rosenthal et al., "Sensitivity to Nonverbal Communication: The PONS Test" (Baltimore: The Johns Hopkins University Press, 1979). See also *Essentials of Behavioral Research: Methods and Data Analysis* (New York: McGraw-Hill, 1991) by Robert Rosenthal and Ralph Rosnow.

p. 161 (It's also about) F. M. Gresham, "Social Skills and Learning Disabilities: Causal, Concomitant, or Correlational?" *School Psychology Review* 21 (1992): 348–360.

p. 163 (Most everyone has) M. S. Alfano, T. E. Joiner Jr., and M. Perry, "Attributional Style: A Mediator of the Shyness-Depression Relationship," *Journal of Research in Personality* 28 (1994): 287–300.

p. 163 (Harvard researcher) Jerome Kagan, *The Nature of the Child* (New York: Basic Books, 1994).

p. 163 (There are many) S. R. Baker and R. J. Edelmann, "Is Social Phobia Related to Lack of Social Skill? Duration of Skill-Related Behaviors and Ratings of Behavioral Adequacy," *British Journal of Clinical Psychology* 41 (2002): 243–257.

p. 168 (Angela teetered) M. Voboril, "A Weighty Issue/Empathy Suit Shows Medical Personnel What It's Like to be Obese," *Newsday*, 16 April 2000, B03.

p. 169 (Disney World's "cast members") Thomas Connellan, *Inside the Magic Kingdom* (Atlanta: Bard Press, 1997).

p. 170 (Goleman cites) R. W. Levenson and A. M. Fuef, "Physiological Aspects of Emotional Knowledge and Rapport," in *Empathic Accuracy*, ed. William Ickes (New York: Guilford Press, 1997).

p. 171 ("When we are caught") Daniel Goleman, *Working with Emotional Intelligence* (New York: Bantam Books, 1998), 136.

p. 172 ("Therefore whatever you") Luke 12:3, NKJV

p. 173 ("A friend loves") Proverbs 17:17

p. 173 (Healthy relationships) See Ephesians 4:15

### Chapter Nine—Loving Like Your Life Depended on It
p. 187 (There is hardly) See Luke 10:30-35

p. 188 (It reveals) R. Hatfield, *The Wealth of Michelangelo* (n.p. available, 2002).

pp. 189–190 ("If somebody asked") "A Natural Woman," interview on *Prime Time Thursday*, September 6, 2001.

p. 190 ("Fifteen, twenty years") From the behind-the-scenes documentary, *Walking the Mile*, Warner Home Video, 1999.

pp. 190–191 ("When I was trying") James M. Kouzes and Barry Posner, *Encouraging The Heart* (Hoboken, N.J.: Jossey-Bass, 1999).

p. 192 (The Jewish poet) Steve Moore, "A Graceful Goodbye," *Leadership* (Summer 2002): 41–42.

pp. 200–201 ("10 gallons of happiness") D. McCafferty, "The Happiest Guy," *USA Weekend*, 7 March 2003, 6.

### A Few Closing Thoughts on Self-Giving Love
pp. 203–204 ("The information confirmed") Lisa Beamer, *Let's Roll!* (Carol Stream, Ill.: Tyndale, 2002), 187.

p. 204 ("It is unquestionable") Lisa Beamer, *Let's Roll!* (Carol Stream, Ill.: Tyndale, 2002), 186.

### Appendix A—Optimizing Your Spirit
p. 216 (But here's) See Matthew 6:20-21

pp. 217–218 (Dr. Herbert Benson) See especially *Timeless Healing* (New York: Fireside, 1996) by Herbert Benson.

p. 219 (Further, some thirty-five) D. A. Matthews et al., "Religious Commitment and Health Status: A Review of Research and Implications for Family Medicine," *Archives of Family Medicine* 7 (1998): 118–124.

p. 219 (One study) Warren Berland, "Unexpected Cancer Recovery: Why Patients Believe They Survive," *The Journal of Mind-Body Health* 11 (1995).

p. 219 (Numerous other studies) For a thorough review of these studies, see Carl E. Thoresen and Alan H. S. Harris, "Spirituality and Health: What's the Evidence and What's Needed?" *Annals of Behavioral Medicine* 24, no. 1 (2002), 3–13, and David N. Elkins, "Spirituality: It's What's Missing in Mental Health," *Psychology Today*, September/October 1999.

pp. 220–221 (In studies) Dianne Hales, "Can Prayer Really Heal?" *Parade*, 23 March 2003, 5.

p. 222 (The two of us) See Luke 15:11-32 for the story of the Prodigal Son.

p. 223 ("the prayer of") James 5:16

p. 224 (One of them) R. B. Byrd, "Positive Therapeutic Effects of Intercessory Prayer in a Coronary Care Unit Population," *Southern Medical Journal* 81 (1988): 826–829.

p. 224 (Another group) W. S. Harris et al., "A Randomized, Controlled Trial of the Effects of Remote, Intercessory Prayer on Outcomes in Patients Admitted to the Coronary Care Unit," *Archives of Internal Medicine* 159 (1999): 2272–2278.

p. 226 (And the specific) See Ephesians 3:14-19

p. 226 (He grants us) See Romans 8:35; Romans 5:5; Ephesians 3:14-19

p. 227 (They attended services) Leila Shahabi et al., "Correlates of Self-Perception of Spirituality in American Adults," *Annals of Behavioral Medicine* 24 no. 1 (2002): 59–68.

p. 229 ("love, joy, peace") See Galatians 5:22-23

**Appendix B—Charting Your Destiny**

pp. 232–233 (Once upon a time) Taken from *Growing Strong in the Seasons of Life,* (Portland, Oreg.: Multnomah Press, 1983) by Charles R. Swindoll. Swindoll found this story in the Springfield, Oregon, public schools newsletter.

p. 234 (As you become) See Psalm 139:1

pp. 234–235 (Take Benjamin Franklin) "Benjamin Franklin: An Enlightened American," July 25, 2000. Located at <http://www.careerplanit.com/resource/article.asp?subid=1&artid=3>.

p. 236 (Howard Figler) Howard Figler, "How to Decide What You Want to Do," July 2000. Located at<http://www.careerplanit.com/resource/article.asp?subid=1&artod=3>.

p. 236 ("Do not store") Matthew 6:19-21

p. 236 ("Examine who") Russ Jones, "Take Charge of Your Destiny by Drawing Up a Career Plan," *National Business Employment Weekly,* July 2000. Located at <http://careerjournal.com>.

p. 237 (One of the most) Paulo Coelho, *The Alchemist* (New York: HarperPerennial, 1994).

p. 237 ("live and move") Acts 17:28

pp. 240–241 (Katharine Graham was) Katharine Graham, *Personal History* (New York: Knopf, 1997).

pp. 241–242 (Renowned author) Parker J. Palmer, *Let Your Life Speak* (Hoboken, N.J.: Jossey-Bass, 2000).

p. 246 ("In the coming world") Martin Buber, *Tales of the Hasidim: The Early Masters* (New York: Schocken Books, 1975), 251.

p. 247 (For instance) See appendix 1 of *Date? . . . or Soul Mate?* or go to the Web site, <http://www.eharmony.com>, for a complete presentation of the twenty-nine dimensions.

p. 252 (And it all) This material is discussed more fully in my (Neil's) chapter "Dream a Dream" from the book *Learning to Live with the Love of Your Life . . . and Loving It!* (Carol Stream, Ill.: Tyndale House, 1995).

**LES PARROTT, PH.D.,** is founder and codirector (with his wife, Dr. Leslie Parrott) of the Center for Relationship Development, a ground-breaking program dedicated to teaching the basics of good relationships, on the campus of Seattle Pacific University (SPU). Les is also a professor of psychology and the author of several best-selling and award-winning books, including *Saving Your Marriage Before It Starts, Becoming Soul Mates, When Bad Things Happen to Good Marriages, The Control Freak,* and *High-Maintenance Relationships.*

Dr. Parrott is a sought-after speaker throughout the country. He has written for a variety of magazines, and his work has been featured in *USA Today* and the *New York Times.* Dr. Parrott's television appearances include CNN, *Good Morning America, The View,* and *The Oprah Winfrey Show.*

**www.RealRelationships.com**

To learn more about
Drs. Les and Leslie Parrott's
relationship resources and
speaking schedule go to:

# www.RealRelationships.com

Drs. Les and Leslie Parrott
*Solving Relationship Problems Before They Begin*

# ALSO FROM LES PARROTT, PH.D.

✦ ✦ ✦

### The Control Freak

Need help coping with control freaks or identifying your own controlling tendencies? Self-tests will help you find out whether you are suffering from a controlling relationship—or how controlling you can be. They'll also help provide a lifelong prescription for healthier relationships. Learn how to relate with a coercive or supervising person, how to relinquish unhealthy control, and how to repair relationships damaged by overcontrol.
0-8423-3792-X *Hardcover*
0-8423-3793-8 *Softcover*

### High-Maintenance Relationships

How do you handle a friend who saps your energy? When do you love without limit? We've all asked these questions. And too often our responses are either to back out of relationships or to give up on impossible people. Dr. Les Parrott shows us other options, including setting boundaries, giving the gift of grace, and leaving room for God. This book will give you practical tools by devoting chapters to the Martyr, The Cold Shoulder, The Critic, the Volcano, The Gossip ... fifteen high maintenance relationships in all.
0-8423-1466-0 *Softcover*

**NEIL CLARK WARREN, PH.D.,** is a practicing clinical psychologist and the founder of eHarmony.com, a relationship Web site. He is the former dean of the Fuller Graduate School of Psychology and the author of the best-seller *Finding the Love of Your Life.* For more than thirty years he has worked closely with individuals and couples, specializing in the complex challenge of finding, attracting, and selecting the right marriage partner.

Dr. Warren, a popular speaker, travels the country sharing his insights with thousands of people each year. He has been featured on more than five thousand radio and television programs, including *The Oprah Winfrey Show,* and his articles have appeared in numerous journals and magazines.

**eHarmony.com**

# Are you seeking a fulfilling relationship? Not just a date, but a lifetime relationship?

## eHarmony.com is the answer.

*This unique on-line service uses an in-depth survey and scientific technology to match users with truly compatible singles for a real chance at making a lasting connection.*

*But it doesn't stop there. Once a match is made, eHarmony guides matched individuals through a five-step communication process to assist them during the awkward "getting to know you" phase. This nonintimidating process allows matched singles to become acquainted with each other from the inside out, so they can make judgments based on what truly matters in a successful relationship.*

*Go to eHarmony.com today for a free personality profile—and a list of relationship resources from Dr. Warren.*

**Founded by Dr. Neil Clark Warren, whose life work in relationship therapy spans more than three decades, eHarmony works!**

e|Harmony™

*fall in love for all the right reasons*

# ALSO FROM NEIL CLARK WARREN, PH.D.

✦ ✦ ✦

### Finding the Love of Your Life
Whether you're starting a relationship, seriously considering marriage, or longing to find that special someone, this best-selling hardcover is for you! Full of practical insights and sage advice, it outlines the 10 proven principles that will guide you through the challenge of choosing a mate you can love *and* live with happily for a lifetime.
*1-56179-088-5 Hardcover*

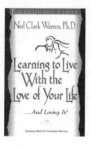

### Learning to Live with the Love of Your Life . . . and Loving It!
Uncover the 10 secrets to staying together in this life-long journey called marriage. Learn practical, proven steps for heightening intimacy, deepening communication, building trust, and simply growing closer along the way. You'll discover how peace and passion, contentment and commitment, and security and satisfaction go hand in hand. But most of all, you'll be inspired and equipped to make your marriage better than ever!
*1-56179-651-4 Softcover*

### Make Anger Your Ally
Anger is powerful. You can suppress it, deny it, and let it control you. Or you can learn how to manage it. Delve into this eye-opening paperback, and discover how to harness anger's energy to cope with pain and resolve problems. Anger—make it work for you, not against you.
*1-56179-707-3 Softcover*